Nirali's New Series

CONCISE STUDY SERIES

(50 Marks)

MATERIAL SCIENCE

Sem. - I

S.E. ELECTRICAL ENGINEERING

As per New Revised Syllabus of University of Pune

(Pattern 2012)

Miss. P. R. Godbole

M. E. (Electrical)

Pune.

N 2838

MATERIAL SCIENCE (S.E. ELECTRICAL)

First Edition : June 2014

© : **Author**

The text of this publication, or any part thereof, should not be reproduced or transmitted in any form or stored in any computer storage system or device for distribution including photocopy, recording, taping or information retrieval system or reproduced on any disc, tape, perforated media or other information storage device etc., without the written permission of Authors with whom the rights are reserved. Breach of this condition is liable for legal action.

Every effort has been made to avoid errors or omissions in this publication. In spite of this, errors may have crept in. Any mistake, error or discrepancy so noted and shall be brought to our notice shall be taken care of in the next edition. It is notified that neither the publisher nor the authors or seller shall be responsible for any damage or loss of action to any one, of any kind, in any manner, therefrom.

Published By :
NIRALI PRAKASHAN
Abhyudaya Pragati, 1312, Shivaji Nagar,
Off J.M. Road, PUNE – 411005
Mumbai
Tel – (020) 25512336/37/39, Fax – (020) 25511379
Email : niralipune@pragationline.com

Printed at
Repro Knowledgecast Limited
India

DISTRIBUTION CENTRES
PUNE

Nirali Prakashan
119, Budhwar Peth, Jogeshwari Mandir Lane
Pune 411002, Maharashtra
Tel : (020) 2445 2044, 66022708, Fax : (020) 2445 1538
Email : bookorder@pragationline.com

Nirali Prakashan
S. No. 28/25, Dhyari,
Near Pari Company, Pune 411041
Tel : (022) 24690204 Fax : (020) 24690316
Email : dhyari@pragationline.com
bookorder@pragationline.com

MUMBAI
Nirali Prakashan
385, S.V.P. Road, Rasdhara Co-op. Hsg. Society Ltd.,
Girgaum, Mumbai 400004, Maharashtra
Tel : (022) 2385 6339 / 2386 9976, Fax : (022) 2386 9976
Email : niralimumbai@pragationline.com

DISTRIBUTION BRANCHES

NAGPUR
Pratibha Book Distributors
Above Maratha Mandir, Shop No. 3, First Floor,
Rani Jhanshi Square, Sitabuldi, Nagpur 440012,
Maharashtra, Tel : (0712) 254 7129

BENGALURU
Pragati Book House
House No. 1, Sanjeevappa Lane, Avenue Road Cross,
Opp. Rice Church, Bengaluru – 560002.
Tel : (080) 64513344, 64513355,
Mob : 9880582331, 9845021552
Email:bharatsavla@yahoo.com

JALGAON
Nirali Prakashan
34, V. V. Golani Market, Navi Peth, Jalgaon 425001,
Maharashtra, Tel : (0257) 222 0395
Mob : 94234 91860

KOLHAPUR
Nirali Prakashan
New Mahadvar Road,
Kedar Plaza, 1st Floor Opp. IDBI Bank
Kolhapur 416 012, Maharashtra. Mob : 9855046155

CHENNAI
Pragati Books
9/1, Montieth Road, Behind Taas Mahal, Egmore,
Chennai 600008 Tamil Nadu, Tel : (044) 6518 3535,
Mob : 94440 01782 / 98450 21552 / 98805 82331, Email : bharatsavla@yahoo.com

RETAIL OUTLETS
PUNE

Pragati Book Centre
157, Budhwar Peth, Opp. Ratan Talkies,
Pune 411002, Maharashtra
Tel : (020) 2445 8887 / 6602 2707, Fax : (020) 2445 8887

Pragati Book Centre
Amber Chamber, 28/A, Budhwar Peth,
Appa Balwant Chowk, Pune : 411002, Maharashtra,
Tel : (020) 20240335 / 66281669
Email : pbcpune@pragationline.com

Pragati Book Centre
676/B, Budhwar Peth, Opp. Jogeshwari Mandir,
Pune 411002, Maharashtra
Tel : (020) 6601 7784 / 6602 0855

PBC Book Sellers & Stationers
152, Budhwar Peth, Pune 411002, Maharashtra
Tel : (020) 2445 2254 / 6609 2463

MUMBAI
Pragati Book Corner
Indira Niwas, 111 – A, Bhavani Shankar Road, Dadar (W), Mumbai 400028, Maharashtra
Tel : (022) 2422 3526 / 6662 5254, Email : pbcmumbai@pragationline.com

Dear Students,

It gives us great pleasure to introduce a New Series "**C**oncise **S**tudy **S**eries" for Second Year Engineering students. These "**CSS**" books are written by Experienced and Eminent Professors of respective subjects.

The specialty of this new Series "**CSS**" is that it:

- Covers full syllabus of University of Pune.
- Contains Matter written in Simple and Lucid language.
- Includes "To the Point" Topics and well arranged articles.
- Includes Most Likely Questions.
- Includes Previous Years University Question Papers.
- Available in all leading stores at Affordable Price.

Happy Studying and Best of Luck!!!

Nirali Prakashan

SYLLABUS

Unit 1 (A) Dielectric Properties of Insulating Materials
Static Field, Parameters of Dielectric material [Dielectric constant, Dipole moment, Polarization, Polarizability], Introduction to Polar and Non-Polar dielectric materials. Mechanisms of Polarizations-Electronic, Ionic and Orientation Polarization (Descriptive treatment only), Clausius Mossotti Equation, Piezo-Electric, Pyro-Electric & Ferro-Electric Materials, Dielectric Loss and loss Tangent, Concept of negative tan.

(B) Optical Properties of Materials & Cells used for Power Generation:
Photo-Conductivity, Photo-Electric Emission, Photo-Voltaic cells [Materials Used, Construction, Equivalent Circuit, Working and Application), materials used for Photo-Conductive cells, Photo-Emissive cells.

Unit 2 (A) Insulating Materials, Properties & Application
Introduction, Characteristics of Good Insulating Material, Classification, Solid Insulating Materials- Paper, Press Board, Fibrous Materials, Ceramics, Mica & Asbestos, Resins, Polymers Ceramics, Enamels. Liquid Insulating Materials such as Transformer Oil, Varnish, Askarel, Insulating Gases like Air, SF6, Insulating Materials for Power & Distribution Transformers, Rotating Machines, Capacitors, Cables, Line Insulators and Switchgears. Crystal defects.

(B) Dielectric Breakdown:
Introduction, Concept of Primary and Secondary Ionization of Gases (Descriptive treatment only), Breakdown Voltage, Breakdown Strength, Factors affecting Breakdown Strengths of Gaseous, Liquid and Solid Dielectric Materials.

Unit 3 Magnetic Materials
Introduction, Parameters of Magnetic material [Permeability, Magnetic Susceptibility, Magnetization], Classification of Magnetic Materials, Diamagnetism, Paramagnetism, Ferromagnetism, Ferri-magnetism, Ferro-magnetic behaviour below Critical Temperature, Spontaneous Magnetization & Curie-Weiss law, Anti-ferromagnetism, Ferrites, Applications of Ferro-magnetic Materials, Magnetic materials for Electric Devices such as Transformer Core, Core of Rotating Machines, Soft Magnetic Materials, Hard Magnetic Materials, Magnetic Recording Materials, Compact Discs. Introduction to laser and magnetic strip technology.

Unit 4 Conducting Materials
General Properties of Conductor, Electrical Conducting Materials - Copper, Aluminium and its applications, Materials of High & Low Resistivity-Constantan, Nickel-Chromium Alloy, Tungsten, Canthal, Silver & Silver alloys, Characteristics of Copper Alloys (Brass & Bronze), Materials used for Lamp Filaments, Transmission Lines, Electrical Carbon Materials, Material used for Solders, Metals & Alloys for different types of Fuses, Thermal Bimetal & Thermocouple. Introduction to Superconductivity and Super Conductors.

Unit 5 Nanotechnology
Introduction, Concepts of Energy bands & various Conducting Mechanism in Nano-structures, Carbon Nano-structures, Carbon Molecules, Carbon Clusters, Carbon Nano-tubes, Applications of Carbon Nano-tubes, Special Topics in Nano Technology such as Single Electron Transistor, Molecular Machines, BN Nanotubes, Nano wires.

Unit 6 Testing of Materials
Explanation of following with objectives, equipments required, circuit diagrams and observations to be taken. 1. Measurement of Dielectric Loss Tangent (tan δ) by Schering Bridge-IS 13585-1994. 2. Measurement of Dielectric Strength of Solid Insulating Material-IS 2584. 3. Measurement of tan delta, resistivity and dielectric Strength of Liquid Insulating Material – IS 6798. 4. Measurement of Dielectric Strength of Gaseous Insulating Material –IS 2584. 5. Measurement of Power factor and partial discharge of high voltage cables. 6. Measurement of Flux Density by Gauss-meter. 7. Measurement of dielectric strength of resins and polymers.

CONTENTS

Unit - I

1. Introduction 1.1-1.24
1.1 Introduction 1.1
1.2 A Dielectric Material 1.1
1.3 Polarization 1.3
    1.3.1 Dielectric Polarization 1.4
    1.3.2 Piezoelectric Material 1.5
    1.3.3 Ferroelectric 1.8
1.4 Loss Tangent 1.9
1.5 Relation Between D.E. and P 1.10
1.6 Clausius Mossoti Equation 1.11
    Solved Examples 1.12
    University Questions 1.22

2. Optical Properties of Materials and Cells Used for Power Generation 2.1-2.14
2.1 Photoelectric Emission 2.1
2.2 The Laws of Photo-Electric Emission 2.2
2.3 Photoconductivity 2.2
    2.3.1 Applications 2.3
2.4 The Photo-Emissive Cell 2.3
    2.4.1 Operating Principles 2.4
    2.4.2 Applications 2.4
2.5 The Photoconductive Cell 2.5
    2.5.1 Photoconductive Cell Circuit 2.6
    2.5.2 Characteristics of a Photoconductive Cell 2.6
2.6 Photovoltaic Technology 2.7
    2.6.1 Mathematical Modeling of Photovoltaic Module 2.8
    2.6.2 Cell Modular Array PV 2.9
2.7 Types of PV Cell Materials 2.9
    2.7.1 Crystalline Materials 2.9

2.7.2	Thin Film Materials	2.11
2.7.3	Copper Indium Diselenide (CuInSe$_2$, or CIS)	2.12
2.8	Advantages and Disadvantages of PV Cell	2.12
University Questions		2.13

Unit - II

3. Insulating Materials, Properties and Application — 3.1-3.28

3.1	Introduction	3.1
3.2	Properties of Insulating Materials	3.2
	3.2.1 Electrical Properties	3.2
	3.2.2 Thermal Properties	3.3
	3.2.3 Chemical Properties	3.4
	3.2.4 Physical/Mechanical Properties	3.5
3.3	Insulating Materials and Their Applications	3.5
	3.3.1 Fibrous Insulating Materials	3.13
	3.3.2 Insulating Resins (Polymers)	3.15
3.4	Liquid Insulating Materials	3.19
	3.4.1 Properties of Good Liquid Insulating Materials	3.19
	3.4.2 Mineral Insulating Oil (Petroleum Oil or Transformer Oil)	3.20
	3.4.3 Synthetic Liquids	3.20
	3.4.4 Askarel	3.20
	3.4.5 Varnish	3.21
	3.4.6 Enamel	3.21
3.5	Gases Insulating Materials	3.22
Solved Examples		3.23
University Questions		3.26

4. Dielectric Breakdown — 4.1-4.28

4.1	Gases as Insulating Media	4.1
4.2	Ionization Process	4.2
4.3	Townsend's Current Growth Equation	4.2
4.4	Current Growth in the Presence of Secondary Processes	4.3
4.5	Townsend's Criterion for Breakdown	4.4
4.6	Breakdown in Electronegative Gases	4.4

4.7	Time Lags for Breakdown	4.5
4.8	Streamer Theory of Breakdown in Gases	4.5
4.9	Paschen's Law	4.7
4.10	Post-Breakdown Phenomena and Applications	4.8
4.11	Breakdown in Solid Dielectrics	4.9
4.12	Breakdown in Liquid Dielectrics	4.17
4.13	Factors Affecting Breakdown Voltage of Solid	4.22
4.14	Factors Affecting Breakdown Strength of Liquid Dielectric Material	4.22
4.15	Factors Affecting Breakdown Strength of Gaseous Dielectric	4.23
4.16	Breakdown in Vacuum	4.23
University Questions		4.26

Unit - III

5. Magnetic Materials — 5.1-5.34

5.1	Introduction	5.1
5.2	Magnetic Store	5.1
5.3	Magnetic and Electric Fields	5.2
5.4	Magnetic Susceptibility	5.3
	5.4.1 Magnetic Moments	5.3
5.5	Types of Magnetism	5.3
5.6	Curie Temperature	5.5
	5.6.1 Curie-Weiss Law	5.7
	5.6.2 Physics of Curie Temperature	5.8
	5.6.3 Factors affecting on Curie Temperature	5.9
	5.6.4 Curie Temperature in Ferroelectric and Piezoelectric Materials	5.10
5.7	Paramagnetic	5.11
	5.7.1 Paramagnetic	5.11
	5.7.2 Ferromagnetic	5.12
	5.7.3 Ferrimagnetic	5.12
	5.7.4 Antiferromagnetic and the Néel temperature	5.12
	5.7.5 Piezoelectric	5.13
5.8	Types of Magnetic Material	5.13
5.9	Applications of Ferromagnetic Materials	5.17
Solved Examples		5.18
University Questions		5.31

Unit - IV

6. Conducting Materials — 6.1-6.30

6.1 Introduction to Electrical Conducting Materials — 6.1
    6.1.1 Copper — 6.1
    6.1.2 Aluminium — 6.2
    6.1.3 Constantan/Eureka — 6.3
    6.1.4 Nichrome — 6.3
    6.1.5 Tungsten — 6.4
6.2 Material Used For Filaments — 6.4
    6.2.1 Materials used for making solders and contacts — 6.5
    6.2.2 Rewireable fuse — 6.5
    6.2.3 Kanthal — 6.6
    6.2.4 Manganin — 6.6
    6.2.5 Silver — 6.7
6.3 Copper Alloys — 6.7
    6.3.1 Brass — 6.7
    6.3.2 Bronze — 6.8
6.4 Electric Field and Semiconductors — 6.8
6.5 Superconductors and Magnetic Fields 6.10
    6.5.1 Type I Superconductors — 6.11
    6.5.2 Type II Superconductors — 6.13
    6.5.3 Applications of Superconductors — 6.14
6.6 Bimetallic Strips — 6.15
6.7 Thermocouple — 6.15
Solved Examples — 6.17
University Questions — 6.27

Unit - V

7. Nanotechnology — 7.1-7.26

7.1 Energy Band Theory of Solids — 7.1
7.2 Nanostructures — 7.4
7.3 Carbon — 7.5
7.4 Isotopes — 7.5

	7.4.1 Fullerenes	7.7
7.5	Carbon Nano Tubes (CNT)	7.9
	7.5.1 Properties of CNT	7.11
	7.5.2 Application of Nanotube	7.15
7.6	Boron nitride Nanotube	7.16
7.7	Single electron Transistor	7.17
7.8	Molecular Machines	7.20
7.9	Nano Wires	7.22
University Questions		7.24

Unit - VI

8. Testing of Materials 8.1-8.28

8.1.	Measurement of Dielectric Loss Tangent (tan δ) by Schering Bridge, IS 13585-1994	8.1
8.2	Measuirement of Dielectric Strength of Solid Insulating Materials IS 2584	8.4
8.3.	Measurement of Dielectric Strength of Liquid Dielectric Material	8.5
8.4.	Measurement of Resistivity of Liquid Dielectric	8.8
8.5.	Measurement of Dielectric Strength of Gases	8.9
8.6.	Measurement of Power Factor and Partial Discharge of High Voltage Cables	8.11
	8.6.1 General Construction of a Cable	8.11
	8.6.2 Tan δ, Or Tan Delta	8.12
	8.6.3 Partial Discharge Testing for Cables	8.15
8.7 Flux density test (gauss meter)		8.16
	8.7.1 Total Flux Test (Flux Meter)	8.18
	8.7.2 Hysteresis Test	8.19
8.8 Resins		8.20
	8.8.1 Materials	8.21
	8.8.2 Specifications	8.22
	8.8.3 Dielectric Strength of Resins	8.22
Solved examples		8.23
University Questions		8.26

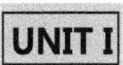

CHAPTER 1
DIELECTRIC PROPERTIES OF INSULATING MATERIALS

1.1 INTRODUCTION

Every material in the world can be defined in terms of how it conducts electricity. Certain things, such as cold glass, do not conduct electricity. They are known as insulators. Materials which do conduct electricity, like copper, aluminum are called conductors. In the middle are materials known as semiconductors, which do not conduct as well as conductors, but can carry current. such materials called superconductors, which when brought down to very low temperatures turn into superhighways of current, they conduct electricity without any resistance.

1.2 A DIELECTRIC MATERIAL

> **Q.** What is dielectric materials ?
> **Q.** What are the different types of dielectric materials.
> **Q.** Define dielectric constant.
> **Q.** Define dipole moment.
> **Q.** Write short note on Dipole Moment.

A dielectric material is an electrical insulator that can be polarized by an applied electric field.

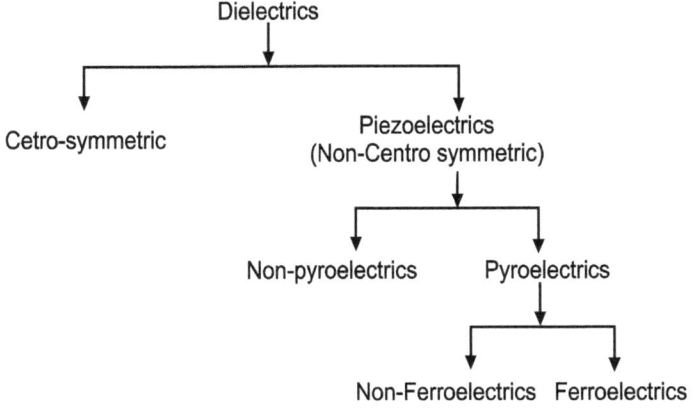

Fig. 1.1

When a dielectric is placed in an electric field, electric charges do not flow through the material as they do in a conductor, but cause dielectric polarization. Because of dielectric polarization, positive charges are displaced toward the field and negative charges shift in the opposite direction. This creates an internal electric field that reduces the overall field within the dielectric. The study of dielectric properties concerns storage and dissipation of electric as well as magnetic energy in materials. It is important to explain various phenomena in electronics, optics, and solid-state physics.

Dielectric constant : The dielectric constant is the ratio of the permittivity of a substance to the permittivity of free space. It is an electrical equivalent of relative magnetic permeability. As the dielectric constant increases, the electric flux density increases, if all other factors remain unchanged. This enables objects of a given size, such as sets of metal plates, to hold their electric charge for long periods of time, and/or to hold large quantities of charge. Materials with high dielectric constants are mainly useful in the manufacture of high-value capacitors.

Electric permittivity, is a constant of proportionality that exists between electric displacement and electric field intensity. This constant is equal to approximately 8.85×10^{-12} farad per meter (F/m) in free space. In other materials, it can be much different, often substantially greater than the free-space value, which is symbolized ε_o. In engineering applications, permittivity is often expressed in relative, rather than in absolute permittivity. If ε_o represents the permittivity of free space (that is 8.85×10^{-12} F/m) and ε represents the permittivity of the substance in question (also specified in farads per metre), then the relative permittivity, also called the dielectric constant ε_r, is given by:

$$\varepsilon_r = \varepsilon/\varepsilon_o$$
$$= \varepsilon (1.13 \times 10^{11})$$

Various substances have dielectric constants ε_r greater than 1. These substances are generally called dielectric materials, or dielectrics. Commonly used dielectrics include glass, various ceramics, paper, mica, polyethylene, and certain metal oxides. Dielectrics are used in capacitors and transmission lines in Alternating Current (AC), Audio Frequency (AF), and radio frequency (RF) applications.

Dipole Moment

$$-q \ominus \uparrow\uparrow$$
$$d \; p$$
$$+q \oplus \downarrow\downarrow$$
$$\vec{p} = q \vec{d}$$

The electric dipole moment for a pair of opposite charges of magnitude q is defined as the magnitude of the charge times the distance between them and the defined direction is toward the positive charge. It is a useful concept in atoms and molecules where the effects of charge separation are important, but the distances between the charges are too small to be easily measurable. It is also very useful concept in dielectrics and other applications in solid and liquid materials. Applications involve the electric field of a dipole and the energy of a dipole when placed in an electric field. As shown in below fig.

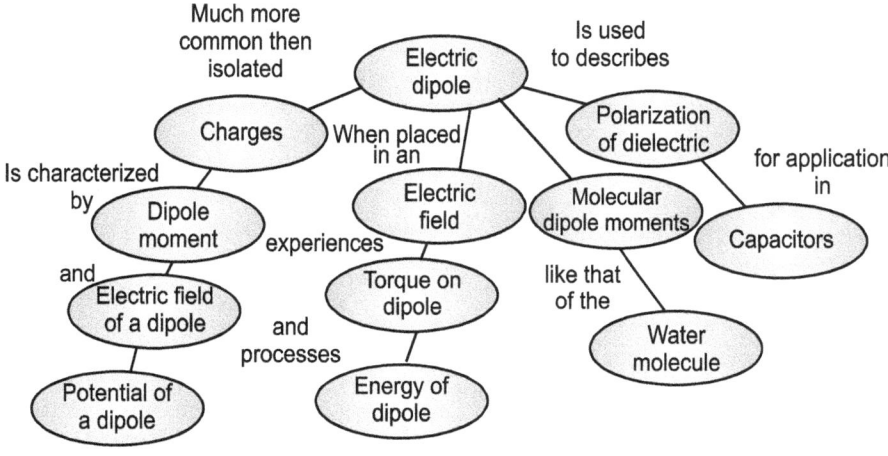

Fig. 1.2

1.3 POLARIZATION

> Q. What is polarization ?
> Q. What are the types of polarization ?
> Q. Write short note on polarization.

Polarization of Dielectric : If a material contains polar molecules, they will generally be in random orientations when no electric field is applied. An applied electric field by orienting the dipole moments of polar molecules which will polarize the material. This decreases the effective electric field between the plates and will increase the capacitance of the parallel plate structure. The dielectric must be a good electric insulator so as to minimize any DC leakage current through a capacitor.

The presence of the dielectric decreases by the electric field produced by a given charge density.

$$E_{effectuve} = E - E_{polarization} = \frac{\sigma}{k\varepsilon_o}$$

The factor k by which the effective field is decreased by the polarization of the dielectric is called the dielectric constant of the material.

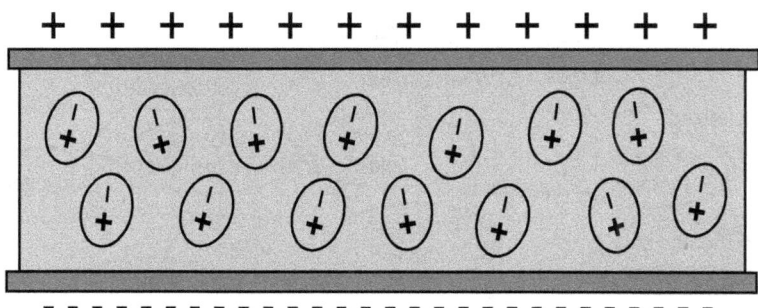

Fig. 1.3
Comparision between Polar Dielectric and Non-polar Dielectric

Polar Dielectric	Non-polar Dielectric
1. The centres of positive and negative charges do not coincide because of the asymmetric shape of the molecules in Polar Dielectric	1. The centre of positive charge coincides with centre of negative charge in the molecule in Non-polar dielectric.
2. It has dipole moment in the application of external electric field.	2. It has very small dipole moment to each molecule in the application of external electric field.

1.3.1 Dielectric Polarization

> **Q.** Explain what is dielectric polarization.
> **Q.** Write short note on Ionic polarization.

(1) Dipolar Polarization

Dipolar polarization is a polarization that is either inherent to polar molecules which is orientation polarization, or can be induced in any molecule in which the asymmetric distortion of the nuclei is possible. Orientation polarization results from a permanent dipole. When an external electric field is applied, the distance between charges within each permanent dipole, which is related to chemical bonding, remains constant in orientation polarization. But in the direction of polarization it rotates. This rotation occurs on a timescale that depends on the torque and surrounding viscosity of the molecules. Because the rotation is not instantaneous, dipolar polarizations lose the response to electric fields at the highest frequencies. The delay of the response to the change of the electric field causes friction and heat. When an external electric field is applied at infrared frequencies or less than it, the molecules are bent and stretched by the field and the molecular dipole moment changes. The molecular vibration frequency is roughly the inverse of the time it takes for the molecules to bend, and this distortion polarization disappears above the infrared.

(2) Ionic Polarization

Ionic polarization is polarization caused by relative displacements between positive and negative ions in ionic crystals (for example, NaCl). If a crystal consists of atoms of more than one kind, the distribution of charges around an atom in the crystal or molecule leans to positive or negative. Because of this, when lattice vibrations or molecular vibrations induce relative displacements of the atoms, the centers of positive and negative charges are also displaced. The locations of these centers are affected by the symmetry of the displacements. When the centers don't correspond, polarizations arise in crystals. This polarization is called ionic polarization. Ionic polarization causes the ferroelectric effect as well as dipolar polarization. In the ferroelectric transition, which is caused by the lining up of the orientations of permanent dipoles along a particular direction, is called an order-disorder phase transition. The transition caused by ionic polarizations in crystals is called a displacive phase transition.

1.3.2 Piezoelectric Material

Piezoelectric Material that possesses the property of converting mechanical energy into electrical energy and vice versa.

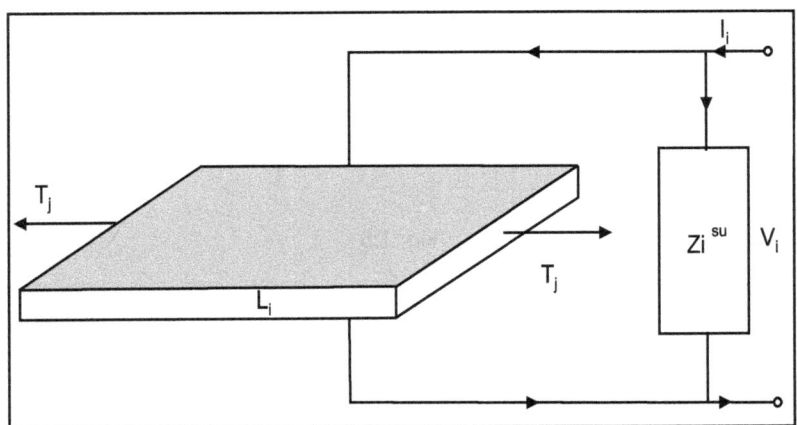

Fig. 1.4 : Piezoelectric materials

- It is reversible an applied mechanical stress will generate a voltage and an applied voltage will change the shape of the solid by a small amount (up to 4% change in volume).

- In physics, the piezoelectric effect can be described as the link between electrostatics and mechanics.

Direct Piezoelectric Effect

Piezoelectric material will generate electric potential when subjected to some kind of mechanical stress.

The direct effect : Strain sensor, gas lighters, microphones, ultrasonic detectors.

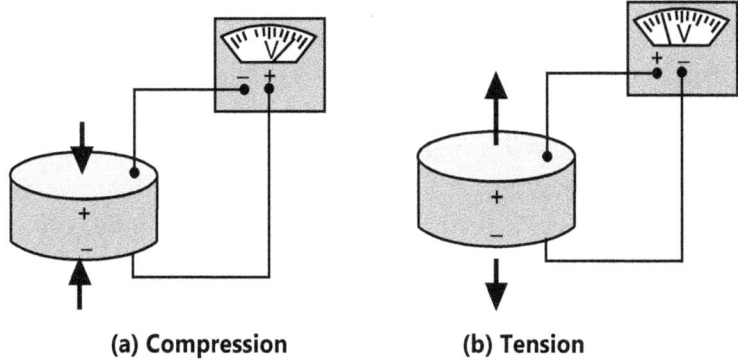

(a) Compression   (b) Tension

Fig. 1.5

Inverse Piezoelectric Effect : If the piezoelectric material is exposed to an electric field it consequently lengthens or shortens proportional to the voltage. E.g. Crystal oscillators, crystal speakers, record player pick ups, actuators etc.

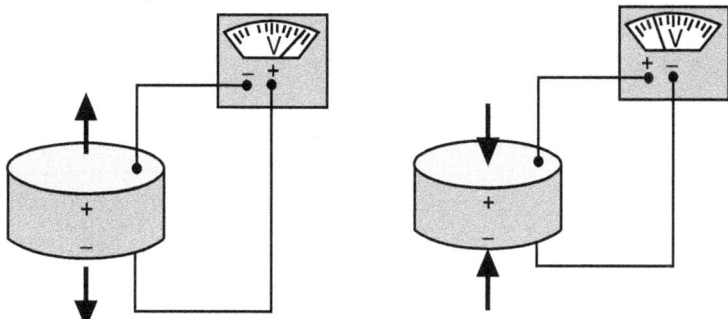

Fig. 1.6

The necessary condition for the piezoelectric effect is the absence of a center of symmetry in the crystal structure. For example: Of the 32 crystals classes 21 lack a center of symmetry, and with the exceptions of one class, all these are piezoelectric. If lead zirconate titanate (PZT), a piezoceramic, is placed between two electrodes and a pressure causing a reduction of only $1/20^{th}$ of one millimeter is applied, a 100,000 volt potential is produced.

The basic equations of piezoelectricity are :

$$P = D \times stress$$

and

$$E = strain/D$$

Where,

P = Polarization

E = Electric field generated

D = Piezoelectric coefficient in metres per volt.

Naturally occurring crystals : $AlPO_4$, Cane sugar, Quartz, Rochelle salt, Topaz, Tourmaline group minerals, and dry bone.

Man-made crystals : Gallium orthophosphate ($GaPO_4$), Langasite ($La_3Ga_5SiO_{14}$).

Man-made ceramics : Barium titanate ($BaTiO_3$), Lead titanate ($PbTiO_3$), Lead zirconate titanate ($Pb[Zr_x Ti_1] O_3\ 0 < x < 1$). More commonly known as PZT, Potassium niobate ($KNbO_3$), Lithium niobate ($LiNbO_3$) Lithium tantalate ($LiTaO_3$), Sodium tungstate ($NaxWO_3$).

Polymers : Polyvinylidene fluoride (PVDF).

Pyroelectric Materials : A special class of material which is subset of piezoelectric material. This are polarized spontaneously but they do not respond to an electric field like ferroelectronics require very high electric field for orienting the dipoles.

The field required for some materials is so high that the material reaches electric breakdown before it can get polarized. But when temperature is changed the polarization of crystal changes e.g. $LiNbO_3$.

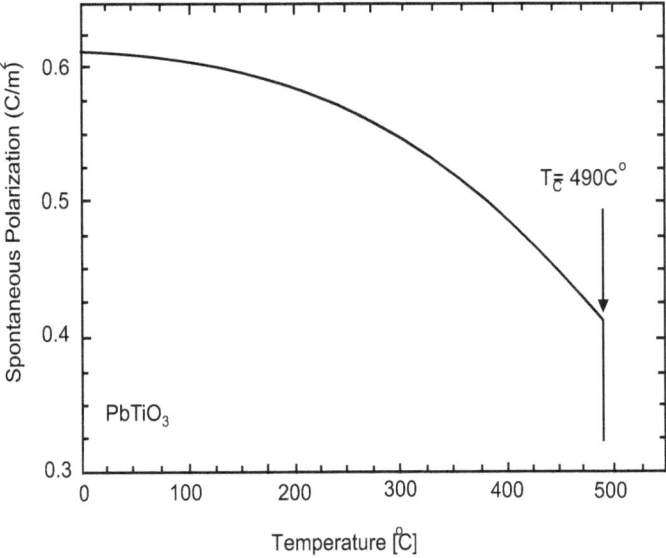

Fig. 1.7

The spontaneous polarization is strongly dependent on the temperature. It disappears completely at the phase transformation temperature T_c. The variation in the polarization effect with respect to the temperature is called the pyroelectric effect.

$$p = \left(\frac{\delta D}{\delta T}\right)_E = \frac{\delta P_s}{\delta T} + \delta \frac{\delta \varepsilon}{\delta T}$$

1.3.3 Ferroelectric

Q. Write short note on ferroelectric.
Q. Give the properties and applications of ferroelectric.

- Some ionic crystals and polymer dielectrics exhibit a spontaneous dipole moment, which can be reversed by an externally applied electric field. This is called the ferroelectric effect. These materials are similar to the ferromagnetic materials behave within an externally applied magnetic field. Ferroelectric materials often have very high dielectric constants, making them very useful for capacitors.
- Ferromagnetism was already known when ferroelectricity was discovered in 1920, in by Valasek. Thus, the prefix ferro, meaning iron, was used to describe the property despite the fact that most ferroelectric materials do not contain iron.
- All Ferroelectric materials exhibit Piezoelectric effect because of lack of symmetry.
- Special class of Piezoelectric material exhibit spontaneous polarization i.e., polarization in the absence of an electric field.
- Ferroelectrics are the electric analog of the ferromagnets, which may show permanent magnetic behaviour.
- Valasek discovered the first ferroelectric material, namely Rochelle salt.
- In ferroelectrics, the polarization can be varied and even reversed by an external electric field.

Properties
- Extremely high dielectric constant (~500-15,000).
- High strain response to applied electrical field → piezoelectricity.
- Strong variation in polarization with temperature → pyroelectricity.
  Strong non-linear dielectric response to an applied electrical field.

Applications of Ferroelectrics
- Non-volatile RAMs
- Dynamic capacitors
- Tunable microwave devices
- Pyroelectric sensors
- Optical waveguides

All ferroelectric materials are Piezoelectric, but all Piezoelectric materials are not Ferroelectric.

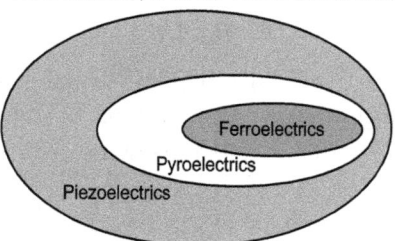

Fig. 1.8

Ferroelectrics are spontaneously polarised, but are also piezoelectric, in that their polarisation changes under the influence of a stress. This is because while all ferroelectrics are piezoelectric, but not all piezoelectrics are ferroelectric.

1.4 LOSS TANGENT

Q. What is loss tangent ?
Q. Explain factors affecting on loss tangent.

Tan δ, or Tan Delta

Tan Delta, also called Loss Angle or Dissipation Factor. tan δ testing, is a indicative method of testing cables to determine the quality of the cable insulation. This is done to predict the remaining life expectancy and in order to prioritize cable replacement. If the insulation of a cable is free from defects, such as water trees, electrical trees, moisture and air pockets, etc., the cable approaches the properties of a perfect capacitor. It is very similar to a parallel plate capacitor with the two plates separated by the insulation material. In a perfect capacitor, the voltage and current phaser are phase shifted 90 degrees and the current through the insulation is capacitive. If there are impurities in the insulation, the resistance of the insulation decreases, resulting in an increase in resistive current through the insulation. It is no longer a perfect capacitor. The current and voltage will no longer be shifted 90 degrees. It will be something less than 90 degrees. The extent to which the phase shift is less than 90 degrees is indicative of the level of insulation contagion, hence quality/reliability. This "Loss Angle" is measured and analyzed. Below is a representation of a cable. The tangent of the angle δ is measured. This will indicate the level of resistance in the insulation of cable. By measuring I_R/I_C (opposite over adjacent – the tangent), we can determine the quality of the cable insulation. In a perfect cable, the angle would be nearly zero. An increasing angle indicates an increase in the resistive current through the insulation, meaning contagion. The greater the angle, the worse the cable condition.

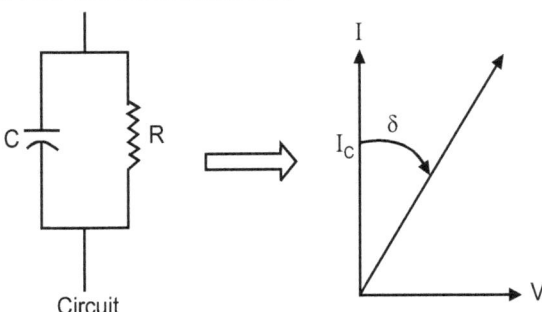

Fig. 1.9

Factors Affecting Dielectric Loss

- **Temperature** : With rise in temperature the dielectric loss also increases.

- **Moisture :** Presence of moisture in the insulating material increases the dielectric loss in the insulating material.
- **Applied voltage :** Dielectric loss increases with rise in the applied voltage. This loss is one factor in limiting the operating voltage of underground cables generally to 100 kV.

1.5 RELATION BETWEEN D.E. & P

> Q. What is relationship between D.E. and P.
> Q. What is relation between x and P.

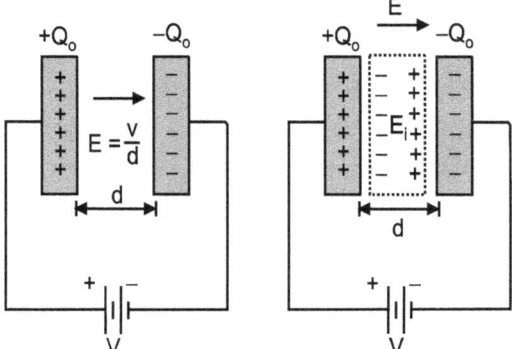

(a) When vacuum as dielectric (b) When dielectric material is present

Fig. 1.10 : Parallel plate capacitor

Consider a parallel plate capacitor having area m² for each plate and distance between it as d m. Battery voltage is V applied across it. Electric field strength is given by when there is vacuum.

$$E = \frac{V}{d} \text{ (V/m)}$$

Surface charge density is given by,

$$\sigma_0 = \frac{Q_0}{A}$$

$$= \frac{C_0 \cdot V}{A}$$

Where, Q_0 is charge.

$$\sigma_0 = \frac{\varepsilon_0 A}{d} \times \frac{V}{A}$$

$$\sigma_0 = \varepsilon_0 \frac{V}{d}$$

$$\sigma_0 = \varepsilon_0 E$$

Surface charge density when dielectric material is introduced between the plates of capacitor.

$$\sigma_1 = \frac{Q}{A}$$

Where, Q is charge.

$$\sigma_1 = \frac{CV}{A}$$

$$\sigma_1 = \frac{\varepsilon_0 \varepsilon_r A}{d} \frac{V}{A}$$

$$\sigma_1 = \varepsilon_0 \varepsilon_r E$$

This shows increase in charge density.

i.e. $\sigma_1 = \sigma_0 + \sigma_P$

Where, σ_P = Charge density due to polarization.

We know that $\sigma_p \cong P$

∴ $\sigma_p = \sigma_0 + P$

$\varepsilon_0 \varepsilon_r E = \varepsilon_0 \cdot E + P$

$P = \varepsilon_0 \varepsilon_r E - \varepsilon_0 E$

$$\boxed{P = D - \varepsilon_0 E} \qquad (\because D = \varepsilon_0 \varepsilon_r E)$$

also, $P = \varepsilon_r E (\varepsilon_0 - 1)$

$P = \varepsilon_r E x_0$

Where, x_0 is called susceptibility of dielectric material.

1.6 CLAUSIUS MOSSOTI EQUATION

Q. What are the assumption in Clausius Mossoti equation.
Q. What is Clausius Mossotti equation.

Assumption in Clausius Mossotti equation. **[Dec. 05, May 07, 10]**

1. It is applicable to elemental solid dielectrics which only having cubic crystal structure.
2. Molecule arrangement is isotropic.
3. Polarizability of molecule isotropic and by elastic displacement only.
4. Absence of short range interactions.

The materials like diamond, silicon exhibit only electronic polarization so for such material, $P_i = P_o = 0$ and total polarization $P = P_e$.

$$P = N \alpha_e E_i$$

where, α_e = electronic polarizability and E_i = internal field.

For cubic symmetry,

$$E_i = E + \frac{P}{3\varepsilon_0}$$

Putting this in equation (1),

$$P = N\alpha_e \left(E + \frac{P}{3\varepsilon_0} \right)$$

We know that,
$$P = \varepsilon_0 (\varepsilon_r - 1) E$$

∴
$$\varepsilon_0 (\varepsilon_r - 1) E = N\alpha_e \left[E + \frac{E_0 (\varepsilon_r - 1) E}{3\varepsilon_0} \right]$$

$$\varepsilon_0 (\varepsilon_r - 1) E = N\alpha_e \left[E + \frac{(\varepsilon_r - 1) E}{3} \right]$$

$$\varepsilon_0 (\varepsilon_r - 1) E = N\alpha_e \left[1 + \frac{(\varepsilon_r - 1)}{3} \right]$$

$$\varepsilon_0 (\varepsilon_r - 1) = N\alpha_e \left[\frac{3 + (\varepsilon_r - 1)}{3} \right]$$

$$\varepsilon_0 (\varepsilon_r - 1) = N\alpha_e \frac{(\varepsilon_r - 2)}{3}$$

$$\boxed{\frac{(\varepsilon_r - 1)}{(\varepsilon_r - 2)} = \frac{N\alpha_e}{3\varepsilon_0}}$$

SOLVED EXAMPLES

Example 1.1 : Argon gas contains 2.7×10^{25} atom at 0°C and 1 atomic pressure. Calculate dielectric constant of argon atom is 3.48 Au. **[Dec. 08]**

Solution : Given : $N = 2.7 \times 10^{25}$ atoms/m³, Diameter $d = 3.48$ Au $= 3.48 \times 10^{-10}$ m,

$$\text{Radius} = \frac{d}{2} = 1.92 \times 10^{-10} \text{ m}$$

Now, Dielectric constant,

$$\varepsilon_r = 1 + 4\pi NR^3$$
$$= 1 + 4 \times \pi \times 2.7 \times 10^{25} \times (1.92 \times 10^{-10})^3$$
$$= 1 + 4\pi \times 2.7 \times 10^{-5} \times (1.92)^3$$
$$= 1 + 4\pi \times 19.11 \times 10^{-5}$$
$$\boxed{\varepsilon_r = 1.0024}$$

Example 1.2 : Calculate the electronic polarizability of argon atom $\varepsilon_r = 1.0024$ and at NTP and $N = 2.7 \times 10^{25}$ atom/m³. **[Dec. 07, May 09]**

Solution : Given : $\varepsilon_r = 1.0024$, $N = 2.7 \times 10^{25}$ atom/m³

We know that, $\quad P = \varepsilon_0 (\varepsilon_r - 1) E$

$$P = N\alpha_e \cdot E$$
$$N\alpha_e \cdot E = \varepsilon_0 (\varepsilon_r - 1) E$$
$$\alpha_e = \frac{\varepsilon_0 (\varepsilon_r - 1) E}{NE}$$
$$\boxed{\alpha_e = 7.9 \times 10^{-40} \text{ Fm}^2}$$

Example 1.3 : The number of atoms in volume of one cubic meter of hydrogen gas is 9.8×10^{26}. The radius of hydrogen atom is 0.53 Au. Calculate the polarizability and relative permittivity. **[Dec 08, 09]**

Solution : Given : $R = 0.53 \text{ Au} = 0.53 \times 10^{-10}$ m, $N = 9.8 \times 10^{26}$ atoms/m^3

Polarizability $= \alpha_e = 4\pi \varepsilon_0 R^3$
$$= 4\pi \times 8.85 \times 10^{-12} \times (0.53 \times 10^{-10})^3$$
$$\boxed{\alpha_e = 1.66 \times 10^{-41} \text{ Fm}^2}$$

Relative permittivity $= \varepsilon_r = 1 + 4\pi N R^3$
$$= 1 + 4\pi (9.8 \times 10^{-12}) \times (0.53 \times 10^{-10})^3$$
$$\boxed{\varepsilon_r = 1.008}$$

Example 1.4 : Prove that the energy stored per unit volume in polarized atom of polarizability is $\frac{1}{2} \alpha E^2$ where E is the homogeneous field applied to the material. **[Dec. 04, May 05]**

Solution : In parallel plate capacitor energy stored in polarizing the dielectric is given as,
$$\omega' = \frac{1}{2}(C - C_0)V^2$$
$$= \frac{1}{2}\left(\frac{a\varepsilon_0 \varepsilon_r}{d} - \frac{a\varepsilon_0}{d}\right)V^2 \quad \ldots (1)$$

where,
a = area of parallel plate.
d = distance between plates.
V = applied voltage.

we know that Polarization, is given by $P = \varepsilon_0 (\varepsilon_r - 1) E$

$\therefore \quad (\varepsilon_r - 1) = \dfrac{P}{\varepsilon_0 E}$

From (1),
$$\omega' = \frac{1}{2} \frac{a\varepsilon_0}{d}(\varepsilon_r - 1)V^2$$
$$= \frac{1}{2} \frac{a\varepsilon_0}{d} \frac{P}{\varepsilon_0 E} V^2$$

$$\omega' = \frac{1}{2}\varepsilon_0 V \left(\frac{V}{d}\right) \times a \times \frac{P}{E}$$

$$= \frac{1}{2}\varepsilon_0 \times V \times E \times \alpha \times \frac{P}{E}$$

$$\omega' = \frac{1}{2} \times V \times a \times P$$

Now, volume of dielectric $= a \times d \text{ m}^3$

$$\frac{\omega'}{\text{Volume}} = \frac{\frac{1}{2} V a P}{ad}$$

$$= \frac{1}{2}\left(\frac{V}{d}\right) P$$

$$= \frac{1}{2} P E$$

We know that, $P = \alpha E$

$$\frac{\omega'}{\text{Volume}} = \frac{1}{2}\alpha E^2$$

Hence Proved.

Example 1.5 : Two parallel plates $0.15 \times 0.30 \text{ m}^2$ in area are separated by a dielectric of thickness 0.06 m dielectric constant $\varepsilon_r = 5.4$ the capacitor so formed is connected to a 400 V D.C. supply. Calculate :

(i) The capacitance of the capacitor.

(ii) The charge on the plates of capacitor.

(iii) The electric field intensity in the dielectric.

(iv) Energy stored in condenser as well as energy stored in polarizing the dielectric.

[Dec. 04]

Solution : Given : $a = 0.15 \times 0.30 \text{ m}^2$, $d = 0.06$ m, $\varepsilon = 5.4$, $V = 400$ V.

(i) Capacitance, $C = \dfrac{a \varepsilon_0 \varepsilon_r}{d}$

$$= \frac{(0.15 \times 0.30) \times (8.85 \times 10^{-12}) \times 5.4}{0.06}$$

$$\boxed{C = 3.585 \times 10^{-11} \text{ F}}$$

(ii) Charge, $Q = CV$

$$= 3.585 \times 10^{-11} \times 400$$

$$\boxed{Q = 1.432 \times 10^{-8} \text{ C}}$$

(iii) Electric field intensity, $E = \dfrac{V}{d}$

$$= \dfrac{400}{0.06}$$

$$\boxed{E = 6666.67 \text{ V/m}}$$

(iv) Energy stored in condenser, $\omega = \dfrac{1}{2}CV^2$

$$= \dfrac{1}{2} \times 3.585 \times 10^{-11} \times 400^2$$

$$\boxed{\omega = 2.864 \times 10^{-6} \text{ J}}$$

We know that, $C_o = \dfrac{C}{\varepsilon_r}$

$$= \dfrac{3.585 \times 10^{-11}}{5.4}$$

$$\boxed{C_o = 0.6638 \times 10^{-11}}$$

Energy stored in polarizing the dielectric is,

$$\omega' = \dfrac{1}{2}(C - C_o)V^2$$

$$= \dfrac{1}{2}(3.585 - 0.6638) \times 10^{-11} \times 400^2$$

$$\boxed{\omega' = 2.336 \times 10^{-6} \text{ J}}$$

Example 1.6 : A solid contains 4×10^{28} atoms each having polarizability of 2.75×10^{-40} F/m^2. Assuming that internal field is given by Lorentz formula. Calculate the ratio of internal field to the applied electric field. **[Dec. 06]**

Solution : Given : $N = 4 \times 10^{28}$; $\alpha = 2.7/\text{F/m}^2$

By using Lorentz formula the internal field is given by,

$$E_i = E + \dfrac{P}{3\varepsilon_o} \qquad \ldots (1)$$

$$\text{Polarization } P = N\alpha E_i \qquad \ldots (2)$$

From equations (1) and (2),

$$E_i = E + \dfrac{N\alpha E_i}{3\varepsilon_o}$$

$$E = E_i - \frac{N \alpha E_i}{3\varepsilon_0}$$

$$E = E_i \left(1 - \frac{N\alpha}{3\varepsilon_0}\right)$$

$$\frac{E_i}{E} = \frac{1}{1 - \left(\dfrac{N\alpha}{3\varepsilon_0}\right)}$$

$$= \frac{1}{\left(1 - \dfrac{4 \times 10^{28} \times 2.75 \times 10^{-40}}{3 \times 8.85 \times 10^{-12}}\right)}$$

$$= \frac{1}{\left(1 - \dfrac{11 \times 10^{-12}}{26.55 \times 10^{-12}}\right)}$$

$$= \frac{1}{1 - 0.414} = \frac{1}{0.5856}$$

$$\boxed{\frac{E_i}{E} = 1.7076}$$

Example 1.7 : A solid contains 10×10^{28} atoms/m³ each having polarizability of 1×10^{-40} Farad m². Assuming that the internal field is given by Lorentz formula. Find the ratio of the internal to the applied field. **[May 07]**

Solution : Given :
$N = 10 \times 10^{28}$ atom/m³
$\alpha = 1 \times 10^{-40}$ Fm²

Using Lorentz formula internal field is given by,

$$E_i = E + \frac{P}{3\varepsilon_0}$$

where, $P = N \alpha E_i$

$$E_i = E + \frac{N \alpha E_i}{3\varepsilon_0}$$

$$E_i \left(1 - \frac{N\alpha}{3\varepsilon_0}\right) = E$$

$$\frac{E_i}{E} = \frac{1}{\left(1 - \dfrac{N\alpha}{3\varepsilon_0}\right)}$$

$$= \frac{1}{\left(1 - \dfrac{10 \times 10^{28} \times 1 \times 10^{-40}}{3 \times 8.85 \times 10^{-12}}\right)}$$

$$= \frac{1}{\left(1 - \frac{10 \times 10^{-12}}{26.55 \times 10^{-12}}\right)}$$

$$\boxed{\frac{E_i}{E} = 1.6042}$$

Example 1.8 : When sodium chloride crystal is subjected to an electric field of 1000 V/m, the resultant polarization is 4.3×10^{-8} C/m². Calculate the relative permittivity of sodium chloride crystal.

[Dec. 07]

Solution : Given :
$$E = 1000 \text{ V/m}$$
$$\alpha = 4.3 \times 10^{-8} \text{ c/m}^2$$

Polarization, $\quad P = \varepsilon_0 (\varepsilon_r - 1) E$

$$(\varepsilon_r - 1) = \frac{P}{\varepsilon_0 E}$$

$$\varepsilon_r = 1 + \frac{P}{\varepsilon_0 E}$$

$$= 1 + \frac{4.3 \times 10^{-8}}{8.85 \times 10^{-12} \times 1000}$$

$$\boxed{\varepsilon_r = 5.86}$$

Example 1.9 : A solid contains 7×10^{26} identical atoms/m² each with polarizability of 2×10^{-38} farad m². Assuming that internal field is given by Lorentz formula. Calculate the ratio of internal field to the applied field.

[May 08]

Solution : Given :
$$E = 7 \times 10^{26} \text{ atoms/m}^2$$
$$\alpha = 2 \times 10^{-38} \text{ Fm}^2$$

The internal field using Lorentz formula is given by,

$$E_i = E + \frac{P}{3\varepsilon_0}$$

where, $\quad P = N \alpha E_i$

$$E_i = E + \frac{N \alpha E_i}{3\varepsilon_0}$$

$$E_i \left(1 - \frac{N\alpha}{3\varepsilon_0}\right) = E$$

$$\frac{E_i}{E} = \frac{1}{\left(1 - \frac{N\alpha}{3\varepsilon_0}\right)}$$

$$= \cfrac{1}{\left(1 - \cfrac{7 \times 10^{26} \times 2 \times 10^{-38}}{3 \times 8.85 \times 10^{-12}}\right)}$$

$$\boxed{\dfrac{E_i}{E} = 2.1155}$$

Example 1.10 : A parallel plate has capacitance of 5 µF. The dielectric has permittivity $\varepsilon_r = 100$; for an applied voltage of 2000 V. Find energy stored in capacitor as well as energy stored in polarizing the dielectric. **[Dec. 08]**

Solution : Given :
$C = 5\,\mu F$
$\varepsilon_r = 100$
$V = 2000\,V$

Energy stored in capacitor,

$$\omega = \tfrac{1}{2} CV^2$$

$$= \tfrac{1}{2} \times 5 \times 10^{-6} \times (2000)^2$$

$$\boxed{\omega = 10\,J}$$

$$C_o = \dfrac{C}{\varepsilon_r}$$

$$= \dfrac{5}{100}\,\mu F$$

$$\boxed{C_o = 0.05 \times 10^{-6}\,F}$$

Energy stored in polarizing the dielectric,

$$\omega' = \tfrac{1}{2} (C - C_o) \cdot V^2$$

$$= \tfrac{1}{2} (5 - 0.05) \times 10^{-6} \times (2000)^2$$

$$\boxed{\omega' = 9.9\,J}$$

Example 1.11 : A solid contains 6×10^{28} atom each having polarizability of $2.85 \times 10^{-40}\,F\,m^2$. Assuming that internal field is given by Lorentz formula. Calculate ratio of internal field to the applied electric field. **[Dec. 08]**

Solution : Given :
$N = 6 \times 10^{28}$ atom
$\alpha = 2.85 \times 10^{-40}\,Fm^2$

We know that,

$$E_i = E + \frac{P}{3\varepsilon_o}$$

Polarization, $\quad P = N \alpha E_i$

$$E_i = E + \frac{N \alpha E_i}{3\varepsilon_o}$$

$$\frac{E_i}{E} = \frac{1}{1 - \frac{N\alpha}{3\varepsilon_o}}$$

$$= \frac{1}{\left(1 - \frac{6 \times 10^{28} \times 2.85 \times 10^{-40}}{3 \times 8.85 \times 10^{-12}}\right)}$$

$$\boxed{\frac{E_i}{E} = 2.8095}$$

Example 1.12 : If sodium chloride crystal is subjected to an electric field of 2000 V/m the resultant polarization is 4.3×10^{-8} C/m². Calculate the relative permittivity of sodium chloride crystal. **[May 09]**

Solution : Given :
$\quad P = 4.3 \times 10^{-8}$ C/m²
$\quad E = 2000$ V/m

Polarization, $\quad P = \varepsilon_o (\varepsilon_r - 1) E$

$$(\varepsilon_r - 1) = \frac{P}{\varepsilon_o E}$$

$$\varepsilon_r = 1 + \frac{P}{\varepsilon_o E}$$

$$\varepsilon_r = 1 + \frac{4.3 \times 10^{-8}}{(8.85 \times 10^{-12}) \times 2000}$$

$$\boxed{\varepsilon_r = 3.429}$$

Example 1.13 : The number of atoms in volume of one cubic meter of hydrogen gas is 9.8×10^{26}. The radius of hydrogen atom is 0.53 Au. Calculate the polarizability and relative permittivity. **[Dec 08, 09]**

Solution : Given : $\quad N = 9.8 \times 10^{26}$, $T = 0.53$ Au

Polarizability $\quad 2e = 4\pi\varepsilon_o R^3$
$$= 4 \times \pi \times 8.85 \times 10^{-12} \times (0.53 \times 10^{-10})^3$$

$$\boxed{2e = 1.66 \times 10^{-41} \text{ Fm}^2}$$

Relative permittivity $= 1 + 4\pi N R^3$
$$= 1 + 4\pi \times (9.8 \times 10^{-12}) \times (0.53 \times 10^{-10})^3$$

$$\boxed{\varepsilon_r = 1.008}$$

Example 1.14 : If sodium chloride crystal is subjected to an electric field of 2000 V/m and the resultant polarization is 4.8×10^{-8} C/m². Calculate the relative permittivity of sodium chloride.

[May 10]

Solution : Given : E = 2000 V/m, P = 4.8×10^{-8} C/m²

We know that $P = \varepsilon_0 (\varepsilon_r - 1) E$

$$\frac{P}{\varepsilon_0 E} = \varepsilon_r - 1$$

$$\varepsilon_r = 1 + \frac{P}{\varepsilon_0 E}$$

$$\varepsilon_r = 1 + \frac{4.8 \times 10^{-8}}{8.85 \times 10^{-12} \times 2000}$$

$$\boxed{\varepsilon_r = 3.71}$$

Example 1.15 : A parallel plate has capacitance of 5 μF. The dielectric has permittivity ε_r = 100 for an applied voltage of 1000 V. Find (i) Energy stored in the capacitor (ii) The energy stored in polarizing electric.

[May 11]

Solution : Given : ε_r = 100, V = 1000 V, C = 5 μF.

Energy stored in capacitor is given as,

$$\omega = \frac{1}{2} CV^2$$

$$= \frac{1}{2} \times 5 \times 10^{-6} \times 1000^2$$

$$\boxed{\omega = 2.5 \text{ J}}$$

$$C_0 = \frac{C}{\varepsilon_r}$$

$$= \frac{5}{100} \times 10^{-6}$$

$$\boxed{C_0 = 0.05 \times 10^{-6} \text{ F}}$$

Energy stored in polarizing the dielectric,

$$\omega' = \frac{1}{2} (C - C_0) V^2$$

$$= \frac{1}{2} (5 - 0.05) \times 10^{-6} \times 1000^2$$

$$\boxed{\omega' = 2.475 \text{ J}}$$

Example 1.16 : A slid contains 4×10^{28} atoms each having polarizability of 2.75×10^{-40} F/m². Assuming that internal field is given by Lorentz formula. Calculate the ratio of internal field to the applied field.

Solution : **Given :** $N = 4 \times 10^{28}$ atoms., $\alpha = 2.75 \times 10^{-40}$ F/m².

We know that,

$$E_i = E + \frac{P}{3\varepsilon_0}$$

Where, $P = N \alpha E_i$

$$\therefore \quad E_i = E + \frac{N \alpha E_i}{3\varepsilon_0}$$

$$E_i \left(1 - \frac{N\alpha}{3\varepsilon_0}\right) = E$$

$$\frac{E_i}{E} = \frac{1}{\left(1 - \frac{N\alpha}{3\varepsilon_0}\right)}$$

$$= \frac{1}{1 - \frac{4 \times 10^{28} \times 2.75 \times 10^{-40}}{3 \times 8.85 \times 10^{-12}}}$$

$$\boxed{\frac{E_i}{E} = 1.70}$$

Example 1.17 : Calculate the electronic polarizability of argon atom if $\varepsilon_r = 1.0024$ at NTP and $N = 2.8 \times 10^{25}$ atom/m². **[May 11, Dec. 11]**

Solution : **Given :** $\varepsilon_e = 1.0023$, $N = 2.8 \times 10^{25}$ atom/m²

We know that, $P = \varepsilon_0 (\varepsilon_r - 1) E$

also, $P = N \alpha_e E$

$$N \alpha_e E = \varepsilon_0 (\varepsilon_r - 1) E$$

$$\alpha_o = \frac{\varepsilon_0 (\varepsilon_r - 1)}{N}$$

$$= \frac{8.85 \times 10^{-12} (1.0024 - 1)}{2.8 \times 10^{25}}$$

$$\alpha_e = 0.007585 \times 10^{-37}$$

$$\boxed{\alpha_e = 7.58 \times 10^{-40} \text{ Fm}^2}$$

REVIEW QUESTIONS

1. Prove that $\rho = \varepsilon_0(\varepsilon_r - 1) E$
2. Define and explain :
   (i) Piezoelectricity
   (ii) Ferroelectricity
   (iii) Relative permittivity
   (iv) Dielectric loss and loss tangent
   (v) Polarization
3. Explain different types of polarization.
4. Explain construction of photo emissive cell.
5. Explain photo conductive cell.
6. Explain PV module.

UNIVERSITY QUESTIONS

May 2008

1. Explain loss tangent and its significance. **(4 Marks)**
2. Write note on piezo electricity. **(4 Marks)**
3. Explain term polarization of dielectric. Explain electronic polarization and orientation polarization. **(8 Marks)**
4. Define : **(4 Marks)**
   (i) Electric Dipole moment
   (ii) Dielectric constant
   (iii) Electric flux density
   (iv) Polarizability

Dec. 2008

5. Derive Clausius Mosotti equation from the first principle applied to dielectric materials. Give Debye's generalization of this relation stating the assumptions to make to draw the relation. **(8 Marks)**
6. Explain : **(6 Marks)**
   (i) Ferro electricity
   (ii) Loss tangent and its significance
7. What is meant by loss tangent as referred to polar directions. Hence give this significance. **(4 Marks)**

May 2009

8. Define: **(8 Marks)**
   (i) Electric dipole moment
   (ii) Dielectric constant
   (iii) Polarizability
   (iv) Pyro electricity

9. Derive Clausius Mosotti equation from the first principle applied to dielectric materials stating the assumptions made to draw the relation. **(8 Marks)**

Dec. 2009

10. Derive Clausius Mosotti equation from the first principle applied to dielectric materials stating the assumptions made to draw the relation. **(8 Marks)**

11. Write a note on piezoelectricity. **(4 Marks)**

May 2010

12. Drive Clausius Mossotti relation from first principle applied to dielectric materials stating the assumptions made to draw the relation. **(8 Marks)**

13. Explain the following: **(12 Marks)**
    (a) Loss tangent and its significance
    (b) Ferro-electricity
    (c) Piezo-electricity

14. If sodium chloride crystal is subjected to an electric field of 2000 V/m and the resultant polarization is 4.8×10^{-8} c/m². Calculate the relative permittivity of sodium chloride. **(4 Marks)**

Dec. 2010

15. Describe the polarization process in detail. Why and how does it occurs? **(8 Marks)**

16. Explain ionic polarization in detail. How is it different from oriental polarization?
    (8 Marks)

May 2011

17. Explain the term polarisation. With neat diagram explain electronic polarisation.
    (6 Marks)

18. Explain the following terms: **(6 Marks)**
    (i) Loss tangent
    (ii) Ferro-electricity

19. A parallel plate has capacitance of 5 µF. The dielectric has permittivity $\varepsilon_r = 100$, for an applied voltage of 1000 V.

Find :
(i) Energy stored in the capacitor
(ii) The energy stored in polarising the dielectric **(6 Marks)**

20. A solid contains 4×10^{28} atoms each having polarizability of 2.75×10^{-40} F/m². Assuming that internal field is given by Lorentz formula. Calculate the ratio of internal field to the applied field. **(4 Marks)**

21. Calculate the electronic polarizability of argon atom if ϵ_r = 1.0024 at NTP and N = 2.8×10^{25} atoms per m³. **(4 Marks)**

Dec. 2011

22. Derive Clausius-Mosotti relation from the first principle applied to dielectric materials. State the assumptions. **(8 Marks)**

23. What is meant by loss tangent as referred to polar dielectrics? Give its significance. **(4 Marks)**

24. Explain the following : **(8 Marks)**
    (i) Ferro-electricity
    (ii) Electronic polarization

25. Calculate the electronic polarizability of ARgon atom. Given ε_r = 1.0024 at NTP and N = 2.8×10^{25} atoms/m³. **(4 Marks)**

May 2012

26. Explain the following terms : **(6 Marks)**
    (i) Electric Dipole Moment
    (ii) Dielectric constant
    (iii) Ferroelectricity

27. Explain the term 'polarization' of dielectric. With neat diagram, explain Electronic Polarization and Orientational Polarization. **(8 Marks)**

28. Write a note on piezoelectricity and pyroelectricity. **(8 Marks)**

Dec. 2012

29. Explain orientation polarization in detail. How is it different than ionic polarization? **(9 Marks)**

Chapter 2
OPTICAL PROPERTIES OF MATERIALS AND CELLS USED FOR POWER GENERATION

2.1 PHOTOELECTRIC EMISSION

Q. What is photoelectric emission ?
Q. What is the law of photoelectric emission ?

Electrons can be emitted from solids under irradiation with photons of sufficiently low wavelength. This process, called photoelectron emission, this played a key role as experimental support for quantum mechanics. Photoelectrons are emitted when a single photon of energy 'hv' is absorbed by the solid, where h is known as Planck's constant and v the frequency of the light used. The energy of the photon must be larger than the energy separation between the top of the valence band. At low temperatures and in metals, this energy is denoted as work function. For non-metals, electrons may exist in the band gap. Thus, in semiconductors, the photoelectric threshold or minimum photon energy is usually larger than the work function. In insulators, the Fermi level is not defined in practice, so the photoelectron threshold is just the energy between the most weakly bound electron state usually known as a band-gap state and the vacuum level. For metals at any finite temperature, there will be electrons in the conduction band above the Fermi level. Because the photon carries essentially no momentum, photoelectron emission cannot result in the "free-electron" model. This is because when a free electron absorbs energy from the photon, its momentum also increases. For the process to be achievable, a third body must absorb the momentum which is most likely participant is the lattice.

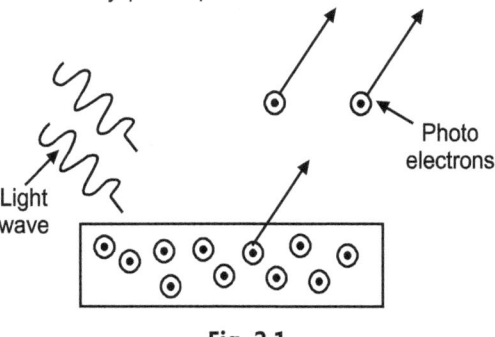

Fig. 2.1

The photoelectric effect is the observation that many metals emit electrons when light shines upon them. Electrons emitted in this manner may be called as photoelectrons.

2.2 THE LAWS OF PHOTO-ELECTRIC EMISSION

There are three laws of Photo-Electric Emission.

(1) The number of electrons emitted per second is directly proportional to the intensity of the radiation.

(2) The maximum kinetic energy of the electrons emitted is increases with the frequency of the radiation.

(3) There is a minimum frequency below which no emission occurs. The minimum frequency for photo-electric emission is called the threshold frequency, f_o which is shown in Fig. 2.2.

A graph of K.E.$_{max}$ of photo-electrons against frequency of radiation has the following form.

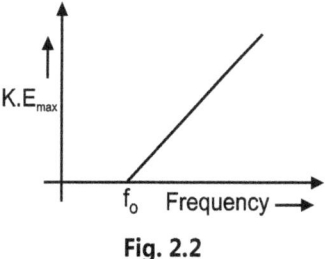

Fig. 2.2

2.3 PHOTOCONDUCTIVITY

> **Q.** Write short note on photo conductivity.
> **Q.** What is photoconductivity and its applications ?

Photoconductivity is an optical and electrical phenomenon in which a material becomes more electrically conductive due to the absorption of electromagnetic radiation such as visible light, ultraviolet light(UV), infrared light, or gamma radiation. When light is absorbed by a material such as a semiconductor, the number of free electrons and pair of electron holes increases and raises its electrical conductivity. To cause excitation, the light that strikes the semiconductor must have enough energy to raise electrons across the band gap. examples of photoconductive materials include the conductive polymer poly-vinylcarbazole, used extensively in photocopying, lead sulfide, used in infrared detection applications. According to electromagnetic theory, this effect can be attributed to the transfer of energy from the light to an electron in the metal. The photons of a light beam have a energy proportional to the frequency of the light. In the photoemission process, if an electron within some material absorbs the energy of one photon and acquires more energy than the work function of the material. If the photon energy is too low, the electron is unable to escape the material. Since an increase in the intensity of low-frequency light will only increase the number of low-energy photons sent over a given interval of time, this change in intensity will not create any single photon with enough energy to dislodge the electron. Thus, the energy of the emitted electrons does not depend on the intensity of the incoming light, but only on the energy of the individual photons. It is an relations between the incident photon and the outermost electrons. Electrons can absorb energy from photons when irradiated. All of the energy from one photon must be absorbed and used to liberate one electron from atomic binding of material, or else the energy is re-emitted. If the photon energy is absorbed, some of the energy liberates the electron from the atom in materials, and the rest contributes to the electron's kinetic energy as a free particle. From this perception, an alteration in either the amplitude or wavelength of light would induce changes in the rate of emission of electrons from the metal. Furthermore, according to this theory, a sufficiently dim light would be expected to show a lag time between the initial shining of its light and the subsequent emission of an electron. However, the experimental results did not associate with either of the two predictions made by this theory.

2.3.1 Applications

When a photoconductive material is connected as part of a circuit, it functions as a resistor whose resistance depends on the light intensity. In this context the material is called a photoresistor it also called light-dependent resistor or photoconductor. The most common application of photoresistors is as photodetectors, i.e. devices that measure light intensity. Photodetector other types include CCDs, photodiodes and phototransistors but they are among the most common photodetectors. Some photodetector applications in which photoresistors are mostly used include camera light meters, street lights, clock radios, and infrared detectors.

2.4 THE PHOTO-EMISSIVE CELL

Q. Write short note on operating principle of photo-emissive cell.
Q. Explain photo-emissive cells with its application.

A phototube or photoelectric cell is a type of gas-filled or vacuum tube that is sensitive to light. Such a tube are called as 'photoemissive cell'. Phototubes were previously more widely used but are now replaced in many applications by solid state photodetectors. The photomultiplier tube, which is one of the most sensitive light detectors, and is still widely used in physics research.

2.4.1 Operating Principles

Phototubes operate according to the photoelectric effect. The photo emissive cell consists of a glass envelope with a vacuum inside of it. The cover also contains a light sensitive cathode and an anode. When light strikes the cathode negative electrons are emitted and are attracted by the positive anode. Thus, current flow is dependent on the frequency and intensity of incoming photons. No amplification takes place in between, so the current that flows through the device is typically of the order of a few microamperes.

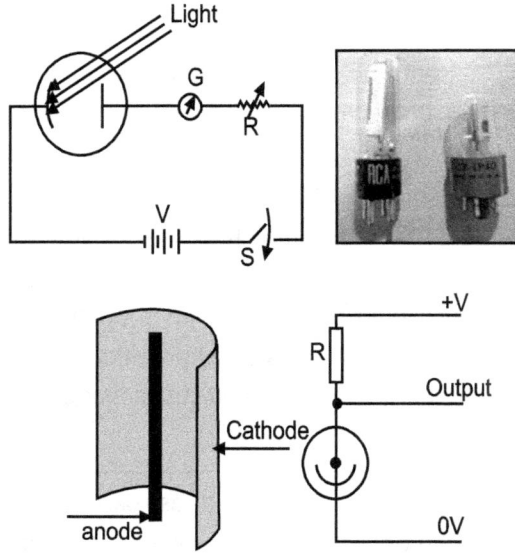

Fig. 2.3 : Photo-emissive Cell

The light wavelength range over which the device is sensitive depends on the material used for the photoemissive cathode. A caesium-antimony cathode gives a device that is very sensitive in the violet to ultra-violet region with sensitivity falling off to blindness to red light. Caesium on oxidised silver gives a cathode that is most sensitive to infra-red to red light, falling off towards blue, where the sensitivity is low but not zero.

Vacuum devices have a nearly constant anode current for a given level of illumination relative to anode voltage. Gas filled devices are more sensitive but the frequency response to modulated illumination falls below at lower frequencies compared to the vacuum devices. The frequency response of vacuum devices is generally limited by the transit time of the electrons from cathode to anode.

2.4.2 Applications

One of the major applications of the phototube is the reading of optical sound tracks for projected films. Phototubes are used in a variety of light-sensing applications until they were superseded.

2.5 THE PHOTOCONDUCTIVE CELL

> Q. What is photoconductive cell ?
> Q. Explain construction of photoconductive cells.

The photoconductive cell is a two terminal semiconductor device whose terminal resistance will vary with the intensity of the incident light. it is frequently called a photoresistive device. The photoconductive materials include cadmium sulphide (CdS) and cadmium selenide (CdSe). Both materials respond rather slowly to changes in light intensity. The peak spectral response time of CdS units is about 100 ms and 10 ms for CdSe cells. Another important difference between the two materials is their temperature sensitivity.

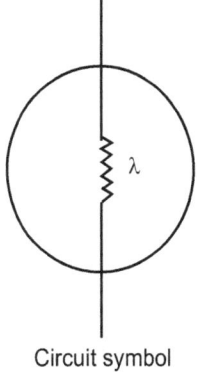

Circuit symbol

Fig. 2.4 : Photoconductive cell circuit symbol

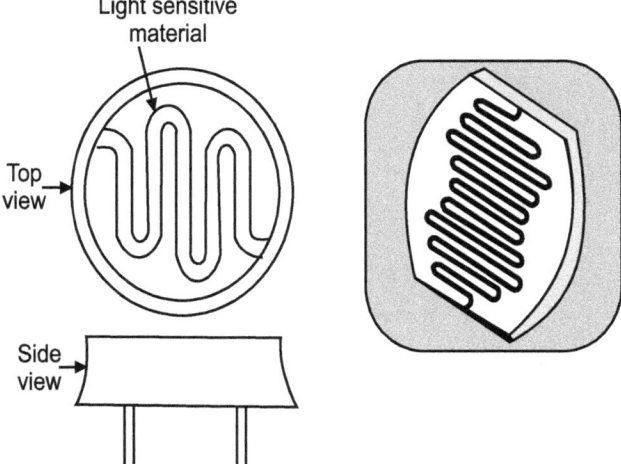

Fig. 2.5 : Photoconductive cell construction

There is large change in the resistance of a cadmium selenide cell with changes in ambient temperature, but the resistance of cadmium sulphide remains relatively stable with changes in ambient temperature. The spectral response of a cadmium sulphide cell closely matches that of the human eye, and the cell is therefore often used in applications where human vision is a important factor, such as street light control or automatic iris control for cameras. The essential elements of a photoconductive cell are the ceramic substrate, a layer of photo conductive material, metallic electrodes to connect the device into a circuit. The circuit symbol and construction of a typical photoconductive cell are as shown Fig. 2.5.

Light sensitive material is arranged in the form of a long strip, zigzagged across a disc shaped base with protective sides. For more protection, a glass or plastic cover may be included. The two ends of the strip are brought out to connecting pins below the base.

2.5.1 Photoconductive Cell Circuit

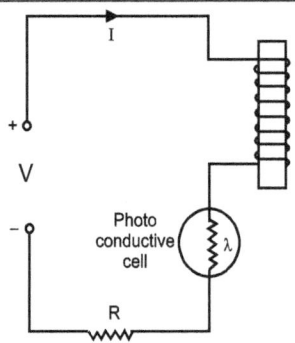

Fig. 2.6 : Photoconductive cell circuit

2.5.2 Characteristics of a Photoconductive Cell

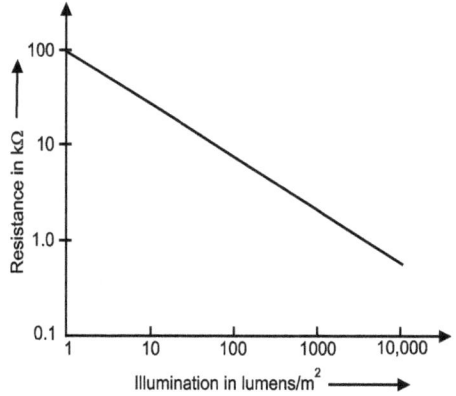

Fig. 2.7 : Photoconductive cell characteristics

The illumination characteristics of a typical photoconductive cell are shown from which it is obvious that when the cell is not illuminated its resistance may be more than 100 kilo ohms. This resistance is called the dark resistance. When the cell is illuminated, the resistance may drop to a few hundred ohms. Note that the scales on the illumination characteristic are logarithmic to cover a wide range of resistance and illumination that are possible. Cell sensitivity is expressed in terms of the cell current for a given voltage and given level of illumination. The major drawback of the photoconductive cells is that temperature variations cause substantial variations in resistance for a substantial variation in resistance for a particular light intensity. Therefore such a cell is unsuitable for analog applications. The photoconductive cell used for relay control is shown as circuit above. When the cell is illuminated, its resistance is low and the relay current is maximum. When the cell is dark, its high resistance reduces the current down to a level too low to energize the relay. Resistance R is included to limit the relay current to the desired level when the resistance of the cell is low. Photoconductive cells are used to switch transistors on and off, as illustrated in figure 2.6. When the cell shown in figure 2.6 is dark, the transistor base is biased above its emitter level, and the device is turned on. When the cell is illuminated, the lower resistance of the cell in series with R biases the transistor base voltage below its emitter level. Thus, the device is turn off.

2.6 PHOTOVOLTAIC TECHNOLOGY

- **Q.** Short note on photovoltaic cell.
- **Q.** What are the materials use of photovoltaic cells ?
- **Q.** Explain mathematical model of photovoltaic cells.

Sunlight is composed of packets of energy, called photons. The photon is the basic unit of light and other electromagnetic radiation. Photons contain various amount of energy corresponding to the different wavelengths of light. The energy can be expressed by the equation

$$E = h\nu$$

Where, h is Planck's constant and ν is the photon's frequency. As the wavelength of light increases, the photon energy of that light decreases.

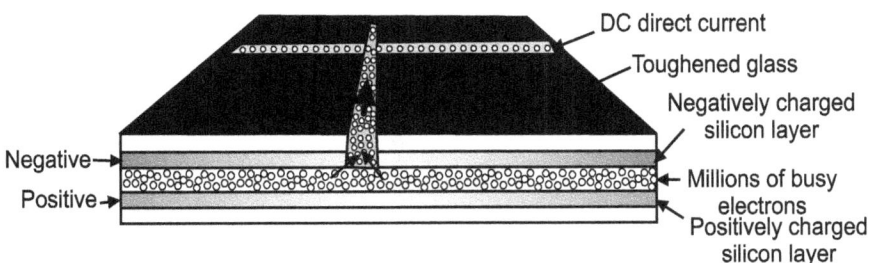

Fig. 2.8

Photovoltaic (PV) cells are made up of two semi-conductor layers. One layer containing a positive charge and the other a negative charge. As a PV cell is exposed to this sunlight, many of the photons are reflected, pass right through, or absorbed by the solar cell. When enough photons are absorbed by the negative layer of the photovoltaic cell, electrons are freed from the negative semiconductor material. Due to the manufacturing process of the positive layer, these freed electrons naturally travel to the positive layer creating a voltage differential, similar to a household battery. When the two layers are connected to an external load, the electrons flow through the circuit. Each individual solar energy cell produces only 1 or 2 watts. To increase power output, cells are combined in a weather-tight package called a solar module. These modules are then wired up in serial and/or parallel with one another called a solar array, to create the desired voltage and amperage output required. This is shown in Fig. 2.10.

2.6.1 Mathematical Modeling of Photovoltaic Module

The symbols used in Fig. 2.9 are abbreviated as follows:

I_{ph} : Photocurrent
I_d : Current through parallel diode
I_{sh} : Shunt current
I : Output current
V : Output voltage
D : Parallel diode
R_{sh} : Shunt resistance
R_s : Series resistance

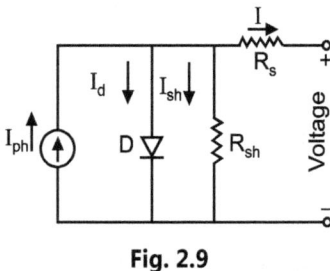

Fig. 2.9

The basic equation from the theory of semiconductors that mathematically describes the I–V characteristic of the ideal PV cell is

$$I = I_{ph} - I_0 \left\{ e^{\frac{q(V + R_s I)}{AKT}} - 1 \right\} - \frac{V + R_s I}{R_{sh}}$$

Where,

I_0 is the reverse saturation current of the diode,

q is the electron charge (1.602×10^{-19} C),

A is the curve fitting factor,

K is Boltzmann constant (1.38×10^{-23} J/K)

2.6.2 Cell Modular Array PV

A complete PV system consists not only of PV modules, but also the "balance of system" (BOS) the support structures, wiring, storage, conversion devices, etc. i.e. everything else in a PV system except the PV modules. Two major types of PV systems are available in the market today flat plate and concentrators. As the most prevalent type of PV systems, flat plate systems build the PV modules on a rigid and flat surface to capture sunlight.

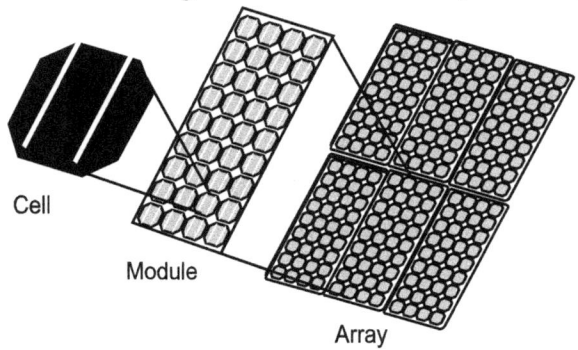

Fig. 2.10

Concentrator systems use lenses to concentrate sunlight on the PV cells and increase the cell power output. Flat plate systems are typically less complicated but employ a larger number of cells while the concentrator systems use smaller areas of cells but require more sophisticated and expensive tracking systems. Unable to focus diffuse sunlight, concentrator systems do not work under cloudy conditions.

2.7 TYPES OF PV CELL MATERIALS

PV cells are made of semiconductor materials. The major types of materials are crystalline and thin films, which vary from each other in terms of light absorption efficiency, energy conversion efficiency, manufacturing technology and cost of production.

2.7.1 Crystalline Materials

Single-Crystal Silicon

Single-crystal silicon cells are the most common in the PV. The main technique for producing single-crystal silicon is the Czochralski (CZ) method. in this High-purity polycrystalline is melted in a quartz crucible. A single-crystal silicon seed is dipped into this molten mass of polycrystalline. As the seed is pulled slowly from the melt, a single-crystal slab is formed. slab is also known as ingots. The ingots are then sawed into thin wafers about 200-400 micrometers thick (1 micrometre = 1/1,000,000 metre). The thin wafers are then polished, doped, coated, interconnected and assembled into modules and arrays. A single-crystal silicon has a uniform molecular structure. Compared to non crystalline materials, its high uniformity results in higher energy conversion efficiency, the ratio of electric power produced by the cell to the amount of available sunlight power i.e. power-out divided by power-in. The higher a PV cell's conversion efficiency, the more electricity it generates for a given area of exposure to the light. The conversion efficiency for single-silicon commercial modules ranges between 15-20%. Not only are they energy efficient, single-silicon modules are highly reliable for outdoor power applications. More than half of the manufacturing cost comes from wafering, a time-consuming and costly batch process in which ingots are cut into thin wafers with a thickness not less than 200 micrometres thick. If the wafers are too thin, the entire wafer will break in wafering and subsequent processing. Due to this thickness requirement, a PV cell requires a significant amount of raw silicon and half of this expensive material is lost as sawdust in wafering process.

Polycrstalline Silicon

Consisting of small grains of single-crystal silicon, polycrystalline PV cells are less energy efficient than single-crystalline silicon PV cells. A common method to produce polycrystalline silicon PV cells is to slice thin wafers from blocks of cast polycrystalline silicon. Another advanced approach is the "ribbon growth" method in which silicon is grown directly as thin ribbons or sheets with the approach thickness for making PV cells. Since no sawing is needed, the manufacturing cost is lower. The most commercially developed ribbon growth approach is Edge-defined Film-fed Growth (EFG). Compared to single-crystalline silicon, polycrystalline silicon material is stronger and can be cut into one-third the thickness of single-crystal material. It also has slightly lower wafer cost and less strict growth requirements. However, their lower manufacturing cost is offset by the lower cell efficiency.

Gallium Arsenide (GaAs)

A compound semiconductor made of two elements: gallium (Ga) and arsenic (As). GaAs has a crystal structure similar to that of silicon. An advantage of GaAs is that it is having high level of light absorptivity. To absorb the same amount of sunlight, GaAs requires only a layer of few micrometers thick while crystalline silicon requires a wafer of about 200-300 micrometers thick. GaAs has much higher energy conversion efficiency than crystal silicon. GaAs is also popular in space applications where strong resistance radiation damage and also high cell efficiency are required. The biggest drawback of GaAs PV cells is the high cost of the single-crystal substrate that GaAs is grown on. Therefore, it is mostly used in concentrator systems where only a small area of GaAs cells is needed.

2.7.2 Thin Film Materials

In a thin-film PV cell, a thin semiconductor layer of PV materials is deposited on low-cost supporting layer such as glass, metal or plastic foil. Since thin-film materials have higher light more absorptive than crystalline materials, the deposited layer of PV materials is extremely thin, from a few micrometers to even less than a micrometer for example a single amorphous cell can be as thin as 0.3 micrometers. Thinner layers of material yield significant cost saving. Also, the deposition techniques in which PV materials are sprayed directly onto glass or metal substrate are cheaper. So the manufacturing process is faster, and mass production is easier than the ingot-growth approach of crystalline silicon. But, thin film PV cells suffer from poor cell conversion efficiency due to non-single crystal structure, requiring larger array areas. Increasing area associated costs such as mountings. Materials used for thin film PV modules are as follows.

Amorphous Silicon (a-Si)

Used mostly in electronic products which require lower power output amorphous silicon is a non-crystalline form of silicon i.e. its silicon atoms are disordered in structure. A significant advantage of a-Si is its high light absorptive, about 40 times higher than that of single-crystal silicon. Therefore, only a thin layer of a-Si is sufficient for making PV cells of about 1 micrometer thick as compared to 200 or more micrometers thick for crystalline silicon cells. Also, a-Si can be deposited on various low-cost substrates such as steel, glass and plastic, and the manufacturing process requires lower temperatures and thus less energy. So the total material costs and manufacturing costs are lesser per unit area as compared to those of crystalline silicon cells. It has low cell energy conversion efficiency and the other is the outdoor reliability problem in which the efficiency degrades within a few months of exposure to sunlight.

Cadmium Telluride (CdTe)

As a polycrystalline semiconductor compound made of cadmium and tellurium, CdTe has a high light absorptive level only about a micrometer thick can absorb 90% of the solar spectrum. Another advantage is that it is relatively easy and cheap to manufacture by various processes such as high-rate evaporation, spraying or screen printing. The conversion efficiency for a CdTe commercial module is much similar to that of a-Si. The instability of cell and module performance is one of the major drawbacks of using CdTe for PV cells. Another disadvantage is that cadmium is a very toxic substance. even though very little cadmium is used in CdTe modules, extra precautions have to be taken in manufacturing process.

2.7.3 Copper Indium Diselenide (CuInSe$_2$, or CIS)

A polycrystalline semiconductor compound of copper, indium and selenium, CIS has been one of the most important research areas in the thin film industry. The reason for it to receive so much attention is that CIS has the highest energy conversion efficiency which is not only the best among all the existing thin film materials, but also came close to the efficiency of the polycrystalline silicon PV cells. Being able to deliver such high energy conversion efficiency without suffering from the outdoor degradation problem, CIS has demonstrated that thin film PV cells are a viable and competitive choice for the solar upcoming industry. CIS is an efficient but complex material. Its complexity makes it difficult to manufacture. Also, safety issues might be another concern in the manufacturing process.

2.8 ADVANTAGES AND DISADVANTAGES OF PV CELL

Q. Give the Advantages and Disadvantages of PV cell.

Advantages :

- The solar energy source is the sun. It is free, sustainable and will never run out.
- No pollution, it doesn't produce carbon dioxide.
- No mechanical moving parts, no noise, as it directs conversion of solar radiation into electricity.
- PV modules have a long lifetime it do not detonate with time.
- Its power out put ranges from microwatts to megawatts.

Disadvantages :

- Toxic chemicals, like cadmium and arsenic, are used in the PV production process but these environmental impacts are minor and can be easily controlled through recycling and proper disposal.
- Solar energy is somewhat more expensive to produce than conventional sources of energy due in part to the cost of manufacturing PV devices and in part to the conversion efficiencies of the equipment.
- Solar power is a variable energy source, with energy production dependent on the sun.
- Solar facilities may produce no power at all some of the time like night time, which could lead to an energy shortage if too much of a region's power come from solar power.

UNIVERSITY QUESTIONS

May 2008

1. State Different types of photoelectric cells. Describe with neat diagram construction and working of a photo voltaic cell. **(8 Marks)**

Dec. 2008

2. State different types of photoelectric cells. Describe with neat diagram construction and working of a photo voltaic cell. **(8 Marks)**

3. With neat diagram, explain construction and working of photovoltaic cell. **(8 Marks)**

May 2009

4. State different types of photoelectric cells. Describe with neat diagram construction and working of a photo voltaic cell. **(8 Marks)**

Dec. 2009

5. With neat diagram, explain construction and working of photovoltaic cell. **(8 Marks)**

May 2010

6. State different types of photoelectric cells. Describe the construction, operating principle and applications of photovoltaic cell. **(8 Marks)**

Dec. 2010

7. Differentiate between photoconductive and photoemissive cells. **(8 Marks)**

8. Write different materials used for photovoltaic materials. Describe the construction and working principle of photovoltaic cell. **(8 Marks)**

May 2011

9. With neat diagram explain construction and working of photoconductive cell. **(6 Marks)**

Dec. 2011

10. Write different materials used for photovoltaic cell. With neat sketch describe its construction and working principle. **(8 Marks)**

May 2012

11. Explain the following terms : Photoconductivity. **(2 Marks)**

12. State different types of photoelectric cells. Describe with neat diagram, construction and working of any one type. **(8 Marks)**

Dec. 2012

13. Differentiate between photoconductive and photoemissive cells. **(9 Marks)**

14. Write different materials used for photovoltaic cell. Describe its construction and working principle. **(9 Marks)**

✵ ✵ ✵

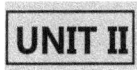

Chapter 3
INSULATING MATERIALS, PROPERTIES AND APPLICATION

3.1 INTRODUCTION

Most substances fall into one of two classes: conductor or insulator. Conductors permit the passage of charge or heat through them, while insulators do not. Associated with the atoms of materials, there is an outer band of electrons called the valence band apart from conduction and insulation bond. When these outer valence electrons can easily become detached from the nucleus and can move freely, the material is said to be a conductor. in an insulator, there are no, or at most very few, free electrons. The actual conductance happens when the electrons change energy levels, or move from one valence band to another. If there are no nearby empty levels, then the electron will not be able to gain any energy and the material behaves like an insulator. These materials have very high resistivity i.e. offers a very high resistance to the flow of electric current. Insulating materials plays an important part in various electrical and electronic circuits. In domestic wiring, insulating material protect us from shock and also prevent leakage current to flow.

Resistivity :

Resistivity is the resistance between the two opposite faces of a cube having each side equal to one meter. Resistivity of conductors is 10^{-8} to 10^{-3} ohm-m, insulators is 10^{10-20} ohm-m, semiconductors is $100^{-0.5}$ ohm-m. So, insulating material offers a wide range of uses in various engineering applications.

Factors affecting selection of an insulating material :

1. **Operating condition :** Before selecting an insulating material for a particular application the selection should be made on the basis of operating temperature, magnitude of voltage and current and pressure.
2. **Easy in shaping :** Shape and size is also important affect.
3. **Availability of material :** The material is easily available.
4. **Cost :** Cost is also a important factor.

    Knowledge of various types of insulating materials is the most powerful tool in selection of right insulating material for proper use.

3.2 PROPERTIES OF INSULATING MATERIALS

> Q. Explain properties of insulating materials.
> Q. Write short notes on :
>   (a) Electrical properties of insulating materials.
>   (b) Chemical properties of insulating materials.
> Q. Explain classification of insulating materials based on temperature.

- Electrical properties
- Thermal properties
- Chemical properties
- Physical/Mechanical properties

3.2.1 Electrical Properties

- Insulation resistance or resistivity
- Dielectric strength or breakdown voltage
- Dielectric constant
- Dielectric loss

Insulation resistance

The resistance offered to the flow of electric current through the material is called insulation resistance. Insulation resistance is of two types :

- Volume insulation resistance.
- Surface insulation resistance.

Volume resistance and resistivity

The resistance offered to current I_v which flows through the material is called volume insulation resistance. For a cube of unit dimensions this is called volume resistivity. As shown in figure 3.1 from A to C.

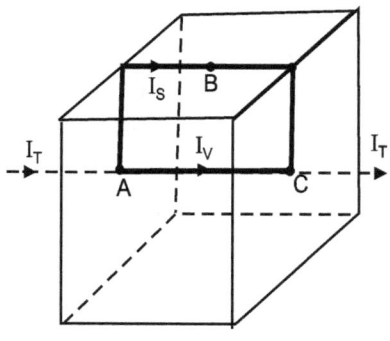

Fig. 3.1

Surface resistance

The resistance offered to current which flows over the surface of the insulating material is called surface insulation resistance. As from A to B and then B to C as shown in figure 3.1.

Factors affecting insulation resistance
- Temperature
- Moisture
- Applied voltage
- Ageing

Temperature

As the temperature of the insulating material rises its insulation resistance keeps on falling.

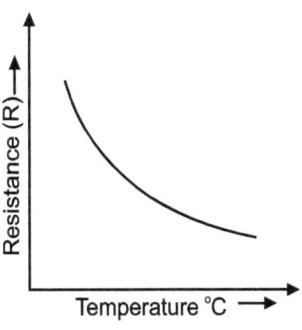

Fig. 3.2

Moisture

Insulation resistance is reduced if the material absorbs moisture, so insulation material should be non-hygroscopic.

Applied voltage

Applied voltage also affects insulation resistance.

Dielectric strength

Dielectric strength is the minimum voltage which when applied to an insulating material will result in the destruction of its insulating properties.

Ageing

Ageing reduces the insulation resistance. As age of insulation material is increased the insulation resistance decreases.

3.2.2 Thermal Properties

- Heat resistance
- Permissible temperature rise
- Effect of overloading on the life of an electrical appliance
- Thermal conductivity

Heat resistance

This is general property of insulating material to withstand temperature variation within desirable limits, without damaging its other important properties.

If an insulator has constructive properties at ambient temperature but, if it is not able to retain these, then it is not a good insulator. The insulator which is capable of withstanding higher temperature without deterioration of its other properties can be used for operation for such higher temperature.

Classification on the basis of operating temperature

Class 'Y' insulation : Material if un-impregnated fall in this category with operating temperature up to 90°C. e.g. paper, cardboard, cotton, poly vinyl chloride etc.

Class 'A' insulation : Insulators of class Y when impregnated fall in class A with operating temperature of about 105°C.

Class 'E' insulation : Insulation of this class has operating temperature of 120°C. Insulators used for enameling of wires fall in this category e.g. PVC etc.

Class 'B' insulation : Impregnated materials fall in class B insulation category with operating temperatures of about 130°C e.g. impregnated mica, asbestos, fiber glass etc.

Class 'F' insulation : Impregnated materials, impregnated or glued with better varnishes e.g. polyurethane, epoxides etc. fall in this category with operating temperature of about 155°C.

Class 'H' insulation : Insulating materials either impregnated or not, operating at 180°C falls in this category e.g. fiber glass, mica, asbestos, silicon rubber etc.

Class 'C' insulation : Insulators which have operating temperatures more than 180°C falls in class C insulation category e.g. glass, ceramics, poly terafluoro ethylene, mica etc.

Permissible temperature

There is always some recommended operating temperature for an insulator. The operating temperature has a bearing on the life of the concerned apparatus. A thumb rule suggested by many experts is that life of insulator is halved for 8-10 degree centigrade rise above the recommended operating temperature for a given apparatus.

3.2.3 Chemical Properties

- Solubility
- Chemical resistance
- Weather ability

Solubility : In certain application insulation can be applied only after it is dissolved in some solvents. In such cases, the insulating material should be soluble in certain appropriate solvent. If the insulating material is soluble in water then moisture in the atmosphere will always be able to remove the applied insulation and cause break down of material.

Chemical resistance : Presence of gases, water, acids, alkalis and salts affects different insulators differently. Chemically, a material is a better insulator if it resists chemical action. Certain plastic are found approaching this condition. thus, their use is very much increase.

Weatherability : Insulators come in contact with atmosphere both during manufacture or operation. The contact of insulation with atmosphere is often so complete that even the less chemically aggressive atmosphere can prove a threat to the smooth running of apparatus.

Hygroscopicity : The property of insulating material by virtue of which it absorbs moisture. The insulating material should be non-hygroscopic. The absorption of moisture reduces the resistivity of the insulator.

3.2.4 Physical/Mechanical Properties

- Mechanical strength
- Porosity
- Machiability and mouldability
- Density
- Brittleness

Mechanical strength : The insulating material should have high mechanical strength to bear the mechanical stresses and strains during operation.

Temperature and humidity are the main factors which reduce the mechanical strength of insulating materials.

Porosity : A material having very small holes in it is called as a porous material. Insulator absorbs moisture if it is porous, which results in reducing its resistivity as will as mechanical strength. Porous materials are impregnated with varnishes or resins to fill their pores which make them non-porous thus better insulating materials.

Machiability and Mouldability : This property of insulating material helps us to give the desired shapes to the insulating materials.

Density : The insulating material should have low density to reduce the weight of equipment in which that insulating material is being used.

Brittleness : The insulating material should not be brittle. Otherwise insulators may fracture easily due to stresses.

3.3 INSULATING MATERIALS AND THEIR APPLICATIONS

Q. Explain selection of insulating material.
Q. Write short notes on :
(1) Mica
(2) Asbestos
(3) Alumina
(4) Rubber

There are thousand of insulating materials available in the market. Insulation technology is one of those few branches where the numbers of materials available for a particular application are more than one. Any special requirement can be served by some special material.

Selection of an insulating material

- **Operating condition :** Operating temperature, pressure, operating voltage and current are to be considered for the selection of a particular material.
- **Easy to shape :** For ease of fabrication of equipment the material should be easy to shape.
- **Availability :** Material should be easily available.
- **Cost :** For cost-effectiveness of the insulating products the material should not have a very high cost compared to the other options available for the same use.

(1) Mica and Mica Products :

Mica is an inorganic mineral. It is one of the best natural insulating materials available.

It is one of the oldest insulating materials of out-standing performance. India fortunately claims the biggest reserves of mica in world.

About 80% of total World requirement of mica for electrical industry is furnished by India.

Chief sources of supply are India, Brazil and U.S.A. But the best quality is available in India. The basic composition is $KH_2Al_3(SiO_4)_3$.

Properties

- Strong, tough and less flexible
- Colorless, Yellow, Silver or Green
- Very good Insulating properties
- High resistance also High chemical Resistance
- Not affected by alkalis
- Specific Gravity : 2.6-3.6 g/cc
- Operating Temperature : 600°C
- Resistivity : 10^{15-16} ohm-m
- Dielectric Strength : 75-80 kV/mm

Applications

- Capacitor
- Commutators of DC machines
- Electric irons
- Electric hot plates
- Electric toasters.

(i) Glass bonded mica

Ground mica and powdered glass when molded makes glass bonded mica. The ratio of mica and glass is 40/60 to 60/40 range.

Properties
- Highly water resistant
- Chemically stable
- Low dielectric loss
- High dielectric strength
- Moldable

Applications
- Capacitors
- The material finds its use in high humidity and high ambient temperature atmospheres.

(ii) Synthetic mica

The development of synthetic mica took place during world war II.

Although synthetic mica possesses many technical defects of natural mica.

Properties
- Operating Temperature : 1200°C
- Dielectric constant : 6-7
- Resistivity : 10^{15-16} ohm-m
- Low-Hygroscopicity
- Low chemical resistance

Applications

Insulation for armature and field coils mainly.

(iii) Manufactured mica

When mica flakes are held together with adhesive the product is called mica plate. The binding material is about 20%. The binding materials are shellac, epoxy and silicon resins etc.

Applications
- Commutators of DC motors and generators.
- Insulation for armature and field coils.
- Heating appliances.
- Transformers.

(iv) Micanite

Very thin mica sheet bound together with adhesives are called micanites.

Applications

Commutators of DC motors and generators.

(2) Asbestos :

Found in veins of serpentine rocks hence the name Serpentine asbestos. Principal sources of supply are Canada and Africa.

(i) It is found in Cuddappah district of Andhra Pradesh in India.
(ii) It is inorganic fibrous material.
(iii) It is neither mechanically strong nor flexible.
(iv) It withstands high temperature of about 400°C so used in electrical equipment as insulator.
(v) Its dielectric strength is 3 to 4.5 kV/mm thickness.

Properties

- Specific Gravity : 1.9-2.7 g/cc.
- Melting Point : 1500°C
- Dielectric Strength : very High
- Hygroscopic
- Bad conductor of heat.

Applications

- It is used in low voltage work in the form of pipe, tape, cloth and board.
- Coil winding and insulating end turns.
- Arc barriers in circuit breakers and switches.
- Transformers

Industrial asbestos products

Asbestos use most because of its utility in engineering applications because of crystalline structure and structural stability at high temperature. However it has limitation because of low tensile strength, high dielectric loss and sensitivity towards moisture. Some of the asbestos are as follows :

(i) Asbestos roving

Asbestos fibers reinforced with cotton or synthetic organic fibers make asbestos roving.

Application

It finds use in insulation of cables and conductors and in heating devices.

(ii) Asbestos paper and board

In actual use asbestos paper is further reinforced with cotton or synthetic fiber or glass fiber.

Applications

- Wrapping material in cables.
- Layer insulation in transformers.

(iii) Asbestos cement

- About 20% asbestos fiber and 80% Portland cement are the main constituents of asbestos cement. Impregnated asbestos cement products are used to overcome its hygroscopic nature.

Properties
- Good mechanical strength.
- High thermal stability.
- Excellent resistance to electrical arcing.
- Hygroscopic

Application
These cements find their use in switch panel construction and in arcing devices.

(3) Ceramics materials
Ceramics are materials made by high temperature firing treatment of natural clay and certain organic matters. Structurally ceramics are crystals bonded together. Other materials used with clay in different type of ceramics are Quartz, Talc, and Magnetite etc.

Properties
- Hard, strong and dense.
- Not affected by chemical action stronger in compression than tension.
- Stability at high temperatures
- Excellent dielectric properties.
- Weak in impact strength.

Applications
- Porcelain insulators
- Line insulators.

Alumina
Aluminium oxide is Al_2O_3 is known as alumina.

Properties
- Specific Gravity : 3.2-4.2 g/cc
- Operating Temperature : 1800 °C
- Dielectric constant : 8-9.5
- Resistivity : 10^{14-16} ohm-m
- Low-Hygroscopicity
- High chemical resistance
- High tensile strength.

Applications
- Circuit Breakers
- Spark Plugs
- Resistor Cores
- Substrates for ICs and Power Transistors

Porcelain

Porcelain are basically clays and quartz embedded in glass matrix. it used as insulators after glazing is done i.e. a thin layer of glass is glazed over the insulator.

Properties
- Specific Gravity : 2.35-5 g/cc
- Operating Temperature : 1200°C
- Dielectric constant : 5-7
- Resistivity : 10^{11-14} ohm-m
- Low-Hygroscopicity
- High chemical Resistance
- High tensile strength

Applications
- Transformer bushings
- Line Insulators
- Switches/ Plugs/ sockets/ Fuse Holders

(4) Steatite

It is basically a mixture of clay and talc i.e. it contains hydrous oxides of magnesium and silicon.

Properties
- Specific Gravity : 2.5-2.9 g/cc
- Operating Temperature : 1200 °C
- Dielectric constant : 5.7-6.5
- Resistivity : 10^{12-15} ohm-m
- Low-Hygroscopicity
- High chemical Resistance
- High tensile strength

Applications

Insulators for High frequency and high thermal shocks.

(5) Glass

It is normally transparent, brittle and hard. It is insoluble in water and the organic solvents. Glass find its use in electrical industry because of its low dielectric loss, slow aging and good mechanical strength. Glass has its limitations because it is not easy to manufacture and is dense and heavy.

Application
- Molded devices such as electrical bushings, fuse bodies, insulators
- Capacitor

- Radio and television tubes
- Laminated boards
- Lamps/ Fluorescent Tubes

(6) Epoxy glass
Insulating material manufactured by bonding multiple layers of glass fibre impregnated with epoxy resins is called epoxy glass.

Properties
- Dielectric constant : 5
- Resistivity : 10^{14} ohm-m
- Dielectric Strength : 0.4 kV/mm
- Non-Hygroscopic
- High chemical resistance

Applications
- Base material in printed circuit boards.
- Cases and terminal posts for instruments.

(7) Silicon grease
Silicon grease is the fluid of silicon oxygen chains with methyl groups. It can be used over a wide range of temperatures.

Properties
- Operating Temperature : 60-200 °C
- Dielectric constant : 2.6
- Resistivity : High
- Non-Hygroscopic

Applications
- Capacitors
- Transformers
- In manufacturing of silicon rubber

(8) Dry paper
The source of dry paper is cellulose obtained mainly from wood. It is obtained by pulping the wood first and then passing it through the rollers to give it the final shape.

Properties
- Resistivity : 10^{5-10} ohm-m
- High hygroscopicity
- Highly inflammable

Applications

It has very limited use as in Telephone cables and Small transformers

Impregnated paper

To improve the properties of dry paper it is impregnated with oils or varnishes.

Properties

It has better properties then the dry paper in terms of mechanical strength, chemical resistance, dielectric constant, operating temperature, hygroscopicity and dielectric loss.

Application

Underground Cables (200-400 V) Capacitors.

(9) Varnishes

Varnishes are obtained by dissolving the materials in oil or alcohol. They are used mainly for impregnation, surface coating and as adhesives.

Properties

- Transparent
- Non-Hygroscopic.

Applications

- Surface coating on windings
- Impregnation of paper, cotton.

(10) Rubber

Natural rubber is obtained from the milky sap of trees. It finds limited applications in the field of engineering. The reasons are rubber is a material which is stretchable to more than twice its original length without deformation.

(i) Natural rubber

Natural rubber is extracted from the milky sap from rubber trees.

Applications

- It finds limited use in covering wires, conductors etc. for low voltage operations.
- Gloves, rubber shoes.

(ii) Hard rubber

Increased sulphur contents and extended vulcanization treatment gives rigid rubber product.

Properties

- Good electrical properties
- High tensile strength.
- Maximum permissible operating temperature is 60°C.
- Continued exposure to sun is harmful.

Applications

- Construction of storage battery housings.
- Panel boards.
- Bushings of various types etc.

3.3.1 Fibrous Insulating Materials

1. Many of them are derived from cellulose which is main constituent of vegetable plants.
2. It consists of elongated particles called fibres.
3. The fibres are mechanically strong and cheaper. But they are Hygroscopic. Hence they are impregnated.
4. Impregnation : It is a process of treating fibrous material with insulating material such as varnishes, resins, oil etc.

Advantages of impregnation :

1. It reduces hygroscopic nature in materials.
2. It helps in filling voids or air pockets in materials and makes them denser (more homogenous).
3. It increases mechanical strength, chemical stability and ability to withstand high temperature.
4. It also reduces chemical and thermal deterioration.
5. Examples of fibrous insulating materials are wood, paper pressboard, asbestos, cotton, silk etc.

(1) Wood

Properties :

1. Cheaper.
2. Easily available.
3. Tensile strength depends on type of wood and it is between 700 – 1200 kg/cm^2.
4. Dielectric constant varies from 2.5 to 7.7.
5. However it is very hygroscopic and hence loses its mechanical properties after absorbing moisture so needs impregnation.

Applications :

1. It is used for slots wedges in motor and generator winding.
2. It is used for making switch boards, terminal boxes, round blocks.
3. It is used as a spacer between HV and LV winding in transformer.

(2) Paper :

Properties :

1. It is easily available and cheaper.
2. It can be easily wrapped around the conductor.
3. Ability to withstand high temperature.
4. Low dielectric loss, density has greater influence on it.
5. Its dielectric strength is 4 to 10 kV/mm thickness.
6. Paper is made from glass or cellulose or asbestos.

7. The base materials for manufacturing insulating paper is coniferous wood.
8. However its major disadvantage is that it is hygroscopic. So to improve electrical properties it is impregnated with mineral oils, varnishes etc.
9. It has good mechanical strength.
10. It has permittivity 2 – 3.
11. It is inflammable.
12. Hygroscopic.
13. Resistivities 10^{5-10} Ωm.

(3) Pressboard :
1. It is less flexible as compared to paper but more mechanical strength.
2. It is similar to paper but is more thicker and denser than paper.
3. Its insulation resistance is 10^7 Ωm.
4. Its dielectric strength is 50 kV/mm.
5. Less hygroscopic than the paper.

Application :
1. For making slot lining.
2. As separator in transformer winding.
3. It is used for making slot wedges for stator and rotor core stacks.

Two important types of pressboard (used in slot lining) :

1. Pressphan :
   (i) It is hygroscopic so needs impregnation.
   (ii) It withstands maximum voltage of 600 V.
   (iii) It has good mechanical and dielectric properties.

2. Leatheroid :
   (i) It is hygroscopic so needs impregnation.
   (ii) It is thicker than pressphan.
   (iii) It is strong, tough and flexible.
   (iv) It is used for low voltages only.

(4) Cotton :

Properties :
1. It is hygroscopic (absorbs moisture quickly).
2. It has low dielectric strength.
3. It can withstand temperature of 100°C.
4. It is made in form of cloth or fibre and tapes.
5. Its properties can be improved by impregnating it with varnish.
6. Inflammable.

7. Density has greater influence on dielectric strength and loss.
8. Permittivity is 2 – 3.

Applications :
1. Cotton covered wire is widely used for winding of small and medium size machine, transformer coils.
2. Chokes.
3. Winding of small magnet coil etc.

(5) Silk :
(i) It is more expensive than cotton.
(ii) It is very thin and mechanically strong.
(iii) It is less hygroscopic, than cotton but like cotton it requires impregnation.
(iv) It has higher dielectric strength than cotton.
(v) It has better space factor than cotton.
(vi) Its thermal conductivity is low.
(vii) Its operating temperature is 100°C.

Application :
Since it takes less space so used for windings in fractional horse power machines.

3.3.2 Insulating Resins (Polymers)

- These are organic substances of higher molecular weight.
- These can be formed into desired shape during or after manufacture.

(a) Natural resins :
1. These are derived from plant and animal sources.
2. Simple purification or slight chemical modifications is made in natural resins so that it can be used as electrical insulation.

Different types of natural resins are :

(i) Amber
1. It is fossil resin.
2. It is light yellow in colour.
3. Its specific gravity is 1.05 to 1.1.
4. It has high electrical resistance.

Application
It is mainly used to make electrical insulating components in measuring instruments.

(ii) Wood resin
1. It is gummy and sticky like material.
2. Its dielectric constant is 2.5 to 3.
3. Its dielectric strength is 10 to 16 kV/mm.

Application

It is used for preparation of paints and varnishes, insulating oils.

(iii) Shellac

1. It is natural resin, obtained from tropical trees and animals.
2. It has high adhesive property.
3. It has less mechanical strength.
4. It has poor resistance to heat, moisture and solvents.
5. Dielectric constant is 3.5.
6. Its dielectric strength is 14 to 50 kV/mm.

Application

It is used for impregnation and manufacture of micanite.

(b) Synthetic resins

1. They are also called plastics.
2. Now-a-days more than 50% insulating material used are from this category.
3. These are organic substances which resemble to natural resins in properties like heat resistance, plasticity.
4. Its chemical composition is different from natural resins.
5. These are obtained by following two methods.

(i) Linear polymerisation :

- It is a chemical reaction in which the reacting materials combine with each other without producing any by-product. Thus here high molecular compound is obtained from low molecular compound. This chemical reaction takes place under the influence of elevated temperature and pressure.

(ii) Condensation polymerization :

- This is irreversible chemical reaction between low molecular weight compounds and produces hydrogen (H_2), hydrogen chloride (HCl), as a by-product.
- Example of this polymer is polyester.

It has the following two types :

(i) Thermoplastic resins : These are the resins which soften and melt on heating and again solidify when they are cooled. Different types of thermoplastic resins are :

(a) Perspex : It is used in model making and decoration purpose.

(b) Polyethylene :

(i) It is also known as polythene.
(ii) It is obtained from polymerization of ethylene.
(iii) It is moisture resistant. It is not soluble in many solvents except benzene and petroleum at high temperature.
(iv) Its melting point is low and it possess good electrical and mechanical properties.

Application :

It is used for insulation of wires, high frequency cables, and television and communication cables.

(c) PVC (Poly Vinyl Chloride) :

(i) It is obtained by polymerization of ethylene dichloride and sodium hydroxide in the presence of catalyst at 50°C.

(ii) Its properties can be improved by adding fillers like cotton, asbestos, powdered mica, stabilizers such as HCl, metal soap, calcium oxide.

Properties of PVC

1. Resist flame and sunlight.
2. High resistance to chemical action.
3. More flexible.
4. Non-hygroscopic.
5. Low weight and reduced size.

Application

It is used for cable insulation, insulation of wires, conduit pipes, insulation for dry batteries.

(d) Poly-tera-fluoro-ethylene :
It is also called Teflon. It is obtained by catalytic polymerization of tetra fluoro-ethylene.

Properties

1. Good mechanical, thermal and electrical proeperties.
2. Insulation resistance is very high.
3. It withstands high temperature (upto 300°C).
4. Water resistant.
5. Specific gravity 2.1 – 2.3.
6. Dielectric strength is 16 – 20 kV/m.
7. Dielectric constant is 2 – 2.2.

Applications :

1. Used as covering for conductors and cables.
2. Used as dielectric material in capacitor.

(ii) Thermosetting resins

1. They can not be softened by heating.
2. They undergo chemical changes when moulded.
3. Different types of thermosetting resins are :

(a) Bakelite

(b) Silicon resin

(c) Epoxy resins

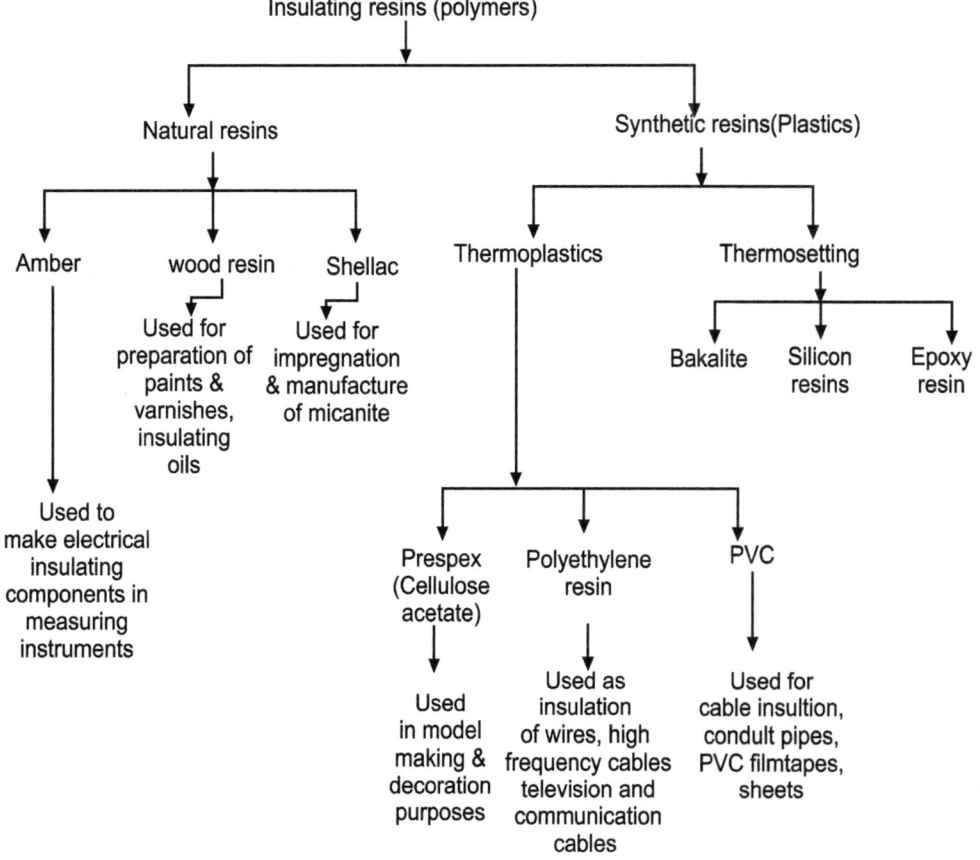

Fig. 3.3 : Classification of insulating resins

(a) Bakelite
1. It is a type of phenol formaldehyde.
2. It is hard, dark coloured thermosetting resins.
3. Low softening temperature.
4. Good electrical properties.
5. Good mouldability, toughness.
6. Good impact strength.

Application :

It is a widely used for manufacturing of lamp holders, switches, plug sockets and bases, and small panel boards.

(b) Silicon resins
1. There are organic compounds of silicon.
2. They are chemically inert and resistant to weather effects.
3. They are heat resistant.
4. Good water repellent.
5. Its dielectric strength is 8 to 12 kV/mm.

Applications :

(i) They are used as cooling and impregnating liquids for capacitors and transformers. They are also used to make silicon rubber when added with rubber.

(ii) Used as mouldings for high temperature applications.

(iii) Used as varnishes.

(c) Epoxy resins

1. They are of transparent light amber colour.
2. They have good mechanical strength, less shrinkage.
3. It is good adhesive metal.
4. As coating material, they shown superior toughness, elasticity and chemical resistance.

Applications :

(i) It is used in manufacturing of laminated insulating boards.

(ii) Used as insulating varnishes.

(iii) Used as insulating material in cable end boxes, cable point boxes, instrument transformer etc.

3.4 LIQUID INSULATING MATERIALS

> Q. Explain various liquid insulating materials.
> Q. Write properties of insulating oil.
> Q. Write short note on enamale.

These are the organic liquids which are used as insulation, coolant and as dielectric.

3.4.1 Properties of Good Liquid Insulating Materials

1. High flash point.
2. Low viscosity.
3. High or low dielectric constant (depending on application).
4. Low dissipation factor (tan δ).
5. Good arc quenching properties.
6. They should have high dielectric strength.
7. High thermal conductivity and specific heat.
8. Resistivity should be high (more than 10^{16} Ωm).
9. Non-inflammable and non-toxic.
10. Low density.
11. Low volatile.

Applications :

It is used in

1. Circuit breakers

2. Capacitors
3. Cables
4. Transformer

Liquid insulating materials have the following types :

3.4.2 Mineral Insulating Oil (Petroleum Oil or Transformer Oil)

1. Most widely used liquid insulation in industry.
2. Dissipation factor (tan δ) at 90°C is 0.001 to 0.005.
3. Its resistivity at 90°C is 22000 Ωm.
4. Permittivity is 2.1 to 2.5.
5. Breakdown voltage is 30 – 50 kV/2.5 mm.
6. These are obtained from crude petroleum by distillation of various by-products obtained.

Applications :

1. Low viscosity oil is used in high tension oil filled cables, transformer.
2. Medium viscosity oil is used in switch gears and cables.
3. High viscosity oil is used in gas filled cables and solid cables.
4. Mostly used as insulation and as coolant in transformer.

3.4.3 Synthetic Liquids

1. These are more expensive than mineral oil due to their high manufacturing cost.
2. It is non-inflammable and non-explosive.
3. Dissipation factor (tan δ) is less than 0.0005
4. Permittivity is 2.1 to 2.2.
5. It has high breakdown strength 40 to 60 kV/2.5 mm.
6. Limitation of mineral oils such as easy oxidation, quick degradation of insulating and chemical properties, inflammable nature are overcome in this.
7. E.g. Askarels, Arodors, Pyranols etc.

Applications :

1. Used in circuit breakers.
2. Used in high pressure gas filled power cables and in D.C. capacitors.
3. Used in high voltage transformer as coolant and insulation.

3.4.4 Askarel

1. It is fire resistant.
2. It has good insulating properties.
3. It is costlier than transformer oil.
4. Its resistivity is 10^{12} Ω-cm.
5. Its permittivity is 4.8 to 5.3.
6. Its breakdown voltage is 20 to 45 kV/2.5 mm.

Applications :
1. Used in circuit breakers.
2. Used as a coolant for transformer and for capacitors operating at higher voltage.

3.4.5 Varnish

1. When varnish is applied to a surface, it dries by either evaporation or by chemical action resulting in hard shining coating which is resistant to air and water.
2. Varnishes protect the materials against moisture, dirt and dust.
3. Varnishes are required in certain insulating system to :
   (i) Give fire proof finish.
   (ii) Protect from atmospheric corrosion and moisture.
   (iii) Reduce degradation caused by oxidation.
   (iv) Improve insulation properties.
   (v) Increase mechanical strength.
4. The raw materials used for manufacture of varnishes are oils, solvents, thinners, resins and dryers.
5. Different type of varnishes are :

(a) Impregnating varnishes :
1. These are used with porous and fibrous insulating materials like paper, fabrics, glass.
2. Used in transformers, capacitors, motor winding etc.

(b) Coating varnishes :
1. These are used when tough, smooth and glossy film is required to protect a substance from oxidation, corrosion, moisture absorption and solvent attract.
2. These varnishes increases the mechanical strength of an assembly and surface leakage resistivity.

(c) Adhesive varnishes :
1. They are used as binders for mica, glass and other insulating systems.

3.4.6 Enamel

1. It is applied on conducting surface.
2. They are also used to furnish a heavy protective coating on electronic equipment.
3. It is a fusible insulated coating of organic base material.
4. The maximum thickness of enamel coating is 0.05 mm.

Applications

The enamel coating is provided on copper or aluminium wires which are used for winding in case of transformer motor etc.

3.5 GASES INSULATING MATERIALS

> **Q.** Explain gases insulating materials.
> **Q.** Write properties of SF_6.

(a) Air
- It is naturally and abundantly available gaseous insulator.
- It needs no processing and can be used directly.
- Its dielectric strength is 30 kV/cm at 50 Hz.
- Its dielectric strength increases linearly with increase in gas pressure.

Applications
1. It provides insulation between overhead transmission lines.
2. Also used for cooling rotating parts of machine.
3. Used in capacitors, as dielectric.
4. Used in small transformers as coolant.

(b) Hydrogen (H_2)
- Very light gas.
- Thermal conductivity is 6.69 times of air.
- It has density 0.07 times that of air, so windage looses in machines can be minimised.

Applicaitons :
- Used as coolant in electric machine due to which efficiency increases.
- Used to reduce windage loss in high speed machines.
- Large turbo-generators and synchronous condensers are now-a-days hydrogen cooled.

(c) Nitrogen (N_2)
- Its density is 0.97 times that of air.
- Its thermal conductivity is 1.08 times that of air.
- In many high voltage applications air is replaced by nitrogen to prevent oxidation of the other insulating materials.
- Under pressure, it is used as the only insulator in certain capacitors.
- In high voltage gas pressure cables, pressurized nitrogen gas is used alongwith oil impregnated paper.

(d) Sulphur Hexafluoride (SF_6)
When sulphur is burnt is an atmosphere of fluorine, sulphur hexafluoride is formed.
It possess following properties :

1. Physical properties :
- Colourless.
- Odourless.

- Non-toxic (pure SF_6 is non-toxic to health).
- Non-inflammable.
- Heat transfer ability is 2.5 times greater than air.

2. **Chemical properties :**
- It is stable upto 500°C.
- It is chemically inert so life of metallic parts, contacts is more.
- It is electro-negative gas.
- It has electron affinity so arc quenches quickly. Thus, it has excellent arc quenching properties.

3. **Dielectric properties :**
- Dielectric strength of SF_6 gas at atmosphere pressure is 2.35 times that of air but less than oil by 30%.
- But when pressure of SF_6 gas is more than 3 kg/cm^2, its dielectric strength is higher than oil.

Applications of SF_6 gas :
- It is widely used in electrical equipments like high voltage switch gears, capacitors, cables, circuit breakers.
- The most important application is Gas Insulated Substation (GIS).

SOLVED EXAMPLES

Example 3.1 : The resistivity of the insulation material in a cable having conductor diameter of 1.8 cm and sheath diameter of 5 cm. If the length of cable is 3000 m and its insulation resistance is 1820 MΩ.

Solution : Given,

$$d_1 = 1.8 \text{ cm}$$
$$d_2 = 5 \text{ cm}$$
$$\therefore \quad R_1 = 1.8/2 = 0.9 \text{ cm}$$
$$R_2 = 5/2 = 2.5 \text{ cm}$$

We know that R_i = Insulation resistance

$$= \frac{\rho_i}{2\pi l} \log_e \left(\frac{R_2}{R_1}\right)$$

$$1820 \times 10^6 = \frac{\rho_i}{2\pi \times 3000} \log_e \left(\frac{2.5}{0.9}\right)$$

$$\rho_i = 33.1 \times 10^{12} \text{ Ωm}$$

Example 3.2 : A parallel plate capacitor is to be made to store 20 μC at a potential of 10 kV. The separation between the plates is 5×10^{-4} m. If the dielectric constant of material is 10 kept between plates, the area that the plates must have is?

Solution : Given,
$$Q = 20 \, \mu C$$
$$V = 10 \, kV$$
$$d = 5 \times 10^{-4}$$
$$\varepsilon_r = 10$$
$$C = \frac{Q}{V}$$
$$= \frac{20 \times 10^{-6}}{10 \times 10^3}$$
$$\boxed{C = 2 \times 10^{-9} \, F}$$

We know that,
$$C = \frac{\varepsilon_0 \varepsilon_r A}{d}$$
$$A = \frac{C d}{\varepsilon_0 \varepsilon_r}$$
$$A = \frac{2 \times 10^{-9} \times 5 \times 10^{-4}}{8.85 \times 10^{-12} \times 10}$$
$$\boxed{A = 10.294 \times 10^{-3} \, m}$$

Example 3.3 : What will be insulation resistance of single core cable having inside diameter 0.03 m outside diameter 0.075 m length 2 km and the resistivity of insulating material 6×10^{12} Ωm.

Solution : Given,
$$d_1 = 0.03$$
$$d_2 = 0.075$$
$$l = 2 \, km$$
$$\rho_i = 6 \times 10^{12} \, \Omega \, m$$

We know that,
$$R_i = \frac{\rho_i}{2\pi l} \log_e \left(\frac{R_2}{R_1}\right)$$
$$R_2 = \frac{d_2}{2} = \frac{0.075}{2} = 0.0375 \, m$$
$$R_1 = \frac{d_1}{2} = \frac{0.03}{2} = 0.015 \, m$$
$$R_i = \frac{6 \times 10^{12}}{2\pi \times 2000} \log_e \left(\frac{0.0375}{0.015}\right)$$
$$= \frac{3 \times 10^9}{2\pi} \log_e \left(\frac{0.0375}{0.015}\right)$$
$$R_i = 4.37 \times 10^8 \, \Omega$$

Example 3.4 : Resistance of conductor for 6.5 km long cable has conductor diameter of 15 mm if specific resistance of conductor material is 0.017 micro Ωm.

Solution : Given,

$l = 6.5$ km

$r = 15$ mm

$\rho = 0.017 \; \mu\Omega$ m

$$\text{Area} = \pi r^2 = \pi \left(\frac{15 \times 10^{-2}}{2}\right)^2$$

$$= 0.01767$$

$$R_c = \frac{\rho l}{\text{Area}} = \frac{0.017 \times 10^{-6} \times 6500}{0.01767}$$

$$\boxed{R_c = 0.3126 \; \Omega}$$

REVIEW QUESTIONS

1. Explain properties of a good insulating materials.
2. Classify insulating materials on the basis of limiting temperature. Give two examples in each class.
3. State the properties and applications of :
   (a) Asbestos
   (b) Ceramics
   (c) Porcelain
   (d) Mica
4. Classify gaseous insulating materials. Give examples in each case.
5. Write short note on 'Impregnation process'.
6. List insulating materials used for :
   (a) power cables
   (b) line insulators
7. Write a short note on 'Crystal defects'.
8. List insulating materials use for power cable and line insulators.
9. Write short note on :
   (i) Mica
   (ii) Asbestos
   (iii) Press board
   (iv) Porcelain
   (v) SF_6

10. Short note on liquid insulating materials.
11. What is thermal classification of insulating materials?

UNIVERSITY QUESTIONS

May 2008

1. What is impregnation process? Why it is necessary? Explain impregnation process for paper and cotton. **(8 Marks)**
2. Sate properties and applications of : **(8 Marks)**
   (a) SF_6
   (b) Transformer oil
   (c) Micanite
   (d) Ceramics
3. Discuss insulating materials used for :
   (a) Rotating machines
   (b) Capacitors **(8 Marks)**
4. Discuss insulating materials used for : **(8 Marks)**
   (a) Power transformer
   (b) Switch gears

Dec. 2008

5. Discuss insulating materials used for : **(8 Marks)**
   (a) Power transformer
   (b) Switch gears
6. Give properties and application of : **(8 Marks)**
   (a) Askarel
   (b) SF_6
   (c) Pressboard
   (d) Mica
7. What are ceramics? Give their properties and applications? What is effect of temperature and moisture on ceramics? **(8 Marks)**

May 2009

8. State the properties and applications of :
   (a) Transformer oil
   (b) SF_6

9. What is impregnation process? Why it is necessary? Explain impregnation process for paper and cotton. **(8 Marks)**
10. Discuss insulating materials used for power capacitors and cables. **(8 Marks)**
11. Discuss insulating materials used for : **(8 Marks)**
    (a) Power transformer
    (b) Line insulators

Dec. 2009

12. State the properties and applications of : **(8 Marks)**
    (a) Transformer oil
    (b) SF_6
13. What do you mean by fibrous insulating material? What is their major drawback? How it can be overcome? **(8 Marks)**
14. Discuss insulating materials used for power and distribution transformer. **(4 Marks)**

May 2010

15. Discuss the insulating materials used for :
    (a) Power transformer
    (b) Power cables
16. State the properties and application of : **(12 Marks)**
    (a) SF_6 gas
    (b) Transformer oil
    (c) Micanate
    (d) Ceramics

Dec. 2010

17. Write down properties and applications of : **(16 Marks)**
    (a) Paper
    (b) Press board
    (c) Fibrous materials
    (d) Ceramics
    (e) Asbestos
    (f) Varnish
    (g) Askarel
    (h) Insulating gases like air
    (i) SF_6 gas
18. Describe the insulating materials used in : **(8 Marks)**
    (a) Switch gears
    (b) Line insulators

May 2011

19. State the properties and applications of : **(6 Marks)**
    (i) Porcelain
    (ii) SF_6 gas

20. Discuss the insulating materials used for power transformers. **(4 Marks)**

21. What is impregnation process? Why is it necessary for fibrous insulating materials? Explain impregnation process for paper and cotton. **(6 Marks)**

22. Discuss the insulating materials used for : **(8 Marks)**
    (i) Power transformer
    (ii) Line insulators

23. State the properties and applications of : **(8 Marks)**
    (i) SF_6 gas
    (ii) Ceramics
    (iii) Asbestos
    (iv) Transformer oil

May 2012

24. State the properties and applications of : **(8 Marks)**
    (i) Mica
    (ii) Transformer oil

25. Discuss insulating materials used for : **(8 Marks)**
    (i) Capacitors
    (ii) Switchgears

Dec. 2012

26. Write down properties and applications of the following : **(16 Marks)**
    (i) Paper and press board
    (ii) SF_6 gas
    (iii) Ceramics
    (iv) Mica and asbestos

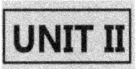

Chapter 4

DIELECTRIC BREAKDOWN

Dielectric strength

Dielectric strength is the minimum voltage which when applied to an insulating material will result in the destruction of its insulating properties. Electrical appliances are designed to operate within a defined range of voltage. If the operating voltage is increased gradually at some value of voltage, the breakdown of the insulating materials will occur. The property which attributes to such type of break down is called the dielectric strength.

4.1 GASES AS INSULATING MEDIA

Q. Write short note on insulating media.

The most common dielectrics are gases. Many electrical apparatus use air as the insulating medium, in a few cases other gases such as CO_2, N_2, CCl_2F_2 (Freon) and SF_6 (hexafluoride) are used.

Various phenomena occur in gaseous dielectrics when a voltage is applied are:

- When low voltage is applied, small current flow between the electrodes and the insulation retains its electrical properties.
- If the applied voltage is huge, the current flowing through the insulation increases very sharply and an electrical breakdown occur. A strongly conducting spark created during breakdown, practically produces a short circuit between the two electrodes. The maximum voltage applied to the insulation at the moment of breakdown is called the breakdown voltage.

In order to understand the breakdown phenomenon in gases, the electrical properties of gases should be considered. The processes by which high currents are produced in gases is essential. The electrical discharges in gases are of two types :

(i) Non-sustaining discharges

(ii) Self-sustaining types

The breakdown in a gas is the conversion of non-sustaining discharges into a self-sustaining discharge. The build up of high currents in a breakdown is due to the ionization in which electrons and ions are created from neutral atoms or molecules, and their movement to the anode and cathode respectively leads to high currents. Townsend theory and Streamer theory are the present two types of theories which explain the mechanism of breakdown under different conditions such as pressure, temperature, and electrode field configuration, nature of electrode surfaces and availability of initial conducting particles.

4.2 IONIZATION PROCESS

> Q. How ionization occur in gaseous materials ?
> Q. What is ionization process ?

Consider a simple electrode arrangement as shown in the Fig 4.1, having two parallel plate electrodes separated by a distance d and immersed in a gas at pressure p. A uniform E is applied between two electrodes. Due to any external radiation free electrons are liberated at the cathode. When an electron, e is placed in an E it will be accelerated with a force eE towards the anode, and it gains an energy

$$u = eEx = \frac{1}{2}mv^2$$

where, x is the distance traveled by the electron from the cathode, m is the mass and v is the velocity of the electron. This electron collides with the other gas molecules while it is traveling towards the anode. If the energy of the electron is adequately large, on collision it will cause a break-up of the atom or molecule into positive ion and electron. As result the new electrons and positive ions are created. Thus created electrons form a group or an avalanche and reach the anode. This is the electric current and if it is adequately large it results in the formation of a conducting path between the electrodes resulting in the breakdown of the gap. Townsend conducted experiments on the growth of these currents which led to breakdown under D.C. voltage conditions, and he proposed a theory to explain this phenomenon.

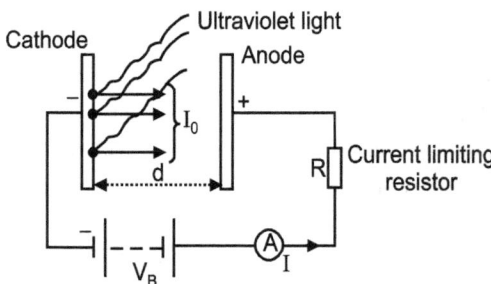

Fig. 4.1 : Arrangement for study to a townsend discharge

4.3 TOWNSEND'S CURRENT GROWTH EQUATION

> Q. Write short note on townsend current growth equation.

Assuming n_0 electrons are emitted from the cathode and when one electron collides with a neutral particle, a positive atom and electron formed. This is called an ionization collision.

Let α be the average number of ionizing collisions made by an electron per centimeter travel in the direction of the field where it depends on gas pressure p and E, this is called the Townsend's first ionization coefficient. At any distance x from the cathode when the number of electrons, n_x, travel a distance of dx they give rise to $\alpha n_x dx$ electrons. Then, the number of electrons reaching the anode at x = d, n_d will be $n_0 = n_x|_{x=0}$

$$\frac{dn_x}{dx} = \alpha n_x \text{ or } n_x = n_0 e^{\alpha x} \qquad ...(4.1)$$

$$n_d = n_0 e^{\alpha x}$$
at x = d ...(4.2)

The number of new electrons created, on the average, by each electron is given by

$$e^{\alpha d} - 1 = \frac{n_d - n_0}{n_0} \qquad ...(4.3)$$

Therefore, the average current in the gap, which is equal to the number of electrons traveling per second, will be as

$$I = I_0 e^{\alpha d} \qquad ...(4.4)$$

where, I_0 is the initial current at the cathode.

4.4 CURRENT GROWTH IN THE PRESENCE OF SECONDARY PROCESSES

Q. Explain current growth in the presence of secondary processes.

When the initial set of electrons reaches the anode the single avalanche process is completed. while the amplification of electrons $e^{\alpha d}$ is occurring in the field, the probability of additional new electrons being liberated by other mechanisms increases. it produced further avalanches and is called as secondary electrons. The other mechanisms are :

(i) The positive ions liberated may have adequate energy to cause liberation of electrons from the cathode when they impose on it.

(ii) The exited atoms or molecules in avalanches may emit photons, and this will lead to the emission odd electrons due to photo-emission.

(iii) The met stable particles may diffuse back causing electron emission.

Defining the Townsend's secondary ionization coefficient γ in the same way as α, then the net number of secondary electrons produced per incident positive ion, photon, excited particle or met stable particle and the total value of γ due to the three different processes is

$\gamma = \gamma_1 + \gamma_2 + \gamma_3$

Following Townsend's procedure for current growth, let us assume n'_0 = number of secondary electrons produced due to secondary γ processes.

Let, $\quad n''_0$ = total number of electrons leaving the cathode.

Then, $\quad n''_0 = n_0 + n'_0$ ...(4.5)

The total number of electrons n reaching to the anode is given as,

$n = n''_0 e^{\alpha d} = (n_0 + n'_0) e^{\alpha d}$ and, $n'_0 = \gamma [n - (n_0 + n'_0)]$

Eliminating n'_0, $n = \dfrac{n_0 e^{\alpha d}}{1 - \gamma(e^{\alpha d} - 1)}$ or $I = \dfrac{I_0 e^{\alpha d}}{1 - \gamma(e^{\alpha d} - 1)}$ ...(4.6)

4.5 TOWNSEND'S CRITERION FOR BREAKDOWN

Q. Explain townsends criterion for breakdown.

Equation 4.6 gives the total average current in a gap before the occurrence of breakdown. As the distance between the electrodes d is increased the denominator of equation tend to zero and at some critical distance $d = d_s$

$$1 - \gamma(e^{\alpha d} - 1) = 0 \qquad ...(4.7)$$

For values of $d < d_s$, I is approximately equal to I_0 and if the external source for the supply of I_0 is removed, I becomes zero. If $d = d_s$, $I \Rightarrow \infty$ and the current will be limited only by the resistance of power supply and the external circuit. This is called Townsend's Breakdown criterion and can be written as

$\gamma (e^{\alpha d} - 1) = 1$.

Normally, $e^{\alpha d}$ is very large, and hence the above equation reduces to

$$\gamma e^{\alpha d} = 1 \qquad ...(4.8)$$

For at a given gap spacing and at a given pressure the value of voltage V which gives the values of α and γ fulfilling the breakdown criterion is called the spark breakdown voltage V, and the equivalent distance d is called the sparking distance. Townsend mechanism explains the phenomena of breakdown only at low pressures, equivalent to $p \times d$ values of 1000 torr-cm and below.

4.6 BREAKDOWN IN ELECTRONEGATIVE GASES

Q. How breakdown occur in electronegative gases ?

One process that gives high breakdown strength to a gas is the electron attachment. In this process free electrons get attached to a neutral atoms or molecules to form negative ions.

Since, negative ions like positive ions are too huge to produce ionization due to collisions, attachment represents an effective way of removing electrons which otherwise would have led to current growth and breakdown at low voltages. The gases in which attachment plays an active role are called electronegative gases. Two types of attachment are encountered in gases as :

(a) Direct attachment : An electron directly attaches to form a negative ion.

$$AB + e \cdots \rightarrow AB^-$$

(b) Dissociative attachment : The gas molecules split into their constituent atoms and the electronegative atom forms a negative ion.

$$AB + e \cdots \rightarrow A + B^-$$

A simple gas for this type is the oxygen and sulphur hexafluoride, freon, carbon dioxide and fluorocarbons. In these gases, 'A' is usually sulphur or carbon atom and 'B' is oxygen atom or one of the halogen atoms or molecules.

The Townsend current growth equation is modified to include ionization and attachment with such gases. The current reaching the anode, can be given as,

$$I = I_0 \frac{\left[\frac{\alpha}{\alpha-\eta} e^{(\alpha-\eta)d}\right] - \left[\frac{\eta}{\alpha-\eta}\right]}{1 - \left[\gamma \frac{\alpha}{\alpha-\eta} e^{(\alpha-\eta)d} - 1\right]} \quad \ldots(4.9)$$

where, η is the number of attaching collisions made by one electron drifting one centimeter in the direction of the field. The Townsend breakdown criterion for attaching gases can also be given as

$$1 - \left[\gamma \frac{a}{a-n} e(a-\eta)d - 1\right] = 0.$$

When $\alpha > \eta$, breakdown is possible irrespective of the values of α, η and γ. If $\alpha < \eta$, then an asymptotic form is approached with increasing value of d, $\gamma \frac{\alpha}{\alpha-\eta} = 1$ or, $\alpha = \frac{\eta}{1-\gamma}$. Normally, γ is very small ($\leq 10^{-4}$) and the above equation can be written as $\alpha = \eta$. This condition puts a limit for E/P below which no breakdown is possible irrespective of the value of d, and the limit value is called the critical E/P.

4.7 TIME LAGS FOR BREAKDOWN

Q. Write short note on time lags for breakdown.

Theoretically, the mechanism of spark breakdown is considered as a function of ionization processes under uniform field conditions. In engineering designs, the breakdown due to rapidly changing voltages or impulse voltages is of great importance. Actually, there is a time difference between the application of a voltage sufficient to cause breakdown and the occurrence of breakdown. This time difference is called as the time lag. The Townsend criterion for breakdown is satisfied only if at least one electron is present in the gap between the electrodes as in the case of applied D.C. or slowly varying A.C. voltages. If The initiatory electron may not be present in the gap than the breakdown can not occur.

4.8 STREAMER THEORY OF BREAKDOWN IN GASES

Q. Explain streamer theory.

According to the Townsend theory :
- Firstly, current growth occurs as a result of ionization process. however in practice, breakdown voltages were found to depend on the gas pressure and the geometry of the gap.

- The mechanism predicts time lags of order of 10^{-5} s, however practically it observed to occur at a very short time of 10^{-8} s.
- Also the Townsend mechanism predicts a much diffused form of discharge that actually discharges is found to be filamentary and irregular.

Townsend mechanism failed to explain all these observed phenomena and as a result The Streamer theory was proposed.

The theory predicts the development of a spark discharge directly from a single avalanche in which the space charge develops by the avalanche itself it is called transform the avalanche into a plasma steamer. In the Fig 4.2, a single electron starting at the cathode by ionization.

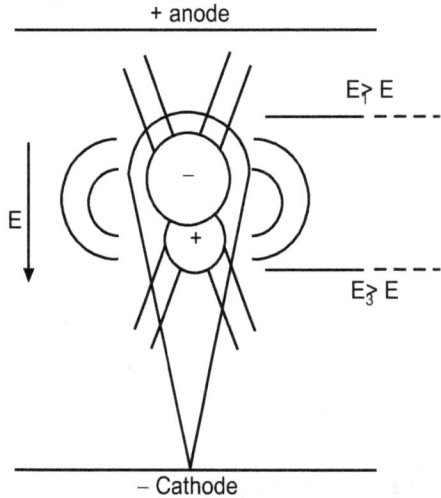

Fig. 4.2 : Effect of space charge produced by an avalanche on the applied electric field

builds up an avalanche that crosses the gap. The electrons in the avalanche move very fast compared with the positive ions. By the time the electrons reach the anode, the positive ions are in their original positions . this form a positive space charge at the anode. This enhances the field, and the secondary avalanches are formed from a few electrons produced due to the photo-ionization in the space charge region. This occurs first near to the anode where the space charge is maximum and a further increase in the space charge. This process is very fast and the positive space charge extends to the cathode very rapidly resulting in the pattern of a streamer. Comparatively narrow luminous tracks occurring at breakdown at pressures are called streamers. As soon as the streamer tip approaches to the cathode, a cathode spot is formed and a stream of electrons charge from the cathode to neutralize the positive space charge in the streamer. this result is a spark and the spark breakdown has occurred. A simple quantitative criterion to calculate approximately the electric field E_r which is produced by the space charge, at the radius r and that transforms an avalanche into streamer is given by

$$E_r = 5.27 \times 10^{-7} \frac{\alpha \, e^{\alpha x}}{\sqrt{\frac{x}{p}}} \frac{V}{cm}$$

where α is the Townsend's first ionization coefficient, p is the gas pressure in torr and x is the distance to which the streamer has extended in the gap.

When,

E_r = E and x = d the equation above simplifies into $\alpha d + \ln \alpha/p = 14.5 + \ln E/p + 0.5 \ln d/p$. This equation is solved between α/p and E/p. The breakdown voltage is given by the corresponding product Ed. It is normally assumed that for pd values below 1000 torr-cm and gas pressures varying from 0.01 to 300 torr. The Townsend mechanism operates, while at higher pressures and pd values the streamer mechanism plays the dominant role in explaining the breakdown phenomena. However controversies still exist in these statements.

4.9 PASCHEN'S LAW

The breakdown criterion

$$1 - \gamma(e^{\alpha d} - 1) = 0 \qquad \ldots (4.10)$$

where α and γ are functions of E/p, i.e.

$$\alpha/p = f_1(E/p)$$

and $\qquad \gamma = f_2(E/p)$

Also, $\qquad E = V/d$

Substituting for E in the expressions α and γ and rewriting equation (4.10) we get

$$f_2(V/pd)[e^{pd\, f_1(V/pd)} - 1] = 1$$

This equation shows a relationship between V and pd, and implies that the breakdown voltage varies as the product pd varies. deliberate the nature of functions f_1 and f_2, we can write the equation

$$V = f(pd)$$

known as Paschen's law and has been experimentally recognized for many gases. Paschen's law is a very important law in high voltage engineering. The relationship between V and pd is not linear for any gas. The minimum breakdown voltages for various gases are as follow :

Gas	V_s min(V)	pd at V_s min (torr-cm)
Air	327	0.567
H_2	273	1.15
CO_2	420	0.51
O_2	450	0.7
SO_2	457	0.33
Helium	156	4.0

The existence of a minimum sparking potential in Paschen's curve may be explained as follows :

- For values pd > (pd)$_{min}$ electrons crossing the gap make more frequent collisions with gas molecules than (pd)$_{min}$, but the energy gained between collisions is lower. Hence to maintain the desired ionization more voltage is to be applied.
- For pd < (pd)$_{min}$ electron may cross the gap without even making a collision or making only less number of collisions. Hence, more voltage has to be applied for breakdown to occur.
- For the effect of temperature, the Paschen's law is generally stated as

$$V = f(Nd)$$

where, N is the density of the gas molecules. This is necessary since the pressure of the gas changes with temperature according to the gas law pv = NRT. The breakdown potential of air is expressed due to the experimental given as :

$$V = 24.22 \left[\frac{293pd}{760T}\right] + 6.08 \left[\frac{293pd}{760T}\right]^{1/2}$$

At 760 torr. and 293 K, $E = \frac{V}{d} = 24.22 + \frac{6.08}{\sqrt{d}}$ kV/cm.

This equation yields a limiting value for E of 24 kV/cm for long gaps and a value of 30 kV/cm for $\left[\frac{293pd}{760T}\right] = 1$, which means a pressure of 760 torr. at 20°C with 1 cm gap. This breakdown strength of air at room temperature and at atmospheric pressure.

4.10 POST-BREAKDOWN PHENOMENA AND APPLICATIONS

Post-Breakdown phenomenon is of technical importance which occurs after the actual breakdown has taken place. Glow and arc discharges are the post-breakdown phenomena and there are many devices that operate in these regions. In a Townsend discharge the current increases gradually as a function of the applied voltage from point A as shown in Fig 4.3. Further to this point B only the current increases and the discharge changes from the Townsend type to Glow type (BC).

Further increase in current results in a very small reduction I voltage across the gap (CD) corresponding to the normal glow region. The gap voltage again increases (DE), when the current increase more, but eventually leads a considerable drop to the applied voltage. This is the region of the Arc discharge (EG). The phenomena occur in the region CG are the post-breakdown phenomena consisting of glow discharge CE and the arc discharge EG.

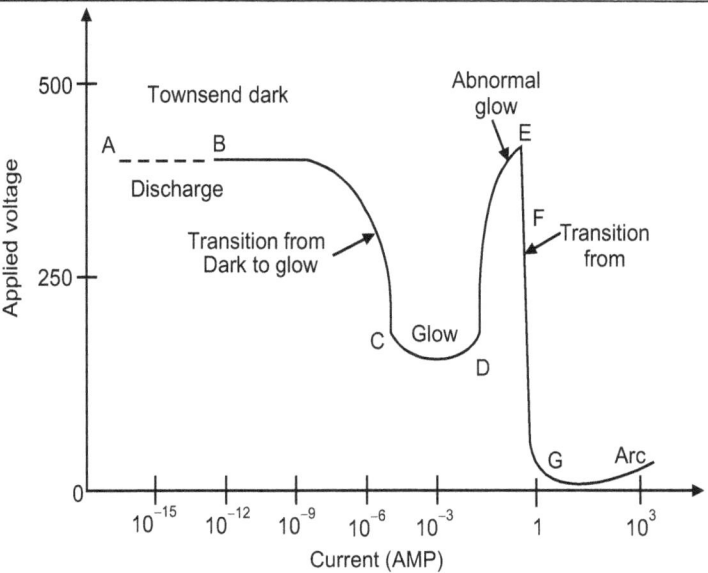

Fig. 4.3 : D.C. Voltage current characteristic at an electrical discharge

Glow Discharge

A glow discharge is characterized by a diffused luminous glow. The colour of the glow discharge depends on the cathode materials and the gas used inside. The glow discharge covers the cathode partially and the space between the cathode and the anode will have intermediate dark and bright regions. In a glow discharge, the voltage drop between the electrodes is significantly constant, ranging from 75 to 300 V over a current range of 1 mA to 100 mA depending on the type of the gas used. The properties of the glow discharge are used such as, voltage regulation (VR) tubes, for rectification and as an amplifier.

Arc Discharge

If the current in the gap is increased to about 1 A or more, the voltage across the gap suddenly reduces to a few volts. The discharge becomes exceptionally luminous and noisy. The current density over the cathode region increases to very high values of 10^3 to 10^7 A/cm^2. Arcing is associated with high temperature, ranging from 1000°C to several thousands degrees celcius. The discharge contains very high density of electrons and positive ions, and called as arc plasma. The study of arcs is significant in circuit breakers and other switch contacts. It is convenient for high temperature high intensity light source. It is used for welding and cutting of metals. It is the light source in lamps such as carbon arc lamp. High temperature plasmas are used for generation of electricity through magneto-hydro dynamic or nuclear fusion processes.

4.11 BREAKDOWN IN SOLID DIELECTRICS

Q. Explain breakdown in solid dielectrics.
Q. Explain various breakdown meahcnisms.

A good dielectric should have low dielectric loss, high mechanical strength, should be free from gaseous inclusion, and moisture, and be resistant to thermal and chemical deterioration. Solid dielectrics have higher breakdown strength compared to liquids and gases. Solid dielectric materials are used in all kinds of electrical circuits and devices to insulate one current carrying part from another when they operate at different voltages. When breakdown occurs, solids get permanently damaged while gases fully and liquids partly recover their dielectric strength after the applied electric field detached. The mechanism of breakdown is a complex phenomenon in the case of solids. it varies depending on the time of application of voltage. The various breakdown mechanisms can be classified as follows :

(a) Intrinsic or ionic breakdown
(b) Electromechanical breakdown
(c) Failure due to treeing and tracking
(d) Thermal breakdown
(e) Electrochemical breakdown, and
(f) Breakdown due to internal discharges

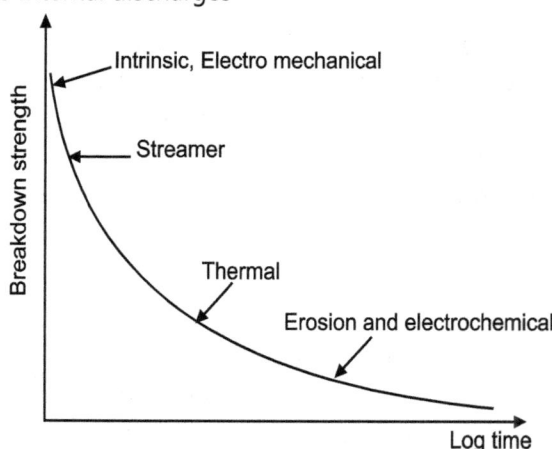

Fig. 4.4 : Variation of breakdown strength with time after application of voltage

(a) Intrinsic breakdown

When voltages are applied only for short durations the dielectric strength of a solid dielectric increases very fast to an upper limit called the intrinsic electric strength. Experimentally, this highest dielectric strength can be obtained only under the best experimental conditions when all inappropriate influences have been isolated and the value depends only on the structure of the material and the temperature. The maximum electrical strength recorder is 15 MV/cm for polyvinyl-alcohol at $-196°C$.

Intrinsic breakdown depends upon the presence of free electrons which are capable of immigration through the lattice of the dielectric. Usually, a small number of conduction electrons are there in solid dielectrics, along with some structural imperfections and small amounts of impurities. The impurity atoms, or molecules or both act as traps for the conduction electrons up to certain level of electric fields and temperatures. When these ranges are exceeded, additional electrons in addition to trapped electrons are released, and these electrons participate in the conduction process. Based on this principle, two types of intrinsic breakdown mechanisms have been proposed as given below.

(i) Electronic Breakdown

Intrinsic breakdown occurs in short time and therefore it is assumed to be electronic in nature. The initial density of conduction electrons is also implicit to be large, and electron-electron collisions occur. When an electric field is applied, electrons gain energy from the electric field and jump to the conduction band. When this process is repeated, more and more electrons become presented in the conduction band, sooner or later leading to breakdown.

(ii) Avalanche or Streamer Breakdown

This is similar to breakdown in gases due to cumulative ionization. Conduction electrons gain sufficient energy above a certain critical electric field and cause deliverance of electrons from the lattice atoms by collision. Under uniform field conditions, if the electrodes are embedded in the specimen, breakdown will occur when an electron avalanche bridges the electrode gap.

An electron within the dielectric, starting from the cathode will drift towards the anode and during this motion it gains energy from the field and loses it during collisions. When the energy gained by an electron exceeds the lattice ionization potential, an additional electron will be liberated due to collision of the first electron. This process repeats itself resulting in the formation of an electron avalanche. Breakdown will occur, when the avalanche exceeds a certain critical size.

In follow, breakdown does not occur by the formation of a single avalanche itself, but occurs as a result of many avalanches formed within the dielectric and extending step by step through the entire thickness of the material.

(b) Electromechanical breakdown

When solid dielectrics are subjected to high electric fields, failure occurs due to electrostatic compressive forces which can exceed the mechanical compressive strength. If the thickness of the specimen is d_0 and is compressed to thickness d under an applied voltage V, then the electrically developed compressive stress is in equilibrium as:

$$\varepsilon_0 \varepsilon_r = \frac{V^2}{2d^2} = Y \ln\left[\frac{d_0}{d}\right]$$

where, Y is the Young's modulus.

$$V^2 = d^2 \left[\frac{2Y}{\varepsilon_0 \varepsilon_r}\right] \ln\left[\frac{d_0}{d}\right]$$

Usually, mechanical instability occurs when $d/d_0 = 0.6$ or $d_0/d = 1.67$
putting this equation the highest apparent electric stress before breakdown,

$$E_{max} = \frac{V}{d_0} = 0.6\left[\frac{Y}{\varepsilon_0 \varepsilon_r}\right]^{1/2}$$

The above equation is only estimated as Y depends on the mechanical stress. Also when the material is subjected to high stresses plastic deformation has to be considered.

(c) Thermal breakdown

In general, the breakdown voltage of a solid dielectric should increase with its thickness. But this is true only up to a certain thickness above which the heat generated in the dielectric due to the flow of current determines the conduction.

When an electric field is applied to a dielectric, conduction current though small it may be, flows through the material. The current heats up the material and the temperature rise. The heat generated is transferred to the surrounding medium by conduction through the solid dielectric and by radiation from its outer surfaces. Equilibrium is reached when the heat used to raise the temperature of the dielectric, addition to that the heat radiated out, equals the heat generated. The heat generated under D.C. stress E is given as

$$W_{d.c.} = E^2 \sigma \text{ W/cm}^3$$

where, σ is the D.C. conductivity of the specimen.

Under A.C. fields, the heat generated is

$$W_{a.c.} = \frac{E^2 f_{\varepsilon r} \tan\delta}{1.8 \times 10^{12}} \text{ W/cm}^3$$

where, f = frequency in Hz, δ = loss angle of the dielectric material, and E = rms value. The heat dissipated (W_r) is given as

$$W_r = C_v \frac{dT}{dt} + \text{div (K grad T)}$$

where,

C_v = specific heat of the specimen

T = temperature of the specimen

K = thermal conductivity of the specimen, and

t = time over which the heat is dissipated

Equilibrium is reached when the heat generated becomes equal to the heat dissipated. Breakdown occurs when $W_{d.c.}$ or $W_{a.c.}$ exceeds W_r. The thermal instability condition is shown in Fig. 4.5. Here, the heat lost is shown by a straight line, while the heat generated at fields E_1 and E_2 is shown by separate curves. At field E_2 breakdown occurs both at temperatures T_A

and T_B heat generated is less than the heat lost for the field E_2, and hence the breakdown will not occur at that point.

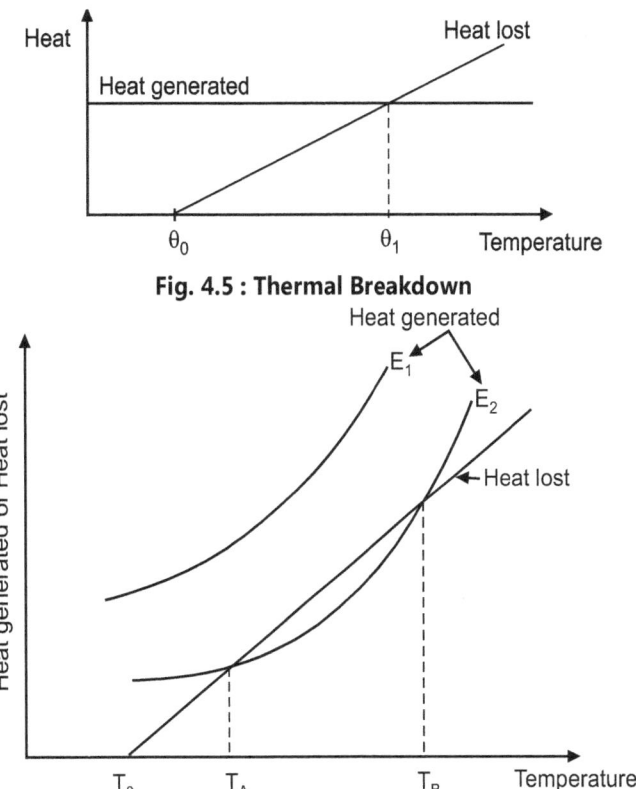

Fig. 4.5 : Thermal Breakdown

Fig. 4.6

(d) Breakdown due to internal discharges

Solid insulating materials sometimes contain voids or cavities in the medium or boundaries within the dielectric and between the dielectric and the electrodes. These voids have a dielectric constant of unity and a lower dielectric strength. Hence the electric field strength in the voids is higher than that across the dielectric surrounded by it. Thus even under normal working voltages, the field in the voids may go beyond their breakdown value and breakdown may occur. The mechanism can be explained by considering the following equivalent circuit of the dielectric with the void, shown in Fig. 4.7.

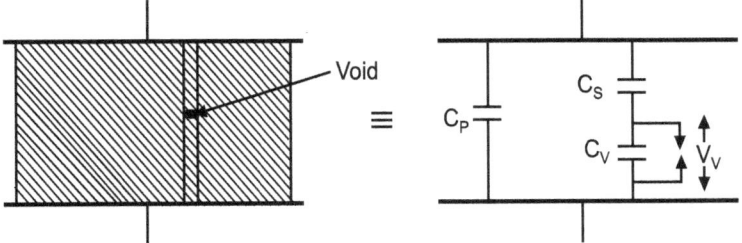

Fig. 4.7 : Equivalent circuit of dielectric with void

When the voltage V_v across the void exceeds the critical voltage V_c, a discharge is initiated and breakdown occur. The discharge extinguishes very rapidly (say 0.1 s). The voltage across the void again builds up and the discharges recur. The number and frequency of the discharges will depend on the applied voltage. The voltage and current waveforms are shown in Fig. 4.7. In the absence of field with applied field in each of the discharges, there will be heat dissipated in the voids which will cause carbonization of the surface of the voids and erosion of the material. The gradual erosion of the material and consequent reduction in the thickness of the insulating material finally leads to breakdown. Breakdown process is slow and may occur in a few days or may take a few years.

Deterioration due to internal discharges

In organic liquid-solid dielectrics, internal discharges produce gradual deterioration because of :

(a) Disintegration of the solid dielectric under the bombardment of electrons set free by the discharges.

(b) High temperatures in the region of the discharges.

(c) Chemical action on the dielectric of the products of ionization of the gas.

All voids in the dielectric can be removed by careful impregnation and these results in an increase in the discharge inception stress E_i. The final value E_i then depends on electrical processes which lead to gas formation.

In oil impregnated paper these are :

(a) Decomposition of moisture in paper.

(b) Local electrical breakdown of the oil.

The stress at which gas is evolved from paper containing significant quantities of moisture can be less than 10 V/m, but increases continuously with increasing dryness and can be higher than 100 V/m when the paper is thoroughly dry. excluding in very dry conditions, the gas first formed arises from electrochemical decomposition of water held in the paper. When a gas bubble is formed in an oil-paper dielectric at the discharge inception stress E_i, discharges in the bubble decompose the molecules of the oil. it resulting in further gas formation and a rapid growth of the bubble. As long as the bubble remains in the dielectric, the inception stress E_i is low, often lower than the rated stress. Although on resting E_i improves, permanent damage has been caused by the discharges and this manifests itself in an increase of loss angle and is due to the formation of ions by the discharges. Also due to the discharges, widespread carbonization occur V applied voltage across void if no discharges occurred.

(e) Surface Breakdown

Surface flashover

Surface flashover is a breakdown of the medium in which the solid is immersed. The role of the solid dielectric is only to deform the field so that the electric strength of the gas is exceeded. If a piece of solid insulation is inserted in a gas so that the solid surface is perpendicular to all points, then the voltage gradient is not affected by the solid insulation. An example of this is a cylindrical insulator placed in the direction of a uniform field. Field intensification consequences if solid insulation departs even in detail from the cylindrical shape. In particular if the edges are chipped, or if the ends of the cylinder are not quite perpendicular to the axis, then an air gap exists next to the electrode and the stress can reach up to 10 times the mean stress in the gap.

The three essential components of the surface flashover phenomena are :

(a) The presence of a conducting film across the surface of the insulation.

(b) A mechanism ofthe leakage current through the conducting film is interrupted with the production of sparks,

(c) Degradation of the insulation must be caused by the sparks.

The conducting film is frequently moisture from the atmosphere absorbed by some form of contamination. Moisture is not essential as a conducting path can also arise from metal dust due to wear and tear of moving parts. Sparks are drawn between moisture films, separated by drying of the surface due to heating effect of leakage current. For a discharge to occur there must be a voltage at least equal to the Paschen minimum for the particular state of the gas. For example, Paschen minimum in air at N.T.P. it is 380 V, whereas tracking can occur at well below 100 V. It does not depend on gaseous breakdown. Degradation of the insulation is almost exclusively the result of heat from the sparks, and this heat either carbonises if tracking is to occur, or volatilises if erosion is to occur. Carbonization results in a permanent extension of the electrodes and usually takes the form of a dendritic growth. Increase of creep age path during design will prevent tracking, but in most practical cases, moisture films can eliminate the designed creep age path.

(f) Breakdown due to Treeing and Tracking

AS we know that the strength of a chain is given by the strength of the weakest link in the chain. Similarly whenever solid materials have some impurities in terms of some gas pockets or liquid pockets in it the dielectric strength of the solid will be more or less equal to the strength of the weakest impurities. assume some gas pockets are trapped in a solid material during manufacture, the gas has a relative permittivity of unity and the solid material £r, the electric field in the gas will be £. As a effect the gas breaks down at a relatively lower voltage. The charge concentration here in the void will make the field more non-uniform. The charge concentration in such voids is found to be quite large to give fields of the order of 10 MV/cm which is higher than even the intrinsic breakdown. These charge concentrations at the voids within the dielectric lead to breakdown step by step and finally lead to complete breakdown of the dielectric as the breakdown is not caused by a single discharge channel and assumes a tree like structure as shown in Fig. 4.8, it is known as breakdown due to treeing. The treeing phenomenon can be verified in a laboratory by applying an impulse voltage between point plane electrodes with the point embedded in a transparent solid dielectric such as Perspex. The treeing phenomenon can be observed in all dielectric wherever non-uniform fields.

Suppose we have two electrodes separated by an insulating material and the assembly is placed in an outdoor environment. Some contaminants in the form of moisture or dust particles will get deposited on the surface of the insulation. this leads leakage current to starts between the electrodes through the contaminants say moisture. The current heats the moisture and causes breaks in the moisture films. These small films then act as electrodes and sparks are drawn between the films. The sparks cause carbonization of the insulation .that lead to formation of permanent carbon tracks on the surface of insulations. Therefore, tracking is the formation of a permanent conducting path across the surface of insulation. For tracking to occur, the insulating material must contain organic substances. For this reason, for outdoor equipment, tracking severely limits the use of insulation having organic substances. The rate of tracking can be slowed down by adding filters to the polymers which inhibit carbonization.

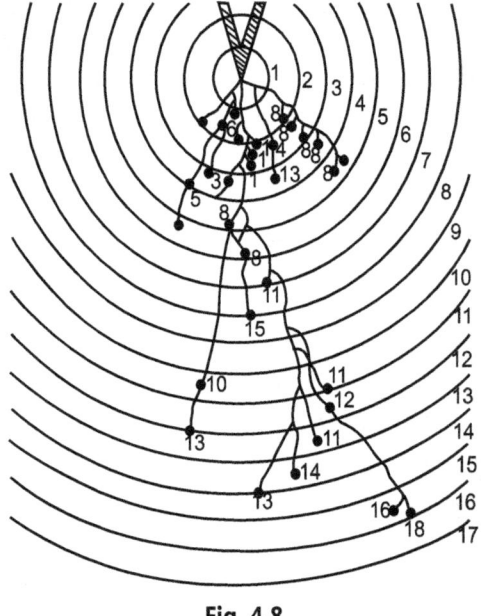

Fig. 4.8

Erosion

In a surface discharge, if the products of decomposition are volatile and there is no residual conducting carbon on the surface, the process is simply one of pitting known as erosion. This is erosion, which again occurs in organic materials. If surface discharges are likely to occur, it is mostly prefer to use materials with erosion properties rather than tracking properties.since tracking makes insulation immediately completely ineffective, whereas erosion only weakens the material but allows operation until replacement can be made.

Breakdown of liquid and solid insulation

The simplest case is where the loss of heat by cooling is linearly related to the temperature rise above surroundings, and the heat generated is independent of temperature. i.e. the resistivity and the loss angle do not much vary with temperature.

4.12 BREAKDOWN IN LIQUID DIELECTRICS

Q. Explain breakdown in liquid dielectries.
Q. Explain suspended solid particle meachanism.

Liquid dielectrics are used for transformers, circuit breakers and as impregnates in high voltage cables and capacitors. For transformer, the liquid dielectric is used both for providing insulation between the live parts of the transformer and the grounded parts besides carrying out the heat from the transformer to the atmosphere thus providing cooling effect. The liquid dielectrics mostly used are petroleum oils. Other oils used are synthetic hydrocarbons and halogenated hydrocarbons and for very high temperature applications sillicone oils and fluorinated hyrocarbons are also used. The three most important properties of liquid dielectric are

(i) The dielectric strength
(ii) The dielectric constant and
(iii) The electrical conductivity.

Other important properties are viscosity, thermal stability, specific gravity, flash point etc. The most significant factors which affect the dielectric strength of oil are the, presence of fine water droplets and the fibrous impurities. The presence of even 0.01% water in oil brings down the dielectric strength to 20% of the dry oil value and the presence of fibrous impurities brings down the dielectric strength much sharply. Therefore, whenever these oils are used for providing electrical insulation, these should always free from moisture, products of oxidation and other contaminants. The main consideration in the selection of a liquid dielectric is its chemical stability. Table 4.1 shows the properties of some dielectrics commonly used in electrical equipments.

Table 4.1 : Dielectric properties of some liquids

Sr. No.	Property	Transformer oil	Capacitor oil	Cable oil	Silicone oil
1.	Relative permittivity 50 Hz	2.2 – 2.3	2.1	2.3 – 2.6	2.7 – 3.0
2.	Breakdown strength at 20°C 2.5 mm 1 min	12 kV/mm	18 kV/mm	25 kV/mm	35 kV/mm
3.	(a) Tan δ at 50 Hz	10^{-3}	2.5×10^{-4}	2×10^{-3}	10^{-3}
	(b) 1 kHz	5×10^{-4}	10^{-4}	10^{-4}	10^{-4}
4.	Resistivity ohm-cm	$10^{12} - 10^{13}$	$10^{13} - 10^{14}$	$10^{12} - 10^{13}$	2.5×10^{14}
5.	Maximum permissible water content (ppm)	50	50	50	< 40
6.	Sponification mg of KOH/gm of oil	0.01	0.01	0.01	< 0.01
7.	Specific gravity at 20°C	0.89	0.89	0.93	1.0 – 1.1

Liquids which are chemically pure, structurally simple and do not contain any impurity even in traces of 1 in 109, are known as pure liquids. In commercial liquids used as insulating liquids are chemically impure and contain mixtures of complex organic molecules. The theory of liquid insulation breakdown is less understood as compared to the gas or even solids. Many aspects of liquid breakdown have been investigated over the last decades but no general theory has been evolved so far to explain the breakdown in liquids insulating material. The first theory of the breakdown in liquids on a model based on the avalanche ionization of the atoms caused by electron collision in the applied field. The electrons are assumed to be ejected from the cathode into the liquid by either a field emission or by the field enhanced thermionic effect. This breakdown mechanism explains breakdown only of highly pure liquid and does not apply to explain the breakdown mechanism in commercially available liquids. It has been experimental that conduction in pure liquids at low electric field (1 kV/cm) is largely ionic due to dissociation of impurities and increases linearity with the field strength. At moderately high fields the conduction saturates but at high field (electric), 100 kV/cm the conduction increases more rapidly and thus breakdown takes place. This is the condition nearer to breakdown. though, if the figure is starting with low fields, a current-electric field characteristic as shown in Fig. 4.9 (b) will be obtained. This curve has three distinct regions as discussed above.

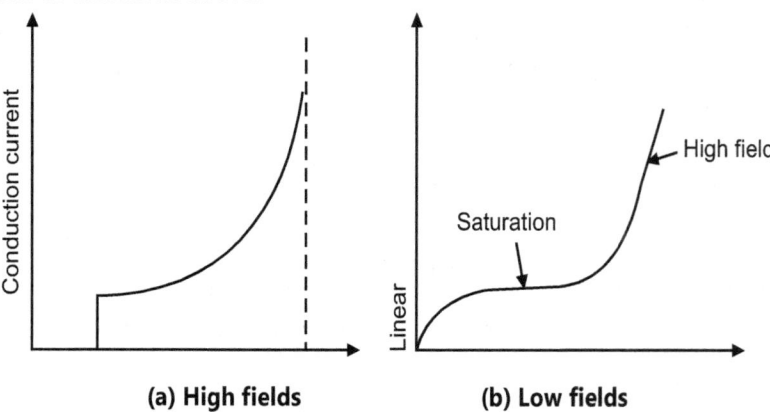

(a) High fields   (b) Low fields

Fig. 4.9 : Variation of current as a function of electric field

The presence of particles in liquid insulations has a marked effect on the dielectric strength of liquid dielectrics. It has been suggested that the suspended particles are polarizable and are of higher permittivity than the liquid. These particles experience an electrical force directed of maximum stress. With uniform field electrodes the movement of particles is presumed to be initiated by surface irregularities on the electrodes, which give rise to local field gradients. The particles thus get accumulated and tend to form a bridge across the gap which leads finally to initiation of breakdown. The impurities could also be in the form of gaseous bubbles which obviously has lower dielectric strength than the liquid itself and hence on breakdown of bubble the total breakdown of liquid may be triggered.

Electronic Breakdown

Once an electron is injected into the liquid, it gains energy from the electric field applied between the electrodes. It is alleged that some electrons will gain more energy due to field than they would lose during collision. These electrons are accelerated under the electric field The threshold condition for the beginning of avalanche is achieved when the energy gained by the electron equals the energy lost during ionization and is given by

$$e\lambda E = Ch\nu$$

where, λ is the mean free path, $h\nu$ is the energy of ionization and C is a constant. The electronic theory whereas relative values of dielectric strength satisfactorily, the formative time lags observed are much longer as compared to the ones predicted by the electronic theory.

Suspended Solid Particle Mechanism

Commercial liquids always contain solid impurities either as fibres or as dispersed solid particles. The permittivity of these solids (E_1) will always be different from that of the liquid (E_2). Let us assume these particles to be sphere of radius r. These particles get polarized in an electric field E and experience a force which is given as

$$F = r^3 \frac{\varepsilon_1 - \varepsilon_2}{\varepsilon_1 + 2\varepsilon_2} E \cdot \frac{dE}{dx}$$

and this force is directed towards a place of higher stress if $\varepsilon_1 > \varepsilon_2$ and towards a place of lower stress if $\varepsilon_1 < \varepsilon_2$ when ε_1 is the permittivity of gas bubbles. The force given above increases as the permittivity of the suspended particles increases. If $\varepsilon_1 \to \infty$, then

$$F = r^3 \frac{1 - \varepsilon_2/\varepsilon_1}{1 + 2\varepsilon_2/\varepsilon_1} E \frac{dE}{dx}$$

Let, $\varepsilon_1 \to \infty$ and, $F = r^3 E \cdot \frac{dE}{dx}$

therefore, the force will tend the particle to move towards the strongest region of the field. In a uniform electric field which usually can be developed by a small sphere gap, the field is the strongest in the uniform field region. Here, the force on the particle is zero and the particle remains in equilibrium. Therefore, the particles will be dragged into the uniform field region. Since the permittivity of the particles is higher than that of the liquid, the presence of particle in the uniform field region will cause flux concentration at its surface. Other particles, if present will be attracted towards the higher flux concentration. If the particles present are large, they become aligned and form a bridge across the gap. The field in the liquid between the gaps will increase and if it reaches critical value, breakdown will take place. If the number of particles is not sufficient to bridge the gap, the particles will give rise to local field enhancement and if the field exceeds the dielectric strength of liquid, local breakdown will occur near the particles and thus result in the formation of gas bubbles which have much less dielectric strength and hence finally lead to the breakdown of the liquid. The movement of the particle under the influence of electric field is opposed by the viscous force posed by the liquid and since the particles are moving into the region of high stress, diffusion must also be taken into account. as We know that the viscous force is given by (Stroke's relation)

$$F_v = 6\pi\eta r v,$$

where η is the viscosity of liquid, r is the radius of the particle and v is the velocity of the particle. Equating the electrical force with the viscous force we have

$$6\pi\eta r v = r^3 E \frac{dE}{dx} \text{ or, } v = \frac{r^2 E}{6\pi\eta} \frac{dE}{dx}.$$ However, if the diffusion process is included, the drift velocity due to diffusion will be given as

$$v_d = -\frac{D}{N}\frac{dN}{dx} = -\frac{KT}{6\pi\eta r}\frac{dn}{Ndx}$$

where, $D = KT/6\pi\eta r$ a relation known as Stokes-Einstein relation. Here K is Boltzmann's constant and T the absolute temperature. At any instant of time, the particle should have one velocity and, therefore, equation $v = v_d$.

$$-\frac{KT}{6\pi\eta r} \cdot \frac{dN}{Ndx} = \frac{r^2 E}{6\pi\eta} \cdot \frac{dE}{dx}$$

$$\frac{KT}{r}\frac{dN}{N} = -r^2 E\, dE$$

$$\frac{KT}{r} \ln N = -\frac{r^2 E^2}{2}$$

It is clear that the breakdown strength E depends upon the concentration of particles N, radius r of particle, viscosity of liquid and temperature T of the liquid. It has been found that liquid with solid impurities has lower dielectric strength as compared to its pure form. Also, it has been observed that bigger the size of the particles impurity the lower the overall dielectric strength of the liquid containing the impurity.

Cavity Breakdown

It has been observed experimentally that the dielectric strength of liquid depends upon the hydrostatic pressure above the gap length. The higher the hydrostatic pressure, the higher the electric strength, this suggests that a change in phase of the liquid is involved in the breakdown process. In fact, smaller the head of liquid, the more are the chances of partially ionized gases coming out of the gap and higher the probability of breakdown. This means a kind of vapour bubble formed is responsible for the breakdown. The following processes might lead to formation of bubbles in the liquids :

(i) Gas pockets on the surface of electrodes.
(ii) Due to irregular surface of electrodes, point charge concentration may lead to corona discharge, thus vapourizing the liquid.

(iii) Dissociation of products by electron collisions giving rise to gaseous products.

(iv) Changes in temperature and pressure. It has been suggested that the electric field in a gas bubble which is immersed in a liquid of permittivity ε_2 is given by

$$E_b = \frac{3E_0}{\varepsilon_2 + 2}$$

Where E_0 is the field in the liquid in absence of the bubble. The bubble under the influence of the electric field E_0 elongates keeping its volume constant. When the field E_b equals the gaseous ionization field, discharge takes place which will lead to decomposition of liquid and breakdown occur. A more accurate expression for the bubble breakdown strength is given as:

$$E_b = \frac{1}{\varepsilon_2 - \varepsilon_1}\left\{\frac{2\pi\sigma(2\varepsilon_2 + \varepsilon_1)}{r}\left[\frac{\pi}{4}\sqrt{\frac{V_b}{2rE_0}} - 1\right]\right\}^{1/2}$$

where σ is the surface tension of the liquid ε_2 and ε_1 are the permittivities of the liquid and bubble, respectively, r is the initial radius of the bubble and V_b is the voltage drop in the bubble. From the expression it can be seen that the breakdown strength depends on the initial size of the bubble which depends upon the hydrostatic pressure above the bubble and temperature of the liquid. as the above formation does not take into account the production of the initial bubble, the experimental values of breakdown were found to be much less than the calculated values. Later on it was suggested that only incompressible bubbles like water bubbles can elongate at constant volume according to the simple gas law pV = RT. Such a bubble under the influence of electric field changes its shape to that of a prolate spheroid and reaches a condition of instability when the ratio of the longer to the shorter diameter of the spheroid is about 1.85 and the critical field producing the instability will be given by

$$E_c = 600\frac{\sqrt{\pi\sigma}}{\varepsilon_2 r}\left[\frac{\varepsilon_2}{\varepsilon_2 - \varepsilon_1} - G\right]H$$

$$G = \frac{1}{\beta^2 - 1}\left[\frac{\beta\cosh^{-1}\beta}{(\beta^2 - 1)^{1/2}} - 1\right]$$

$$H^2 = 2\beta^{1/3}\left[2\beta - 1 - \frac{1}{\beta^2}\right]$$

Electroconvection Breakdown

It has been recognized that the electroconvection plays an important role in breakdown of insulating fluids subjected to high voltages. When a highly pure insulating liquid is subjected to high voltage, electrical conduction results from charge carriers injected into the liquid from the electrode surface. The resulting space charge gives rise to coulombic forces which under certain conditions causes hydrodynamic instability, yielding convecting current. As the applied voltage approaches the critical voltage. Thus, interaction between the space charge and the electric field gives rise to forces creating an eddy motion of liquid. It has been shown that when the voltage applied is near to breakdown value, the speed of the eddy motion is given by,

$$v_e = \sqrt{\varepsilon_2/\rho}$$

where ρ is the density of liquid. In liquids, the ionic drift velocity is given by,

$$v_d = KE \text{ where K is the mobility of ions.}$$

$$M \frac{v_e}{v_d} = \sqrt{\frac{\varepsilon_2}{\rho}} / KE$$

Let, the ratio M is usually greater than unity and sometimes much greater than unity.

4.13 FACTORS AFFECTING BREAKDOWN VOLTAGE OF SOLID

Q. Explain factors affecting on breakdown of solid, liquid materials.

Different factors affect on breakdown strength of solid dielectric are :
1. Temperature.
2. Shape of electrodes.

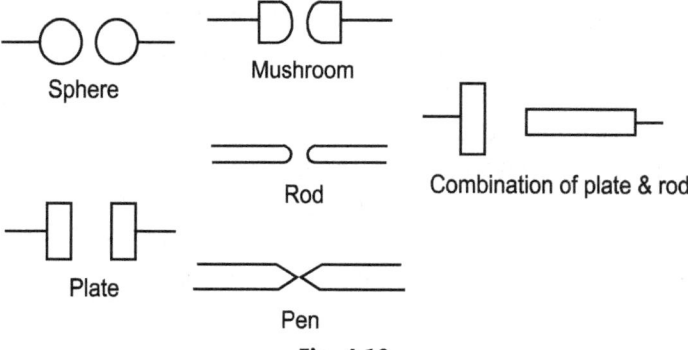

Fig. 4.10

If shape of electrode gives non-uniform field breakdown voltage reduces.
3. Defects of non-homogeneity of material.
4. Thickness of specimen.
5. Time of applied voltage.
6. Electrode surface condition.
7. Moisture and other contaminations.

4.14 FACTORS AFFECTING BREAKDOWN STRENGTH OF LIQUID DIELECTRIC MATERIAL

1. **Distance between electrodes :** Distance between electrodes is directly proportional to the breakdown voltage. As distance between electrodes increases breakdown voltage increase.

2. **Dissolved gasses :** Breakdown voltage is decreases as dissolved gases in liquid increases.
3. **Moisture or water particles :** If moisture in liquid dielectric increases by 0.01% the breakdown voltage reduces from 50 kV to 10 kV.
4. **Impurities :** As impurities increase the breakdown voltage decreases.

Other factor which affect are :

1. Temperature.
2. Viscosity of liquid.
3. Electrode material.
4. Shape of electrode.

4.15 FACTORS AFFECTING BREAKDOWN STRENGTH OF GASEOUS DIELECTRIC

1. Electrode configuration.
2. Gap spacing.
3. Moisture and humidity.
4. Effect of atmospheric conditions.
5. Pressure.

As per Paschen's law product of pressure and distance increases breakdown voltage decreases initially but after certain value it goes on increasing.

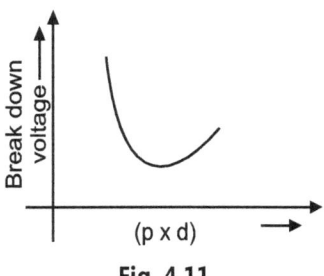

Fig. 4.11

4.16 BREAKDOWN IN VACUUM

Q. Write short note on breakdown in vacuum.

In vacuum system pressure is maintained at below the atmospheric pressure. Unit of vacuum is 'Torr'.

There are three classified vacuums :

1. High vacuum → 1×10^{-3} to 1×10^{-6} Torr.
2. Very high vacuum → 1×10^{-6} to 1×10^{-8} Torr.

3. Ultra high vacuum → 1×10^{-9} and below.

The different mechanisms for breakdown in vacuum have been proposed as follows :

1. Particle exchange mechanism.
2. Field emission mechanism.
3. Clump theory.

Particle exchange mechanism

In this it is assumed that charged particle would be emitted from one electrode under high electric field. It collides with other electrode and liberates oppositely charge particles. This process become cumulative and chain reaction occurs which leads to breakdown of the gap.

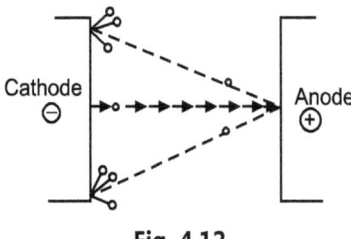

Fig. 4.12

It involves electron photons positive ion and absorbed gases at electrode surface.

Field emission theory

This have two type :

(i) Anode heating mechanism.
(ii) Cathode heating mechanism.

Anode heating mechanism

According to this theory electrons are produced on cathode due to field emission bombarded to anode cause local rise in temperature. This release gases in vacuum. This electron ionizes this gas. This process continues to cause breakdown.

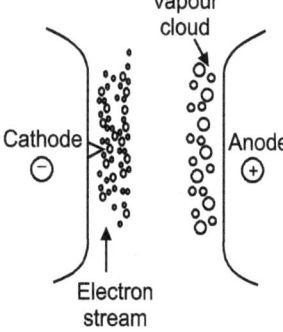

Fig. 4.13

Cathode heating mechanism

According to this theory pre breakdown current causes resistive heating at the tip of a point and when critical current density reached the tip melts and breakdown occurs.

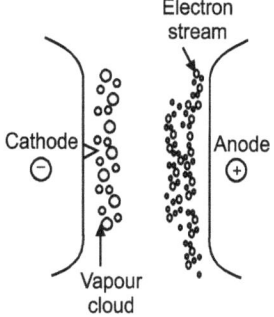

Fig. 4.14

Clump mechanism

This theory has been developed by the following assumption :

1. Clump is exists on one of the electrode surfaces.
2. On the application of high voltage it get charged and detached from originated electrode.
3. Breakdown occurs due to discharge in the vapour or gas released by the impact of clump at the target electrode as shown in Fig. 4.15.

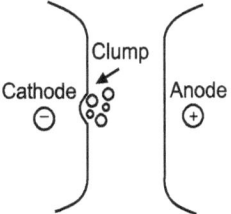

(a) Clamp is loosely attached to surface

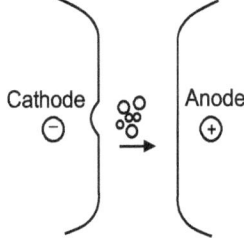

(b) Clump is detached from cathode due to high voltage

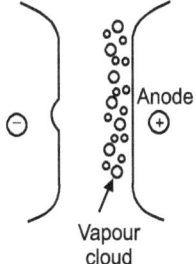

(c) Impact of the clump on anode gives vapours cloud

Fig. 4.15

REVIEW QUESTIONS

1. What is dielectric strength?
2. Explain factors affecting on breakdown voltage of gasses, liquid and solid.

UNIVERSITY QUESTIONS

May 2008

1. What do you understand by : **(8 Marks)**
   (i) Contaminated liquid
   (ii) Technically pure liquid
   (iii) Highly purified liquid
2. State different mechanisms of breakdown in vacuum. Explain any one. **(8 Marks)**

Dec. 2008

3. What do you understand by : **(8 Marks)**
   (i) Contaminated liquid
   (ii) Technically pure liquid
   (iii) Highly purified liquid
4. What is meant by Townsends primary and secondary ionization coefficients? **(8 Marks)**
5. State different mechanisms of breakdown in Vacuum. Explain particle exchange mechanism. **(8 Marks)**

May 2009

6. What do you understand by : **(8 Marks)**
   (i) Contaminated liquid
   (ii) Technically pure liquid
   (iii) Highly purified liquid
7. What are the inferences of breakdown in transformer oil? **(8 Marks)**
8. State different mechanisms of breakdown in vacuum. Explain any one. **(8 Marks)**
9. What is meant by Townsends primary and secondary ionization coefficients? **(8 Marks)**

Dec. 2009

10. State different mechanisms of breakdown in vacuum. Explain any one. **(8 Marks)**
11. What is meant by Townsends primary and secondary ionization coefficients? **(8 Marks)**
12. Define breakdown voltage in connection with dielectric materials. Explain various factors affecting breakdown strength of liquid dielectric materials. **(8 Marks)**

May 2010

13. State different mechanisms of breakdown in vacuum. Explain any one in detail.
    (8 Marks)

14. What is meant by Townsends primary and secondary ionization co-efficient? Explain various factors affecting breakdown strength of gaseous insulating materials.
    (8 Marks)

Dec. 2010

15. Differentiate between : **(4 Marks)**
    (i) Breakdown voltage and breakdown strength.
    (ii) Primary ionization and secondary ionization.

May 2011

16. Explain the factors on which breakdown in gaseous insulating materials depends.
    (6 Marks)

17. With neat diagram explain particle exchange mechanism in connection with vacuum breakdown. **(6 Marks)**

18. Explain : **(4 Marks)**
    (i) Townsend's primary ionization co-efficient
    (ii) Townsend's secondary ionization co-efficient.

Dec. 2011

19. State different mechanisms of breakdown in vacuum. Explain any one in detail.
    (8 Marks)

20. What is meant by Townsend's primary and secondary ionization co-efficient? Explain various factors affecting the breakdown strength of solid insulating materials.
    (8 Marks)

May 2012

21. Explain various factors that affect breakdown in gaseous insulating materials.
    (8 Marks)

22. Explain the following terms : **(8 Marks)**
    (i) Breakdown voltage and breakdown strength.
    (ii) Breakdown in solid insulating materials.
    (iii) Townsend's primary ionization co-efficients.
    (iv) Townsend' secondary ionization co-efficients.

Dec. 2012

23. Define :
    (i) Breakdown voltage
    (ii) Breakdown strength
    (iii) Primary ionization
    (iv) Secondary ionization

UNIT III

CHAPTER 5
MAGNETIC MATERIALS

5.1 INTRODUCTION

A magnetic field consists of imaginary lines of flux coming from moving or spinning electrically charged particles. What a magnetic field actually consists of is somewhat of a mystery, but we do know it is a special property of space.

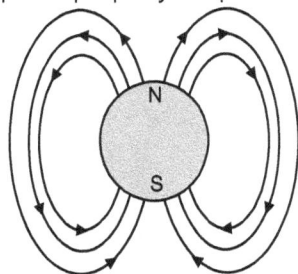

Fig. 5.1 : Magnetic field or lines of flux of a moving charged particle

Names of Poles

The lines of magnetic flux flow from one end of the object to the other. By convention, we call one end of a magnetic object the North-seeking pole and the other the South-seeking pole, as refferd to the Earth's North and South magnetic poles. The magnetic flux is defined as moving from N to S.

Magnets

Although individual particles such as electrons can have magnetic fields, larger objects such as a piece of iron also have a magnetic field. If a larger object exhibits a sufficiently great magnetic field, it is called a magnet.

5.2 MAGNETIC STORE

The magnetic field of an object can create a magnetic force on other objects with magnetic fields. That force is call magnetism.

When a magnetic field is applied to a moving electric charge, such as a moving proton or the electrical current in a wire, the force on the charge is called a Lorentz force.

Attraction

When two magnets or magnetic objects are close to each other, there is a force that attracts the poles together.

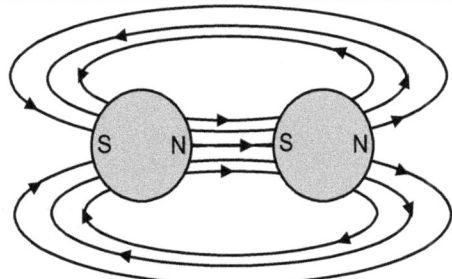

Fig. 5.2 : Force attracts N to S

Magnets also strongly attract ferromagnetic materials such as iron, nickel and cobalt.

Repulsion

When two magnetic objects have like poles facing each other, the magnetic force pushes them apart.

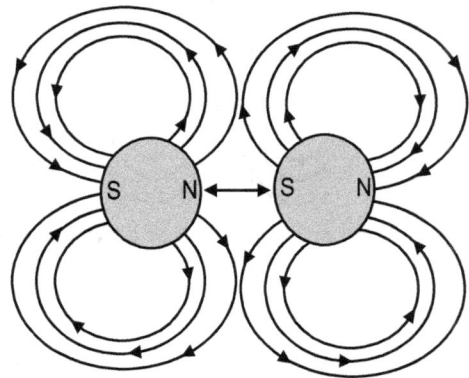

Fig. 5.3 : Force pushes magnetic objects apart

Magnets can also weakly repel diamagnetic materials.

5.3 MAGNETIC AND ELECTRIC FIELDS

Electric charges and magnetism similar

Just as the positive and negative electrical charges attract each other, the N and S poles of a magnet attract each other.

In electricity like charges repel, and in magnetism like poles repel.

Electric charges and magnetism different

The magnetic field is a dipole field. That means that every magnet must have two poles.

On the other hand, a positive (+) or negative (−) electrical charge can stand alone. Electrical charges are thus called monopoles, since they can exist without the opposite charge. Define magnetic susceptibility magnetic moment.

5.4 MAGNETIC SUSCEPTIBILITY

Magnetic susceptibility is the degree to which a material can be magnetized in an external magnetic field. If the ratio between the induced magnetization and the inducing field is expressed per unit volume this volume susceptibility (k) is defined as

$$k = M/H,$$

where M is the volume magnetization induced in a material of susceptibility k by the applied external field H. Volume susceptibility is a dimensionless quantity.

5.4.1 Magnetic Moments

Magnetic moments are permanent dipole moments within the atom which are made up from electrons angular momentum and spin.

Electrons inside atoms contribute magnetic moments from their angular momentum and from their orbital momentum around the nucleus. Magnetic moments from the nucleus are insignificant in contrast to magnetic moments from electrons. Thermal contribution in this will result in higher energy electrons causing disruption to their order and alignment between dipoles to be destroyed.

5.5 TYPES OF MAGNETISM

Q. Explain different type of magnetism.
Q. Write short note on paramagnetism.

All magnetic materials contain *magnetic moments*, which behave in a way similar to microscopic bar magnetis These are principally: paramagnets, ferromagnets, antiferromagnets and ferrimagnets.

Paramagnetism

In a paramagnet, the magnetic moments tend to be randomly orientated due to thermal fluctuations when there is no magnetic field. In an applied magnetic field these moments start to align parallel to the field such that the magnetisation of the material is proportional to the applied field.

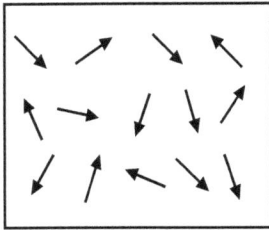

Fig. 5.4 (a) : Schematic showing the magnetic dipole moments randomly aligned in a paramagnetic sample

Ferromagnetism

The magnetic moments in a ferromagnet have the tendency to aligned parallel to each other under the influence of a magnetic field. though, unlike the moments in a paramagnet, these moments will then remain parallel when a magnetic field is not applied.

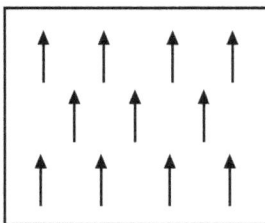

Fig. 5.4 (b) : Schematic showing the magnetic dipole moments aligned parallel in a ferromagnetic material

Antiferromagnetism

Adjacent magnetic moments from the magnetic ions tend to align anti-parallel to each other without an applied field. In case, adjacent magnetic moments are equal in magnitude and opposite therefore there is no overall magnetisation.

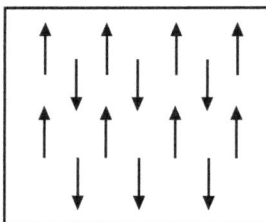

Fig. 5.4 (c) : Schematic showing adjacent magnetic dipole moments with equal magnitude aligned anti-parallel in an antiferromagnetic material. This is only one of many possible antiferromagnetic arrangements of magnetic moments.

Ferrimagnetism

The aligned magnetic moments are not of the identical size; that is more than one type of magnetic ion. An overall magnetisation is produced but not all the magnetic moments may give a positive contribution to the overall magnetisation.

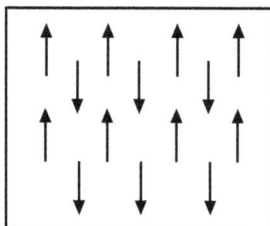

Fig. 5.4 (d) : Schematic showing adjacent magnetic moments of different magnitudes aligned anti-parallel.

Below is a periodic table showing the elements and the types of magnetism at room temperature:

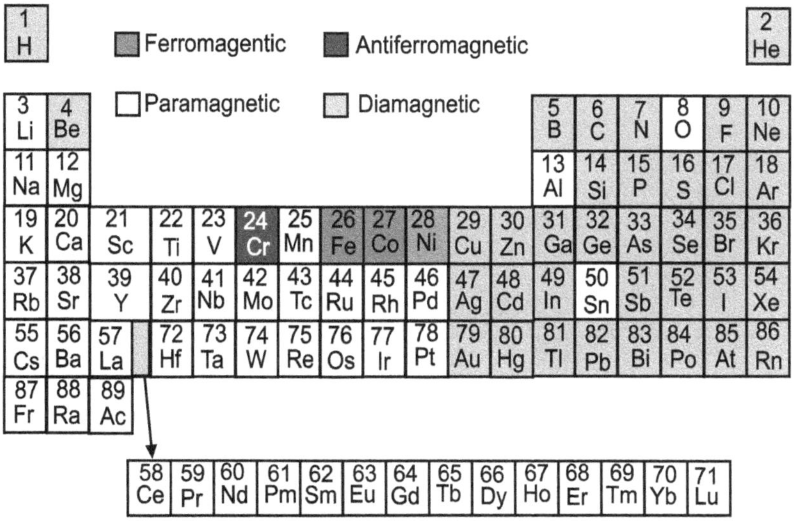

Fig. 5.4 (e) : Diagram of a periodic table showing elements coloured according to the type of magnetism they show at room temperature.

5.6 CURIE TEMPERATURE

Q. Write short note on curie temperature.

In physics and materials science, the **Curie temperature** (T_c), or **Curie point**, is the temperature where a material's permanent magnetism changes to induced magnetism. The force of magnetism is determined by magnetic moments.

The Curie Temperature is the critical point where a material's intrinsic magnetic moments change direction. Magnetic moments in material are permanent dipole moments within the atom which originate from electrons angular momentum and spin. At a material's Curie Temperature those intrinsic magnetic moments change direction.

Permanent magnetism is caused by the alignment of magnetic moments and induced magnetism is created when disordered magnetic moments are forced to align in an applied magnetic field. For example, the ordered magentic moments (ferromagnetic, Fig. 5.5) change and become disordered (paramagnetic Fig. 5.6) at the Curie Temperature.

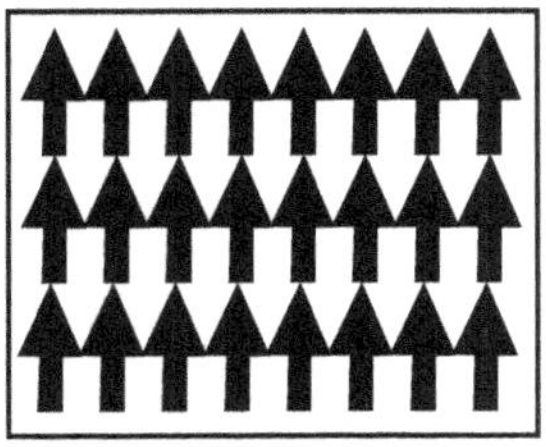

Fig. 5.5. : Below the Curie temperature, neighbouring magnetic spins align in a ferromagnet in the absence of an applied magnetic field

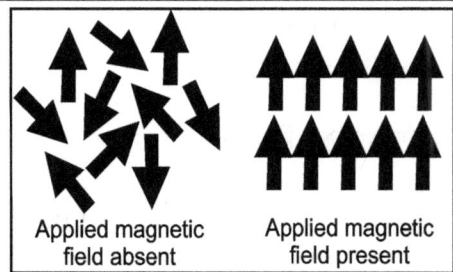

Fig. 5.6 : Above the Curie temperature, the magnetic spins are randomly aligned in a paramagnet unless a magnetic field is applied

Table 5.1 : Curie Temperature of Materials

Material	Curie Temperature (K)
Iron (Fe)	1043
Cobalt (Co)	1400
Nickel (Ni)	631
Gadolinium (Gd)	292
Dysprosium (Dy)	88
MnBi	630
CrO_2	386
MnAs	318
EuO	69
Iron (III) Oxide (Fe_2O_3)	948
Iron (II, III) oxide (FeO Fe_2O_3)	858
$NiOFe_2O_3$	858
$CuOFe_2O_3$	728
$MgOFe_2O_3$	713
$MnOFe_2O_3$	573
$Y_3Fe_5O_{12}$	560

Higher temperatures compose magnets weaker as spontaneous magnetism only occurs below the Curie Temperature. Magnetic susceptibility only occurs above the Curie Temperature and can be calculated from the Curie-Weiss Law which is derived from Curie's Law.

In analogy to ferromagnetic and paramagnetic materials, the Curie temperature can also describe the temperature where a material's spontaneous electric polarisation changes to induced electric polarisation or the reverse upon reduction of the temperature below the Curie temperature.

The Curie temperature is named after Pierre Curie who showed that magnetism was lost at a critical temperature.

5.6.1 Curie-Weiss law

The Curie-Weiss law is model derived from a mean-field approximation, this means it works well for the materials temperature,T, much greater than their corresponding Curie Temperature,T_c, i.e. $T >> T_c$; however fails to describe the magnetic susceptibility, χBoth Curie's law and the Curie-Weiss law do not hold for $T < T_c$.

Curie's law for a paramagnetic material;

$$\chi = \frac{M}{H} = \frac{M\mu_o}{B} = \frac{C}{T}$$

where,

χ : The magnetic susceptibility; the influence of an applied magnetic field on a material.
M: The magnetic moments per unit volume.
H : The macroscopic magnetic field.
B : The magnetic field.
C : The material-specific curie constant.

$$C = \frac{m_o \mu_B^2}{3k_B} Ng^2 J(J+1)$$

where,

m_o : The permeability of free space. Note – in CGS units is taken to equal one.
g : The Lande g-factor.
$J(J+1)$: The eigenvalue for eigenstate J^2 for the stationary states within the incomplete atoms shells (electrons unpaired.
m_B : the Bohr Magneton
k_B : Boltzmann's constant

total magnetism : is N number of magnetic moments per unit volume.

The Curie-Weiss law is then derived from Curie's law to be

$$\chi = \frac{C}{T - T_c}$$

where, $$T_C = \frac{C\lambda}{mo}$$

λ is the Weiss molecular field constant.

Materials with magnetic moments that change properties at the Curie temperature

Ferromagnetic, paramagnetic, ferrimagnetic and antiferromagnetic structures are made up of intrinsic magnetic moments. If all electrons within the structure are paired, these moments cancel out due to having opposite spins and angular momentum with in them. Thus even with an applied magnetic field will have different properties and no Curie Temperature.

Below T_c	Above T_c
Ferromagnetic	↔ Paramagnetic
Ferrimagnetic	↔ Paramagnetic
Antiferromagnetic	↔ Paramagnetic

5.6.2 Physics of Curie Temperature

As the Curie-Weiss Law is an approximation a more accurate model is needed when the temperature, approaches the materials Curie Temperature, T_C.

Magnetic susceptibility occurs above the Curie Temperature.

An accurate model of critical behaviour for magnetic susceptibility with critical exponent γ;

$$X \sim \frac{1}{(T - T_c)^\gamma}$$

The critical exponent differs between materials and for the mean-field model is taken as $\gamma = 1$.

As temperature is inversely proportional to magnetic susceptibility when T approaches T_C the denominator tends to zero and the magnetic susceptibility approaches infinity allowing magnetism to occur. This is a spontaneous magnetism which is a property of ferromagnetic and ferrimagnetic materials.

Approaching Curie temperature from below

Magnetism depends on temperature and spontaneous magnetism occurs below the Curie Temperature. An accurate model of critical behaviour for spontaneous magnetism with critical exponent β;

$$M \sim (T - T_C)^\beta$$

The critical exponent differs between materials and for the mean-field model as taken as β = 0.5 where $T \ll T_C$.

The spontaneous magnetism approaches zero as the temperature increases towards the materials Curie Temperature.

Approaching absolute zero (0 Kelvin)

The spontaneous magnetism, occurring in ferromagnetic, ferrimagnetic and antiferromagnetic materials, approaches zero as the temperature increases towards the Curie Temperature. Spontaneous magnetism is at its maximum as the temperature approaches 0. the magnetic moments are completely aligned and at their strongest magnitude of magnetism due to no thermal disturbance.

In paramagnetic materials temperature is sufficient to overcome the ordered alignments. As the temperature approaches 0 K the entropy decreases to zero. Both Curie's Law and the Curie-Weiss law fail as the temperature approaches 0 K. This is because they depend on the magnetic susceptibility which only applies when the state is disordered.

Gadolinium Sulphate continues to satisfy Curie's law at 1 K. Between 0-1 K the law fails to hold and a sudden change in the intrinsic structure occurs at the Curie Temperature.

Weiss domains and surface and bulk Curie temperatures

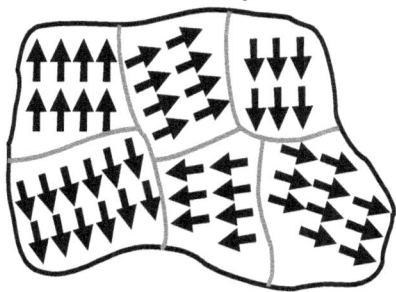

Fig. 5.7 : The Weiss domains in a ferromagnetic material; the magnetic moments are aligned in domains

Materials structures consist of intrinsic magnetic moments which are separated into domains called Weiss domains. This can result in ferromagnetic materials having no spontaneous magnetism as domains. The position of particles can therefore have different orientations around the surface than the main part of the material. This property directly affects the Curie Temperature as there can be a bulk Curie Temperature T_B and a different surface Curie Temperature T_S for a material.

This allows for the surface Curie Temperature to be ferromagnetic above the bulk Curie Temperature when the main state is disordered, i.e. Ordered and disordered states occur simultaneously.

5.6.3 Factors affecting on Curie temperature

Composite materials

Composite materials, other materials with different properties, can change the Curie Temperature. For example, a composite which has silver it can create spaces for oxygen molecules in bonding which decreases the Curie Temperature as the crystal lattice will not be as compact.

The alignment of magnetic moments in the composite material affects the Curie Temperature. If the materials moments are parallel with each other the Curie Temperature will increase and if perpendicular the Curie Temperature will decreaseas either more or less thermal energy will be needed to destroy the alignments.

Particle size

The size of particles in a material's crystal lattice changes the Curie Temperature. Due to the small size of particles the fluctuations of electron spins become more prominent, this results in the Curie Temperature drastically decreasing when the size of particles decrease as the fluctuations cause disorder. The size of a particle also affects the anisotropy causing alignment to become less stable and thus lead to confusion in magnetic moments.

The extreme of this is super magnetism which only occurs in small ferromagnetic particles and is where fluctuations are very influential causing magnetic moments to change direction randomly and thus create disorder.

Pressure

Pressure changes a material's Curie Temperature. Pressure directly affects the kinetic energy in particles as movement increases causing the vibrations to disrupt the order of magnetic moments. This is similar to temperature as it also increases the kinetic energy of particles and destroys the order of magnetic moments and magnetism.

Orbital ordering

Orbital ordering changes the Curie Temperature of a material. Orbital ordering can be controlled through applied strains. This is a function that determines the wave of a single electron or paired electrons inside the material. Having control over the probability of where the electron will be allows the Curie Temperature to be altered. For example, the delocalised electrons can be moved onto the same plane by applied strains within the crystal lattice.

The Curie Temperature is seen to increase greatly due to electrons being packed together in the same plane, they are forced to align due to the exchange interaction and thus increases the strength of the magnetic moments which prevents thermal disorder at lower temperatures.

5.6.4 Curie temperature in ferroelectric and piezoelectric materials

In analogy to ferromagnetic and paramagnetic materials, the Curie Temperature can also used to describe the temperature where a material's spontaneous electric polarisation changes to induced electric polarisation, or vice versa.

Electric polarisation is a result of aligned electric dipoles. Aligned electric dipoles are composites of positive and negative charges The charges are separated from their stable placement in the particles and can occur spontaneously, from pressure or an applied electric field.

Ferroelectric, dielectric (paraelectric) and piezoelectric materials have electric polarisation. In ferroelectric materials, there is a spontaneous electric polarisation in the absence of an applied electric field. In dielectric materials, there is electric polarisation aligned only when an electric field is applied. Piezoelectric materials have electric polarisation due to applied mechanical stress distorting the structure from pressure.

T_0 is the temperature where ferroelectric materials lose their spontaneous polarisation as a first or second order phase change occurs, that is the internal structure changes or the internal symmetry changes. In certain cases, T_0 is equal to the Curie Temperature.

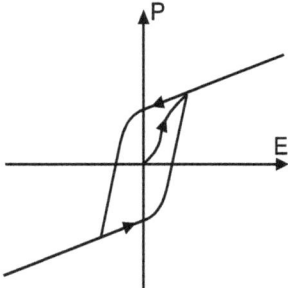

Fig. 5.8 : Ferroelectric polarisation P in an applied electric field E.

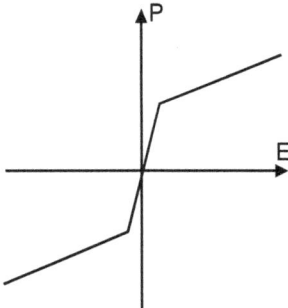

Fig. 5.9 : Dielectric polarisation P in an applied electric field E.

Below T_0	Above T_0
Ferroelectric	↔ Dielectric

5.7 PARAMAGNETIC

Q. Explain paramagnetic, ferromagnetic and ferrimagentic.

5.7.1 Paramagnetic

A material is paramagnetic only above its Curie Temperature. Paramagnetic materials are non-magnetic when a magnetic field is absent and magnetic when a magnetic field is applied. When the magnetic field is missing the material has disordered magnetic moments; that is, the atoms are unsymmetrical and not aligned. When the magnetic field is present the magnetic moments are provisionally realigned parallel to the applied field; the atoms are symmetrical and aligned. The magnetic moment in the same direction is what causes an induced magnetic field.

For paramagnetism The magnetic susceptibility only applies above the Curie Temperature for disordered states.

Sources of Paramagnetism (Materials which have Curie Temperatures) :
- All atoms which have unpaired electrons.
- Atoms where inner shells are incomplete in electrons.
- Free radicals.
- Metals

Above the Curie Temperature the atoms are excited, the spin orientation becomes randomised but can be realigned in an applied field and the material paramagnetic. Below the Curie Temperature the intrinsic structure gone a phase transition, the atoms are ordered and the material is ferromagnetic. The paramagnetic materials induced magnetic fields are very weak in comparison to ferromagnetic materials magnetic fields.

5.7.2 Ferromagnetic

Materials are only ferromagnetic below their corresponding Curie temperatures. Ferromagnetic materials are magnetic in the absence of an applied magnetic field.

The magnetic interactions are held together by exchange interactions; otherwise thermal disorder would overcome the weak interactions of magnetic moments. The exchange interaction has a zero probability of parallel electrons occupying the same point in time, implying a preferred parallel alignment in the material. The Boltzmann factor contributes heavily prefers interacting particles to be aligned in the same direction. This causes ferromagnets to have strong magnetic fields and high Curie temperatures .

Below the Curie temperature, the atoms are aligned and parallel, causing spontaneous magnetism; the material is ferromagnetic. Above the Curie temperature the material is paramagnetic, as the atoms lose their ordered magnetic moments when the material undergoes a phase transition.

5.7.3 Ferrimagnetic

Materials are only ferrimagnetic below their materials corresponding Curie Temperature. Ferrimagnetic materials are magnetic in the absence of an applied magnetic field and are made up of two different ions.

When a magnetic field is absent the material has a spontaneous magnetism which is of ordered magnetic moments; that is, for ferrimagnetism one ion's magnetic moments are aligned facing in one direction with certain magnitude and the other ion's magnetic moments are aligned facing in the opposite direction with a different magnitude. As result there is still a spontaneous magnetism and a magnetic field is present.

5.7.4 Antiferromagnetic and the Néel temperature

Antiferromagnetic materials are weakly magnetic in the absence or presence of an applied magnetic field.Materials are only antiferromagetic below their corresponding Néel Temperature. This is similar to the Curie Temperature as above the Néel Temperature the material undergoes a phase transition and becomes paramagnetic.

The material has equal magnetic moments aligned in opposite directions resulting in a zero magnetic moment and a net magnetism of zero at all temperatures below the Neel

Temperature. Antiferromagnetic materials are weakly magnetic in the absence or presence of an applied magnetic field.

Similar to ferromagnetic materials the magnetic interactions are held together by exchange interactions preventing thermal disorder from overcoming the weak interactions of magnetic moments.

5.7.5 Piezoelectric

An external force applies pressure on particles inside the material which affects the structure of the crystal lattice. Particles become unsymmetrical which allows a net polarisation from each particle. Symmetry would cancel the opposing charges out and there would be no net polarisation. Below the transition temperature T_0 displacement of electric charges causes polarisation. Above the transition temperature T_0 the structure is cubic and symmetric, causing the material to become dielectric. Electric charges are also agitated and disordered causing the material to have no electric polarisation in the absence of an applied electric field.

Ferroelectric and Dielectric

Materials are only ferroelectric below their corresponding transition temperature T_0. Ferroelectric materials are all piezoelectric and therefore have a spontaneous electric polarisation as the structures are unsymmetrical.

Materials are only dielectric above their corresponding transition temperature T_0. Dielectric materials have no electric polarisation in the absence of an applied electric field. The electric dipoles are unaligned and have no net polarisation. In analogy to magnetic susceptibility, electric susceptibility only occurs above T_0.

Ferroelectric materials when polarised are influenced under hysterisis Fig. 5.8 that is they are dependent on their past state as well as their current state. As an electric field is applied the dipoles are forced to align and polarisation is created, when the electric field is removed polarisation remains. The hysteresis loop depends on temperature and as a result as the temperature is increased and reaches T_0 the two curves become one curve as shown in the dielectric polarisation Fig. 5.9.

Relative Permittivity

A modified version of the Curie Weiss law applies to the dielectric constant, also known as the relative permittivity:

$$\varepsilon = \varepsilon_0 + \frac{C}{T - T_c}$$

5.8 TYPES OF MAGNETIC MATERIAL

Q. Explain Hard and Soft magnetic materials.

Most of magnetic materials of industrial interests are ferromagnetic materials. The ferromagnetic materials can be categorized into two; one is **soft magnetic materials** and the other is **hard magnetic materials**. As shown in the magnetization curve, ferromagnetic materials with the demagnetized state does not show magnetization even though they have spontaneous magnetization. This is because the ferromagnetic materials are divided into many magnetic domains. Within the magnetic domains, the direction of magnetic moment is aligened. though, the direction of magnetic moments vary at magnetic domain walls so that it can reduce the magnetostatic energy in the total volume. In the demagnetized state, total magnetization is cancelled because of the random orientation of the magnetizations in magnetic domains. When external magnetic field is applied, domain walls migrate and disappear when all magnetic moments are aligened to the direction of the magnetic field. When all magnetic domains are wiped away and magnetizations are all aligned to the direction of the magnetic field, magnetization is saturated. This magnetization is called saturation magnetization M_s.

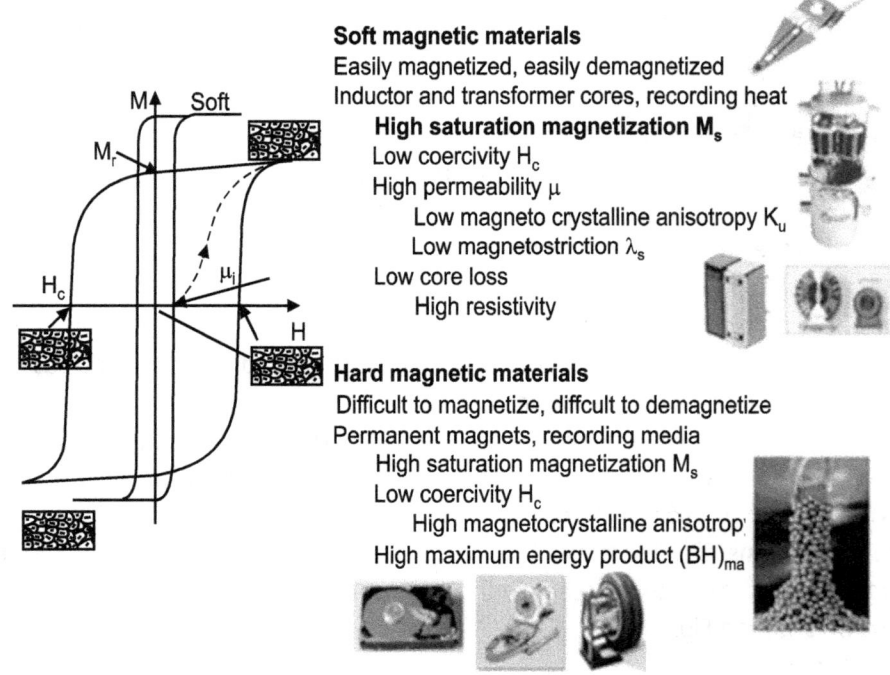

Fig. 5.10

When domain wall can easily migrate, the ferromagnetic material can be easily magnetized at low magnetic filed. This type of ferromagnetic materials are called **soft magnetic material**. Since soft magnetic materials can be demagnetized at low magnetic field, coercivity H_c is low. As they can be easily magnetized, permeability is high. For ferromagnetic materials to be soft, their magnetocrystalline anisotropy and magnetostriction constant must be low. In addition, for easy migration of magnetic domains, they must have small number of defects such as crystal grains.

When domain wall is difficult to migrate, magnetization of the ferromagnetic material occurs only when large magnetic field is applied. In other words, this type of ferromagnetic materials are difficult ot magnetize, but once magnetized, it is difficult to demagnetize. These materials are called **hard magnetic materials**, and are suitable for applications such as permanent magnets and magnetic recording media. Hard magnetic materials have high magnetocrystalline anisotropy. Since large magnetic field is required to demagnetize, their coercivity H_c is usually high, but coercivity is highly sensitive to the microstructurure.

Differences between Hard and Soft Magnetic Materials

Sr.No.	Hard Magnetic Materials	Soft Magnetic Materials
1	Materials which retain their magnetism and are difficult to demagnetize are called hard magnetic materials. These materials retain their magnetism even after the removal of the applied magnetic field. Hence these materials are used for making permanent magnets. In permanent magnets the movement of the domain wall is prevented. They are prepared by heating the magnetic materials to the required temperature and then quenching them. Impurities increase the strength of hard magnetic materials.	Soft magnetic materials are easy to magnetize and demagnetize. These materials are used for making temporary magnets. The domain wall movement is easy. Hence they are easy to magnetize. By annealing the cold worked material, the dislocation density is reduced and the domain wall movement is easier. Soft magnetic materials should not possess any void and its structure should be homogeneous so that the materials are not affected by impurities.
2	They have large hysteresis loss due to large hysteresis loop area.	They have low hysteresis loss due to small hysteresis area.
3	Susceptibility and permeability are low.	Susceptibility and permeability are high.
4	Coercivity and retentivity values are large.	Coercivity and retentivity values are less.
5	Magnetic energy stored is high.	Since they have low retentivity and coercivity, they are not used for making permanent magnets.
6	They possess high value of BH product.	Magnetic energy stored is less.
7	The eddy current loss is high.	The eddy current loss is less because of high resistivity.

Table 5.2 : Applications of magnetic materials

Field of application	Products	Requirements	Materials
Soft Magnets			
Power Conversation Electrical Mecahnical	Motors generators electromagnets	Large M_R Small H_C Low losses = small conductivity low ·	Fe based materials, e.g. Fe + ≈ (0.7 – 5)% Si Fe + ≈ (35 – 50)% Co
Power adaption	(Power) Transformers Transformer	Linear M – H curve	
Signal transfer	LF ("low" frequency; up to ≈ 100 kHz)	Small conductivity medium ·	Fe + ≈ 36% Fe/Ni/Co
	HF ("high" frequency up to ≈ 100 kHz)	Very small conductivity high ·	≈ Ni-Zn ferrites
Magnetic field screening	"Mu-metal"	Large dM/dH for H ≈ 0 ideally	Ni/Fe/Cu/Cr≈ 77/16/5/2
Hard Magnets			
Permanent magnets	small Loudspeaker	Large H_c (and M_R)	Fe/Co/Ni/Al/Cu ≈50/24/14/9/3
	small generators motoers sensors		$SmCo_5$ Sm_2CO_{17} "NdFeB" ($Nd_2Fe_{14}B$)
Data storage analog	Video tape audito tape Ferrite core memory drum	Medium H_c (and M_R) hystereses loop as rectangular as possible	NiCo CuNiFe CrO_2 Fe_2O_3
	Bubble memory	Special domain structure	Magentic garnets or $Gd_3 Ga_5O_{12}$
Specialities			
Quantum devises	GMR reading head MRAM	Special spin structurs in multilayered materials	

5.9 APPLICATIONS OF FERROMAGNETIC MATERIALS

Q. Write short note on (1) Magnetic recording materials. (2) Compact disc. (3) Laser and magnetic strip.

Magnetic recording materials :

Magnetic materials like CrO_2 or Fe_2O_3 are use for recording. In this one is recording head which is consists of toroidals core made up of soft ferrite with coil and having air gap of 5 to 15 mm as shown in Fig. 5.10 This air gap responds to electrical signal and creates magnetic pattern on tape.

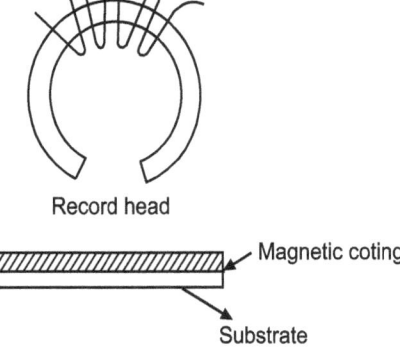

Fig. 5.11 : Magnetic tape

Compact disc

Compact disc also known as CD which is optical disc used to store digital data. In this, data is stored as a series of tiny indentations known as pits area between pits known as lands. Different types of CDs are :
1. Video CD (VCD)
2. Super Audio CD
3. Recordable CD
4. Recordable Audio CD
5. Re-writable CD (CD-RW)

Introduction to laser and magnetic strip

Laser is stands for light amplification by stimulated emission of radiation. Laser light is concentrated and travels as tight unbroken beam. This light does not disperse as it moves from origin of it. Laser light is monochromatic having single wavelength which corresponds to one specific colour.

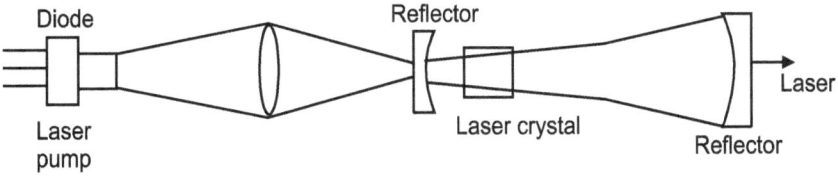

Fig. 5.12

Applications
1. Bore holes in the harder substance like diamond.
2. Use for delicate surgeries.
3. Use at NASA for remote sensing.
4. Use as cutting tool for other substance.

Magnetic strip technology
1. This is a technology carries data stored within a thin strip of magnetic media.
2. Strip is adhered to the paper or plastic card.
3. It is swiped through a magnetic reader to get back data stored in it.
4. It has two tracks. Track 1 has 79 characters and Track 2 has 40 characters at the maximum.

Applications
1. Swap card.
2. ATM card.
3. Card key's of hotels.

SOLVED EXAMPLES

Example 5.1 : Determine the percentage change in hysteresis and eddy current of a ferromagnetic material loss if supply frequency is increased by 10% the supply voltage and size of the specimen remaining unchanged. **(Dec. 05)**

Solution : Hysteresis loss at frequency f

$$W_h = A \cdot f$$

When f is increased by 10%

$$W_h = A(f + 0.1f) = 1.1 \, A \cdot f$$

Change in W_h = $0.1 \, A \cdot f$

$\therefore$ % change in W_h = $\dfrac{0.1 \, A \cdot f \times 100}{A \cdot f} = 10\%$

Eddy current loss at frequency f,

$$W_e = B \cdot f^2$$

When f is increased by 10%

$$W'_e = B \cdot (1.1 \, f)^2$$
$$= 1.21 \, B \cdot f^2$$

$\therefore$ % change in W_e = $\dfrac{1.21 \, Bf^2 - Bf^2}{Bf^2} = 21\%$

Example 5.2 : Calculate hysteresis loss in a specimen of iron subjected to a magnetization of 60 Hz. The weight of the specimen is 40 kg and its density is 8000 kg/m^3. Hysteresis loop area is equivalent to 200 J/m^3. What will be hysteresis loss of the specimen at 50 Hz.

Solution : Given : $w_t = 40$ kg, density = 8000 kg/m², a = 200 J/m², f = 50 Hz

$$\text{Volume of the specimen} = \frac{W_t}{\text{density}} = \frac{40}{8000} = 0.005 \text{ m}^3$$

∴ Hysteresis loss (W_h) = 200 × 0.005 = 1 J ... (1)

Also, $W_h = A \cdot f$

At 60 Hz the hysteresis loss is given by

$$W_h = A \times 60 \quad\quad ... (2)$$

From equation (1) and (2)

∴ $60 A = 1$

∴ $A = \dfrac{1}{60}$

At 50 Hz, the hysteresis loss is given by,

$$W_h = Af$$

∴ $W_{h(50)} = A \times 50$

$$= \frac{1}{60} \times 50 = 0.833 \text{ J}$$

Example 5.3 : In an iron specimen hysteresis loss is 300 W when maximum flux density B_{max} is 0.9 Wb/m² and frequency is 50 Hz. What would be hysteresis loss if B_{max} is increased to 1.1 Wb/m² and frequency decreased to 40 Hz. Assume that hysteresis loss is proportional to $(B_{max})^{1.7}$ **(Dec. 07)**

Solution : Given $P_{h(50)} = 300$, $B_{max(40)} = 1.1$ Wb/m² $B_{max(50)} = 0.9$ Wb/m²

Hysteresis loss, $P_h \propto (B_{max})^{1.7} \cdot f$

At 50 Hz, $P_{h(50)} \propto (0.9)^{1.7} \times 50$

∴ $300 \propto (0.9)^{1.7} \times 50$ ... (1)

At 40 Hz,

$$P_{h(40)} \propto (1.1)^{1.7} \times 40 \quad\quad ... (2)$$

From equations (1) and (2),

$$\frac{P_{h(40)}}{P_{h(50)}} = \left(\frac{1.1}{0.9}\right)^{1.7} \times \left(\frac{40}{50}\right)$$

∴ $$P_{h(40)} = \left(\frac{1.1}{0.9}\right)^{1.7} \times \left(\frac{40}{50}\right) \times 300$$

∴ $P_{h(40)} = 337.57$ watts

Example 5.4 : The core of transformer has an iron loss of 100 W at 40 Hz and 70 W at 30 Hz. Find the hysteresis loss at 50 Hz. **(Dec. 07)**

Solution :

$$P_h = \text{Hysteresis loss} = A \cdot f$$
$$P_e = \text{Eddy current loss}$$
$$P_e = B \cdot f^2 \text{ (where, A and B are constants.)}$$
$$\therefore \text{Iron loss, } P_i = P_h + P_e$$
$$P_i = A \cdot f + B \cdot f^2$$

At 40 Hz,
$$100 = 40A + (40)^2 B$$
$$\therefore 100 = 40A + 1600 B$$
$$\therefore A + 40 B = 2.5 \qquad \ldots (1)$$

At 30 Hz,
$$70 = 30A + (30)^2 \cdot B$$
$$\therefore 70 = 30 A + 900 B$$
$$\therefore 3 A + 90 B = 7 \qquad \ldots (2)$$

Solving equations (1) and (2), we get : $A = \dfrac{11}{6}$, $B = \dfrac{1}{60}$

$\therefore$ Hysteresis loss at 50 Hz $= A \cdot f = \dfrac{11}{6} \times 50$

$$= 91.67 \text{ watts}$$

Example 5.5 : The magnetic field in a piece of copper and another piece of Fe_2O_3 is 10^6 A/m. Their magnetic susceptibilities are -0.5×10^{-5} and 1.4×10^{-3} respectively. Compare the flux density and magnetization in the two pieces. **(May 08)**

Solution : We know that, $B = \mu_0 \mu_r H$
and $M = \chi_m \cdot H$

$\therefore$ For copper, $\quad B_{cu} = \mu_0 \cdot \mu_{rcu} \cdot H_{cu}$
and, $\qquad M_{cu} = \chi_{mcu} H_{cu}$
But, $\qquad \chi_{mcu} = \mu_{rcu} - 1$
$\therefore \qquad -0.5 \times 10^{-5} = \mu_{rcu} - 1$
$\therefore \qquad \mu_{rcu} = 1 - 0.5 \times 10^{-5}$
$\therefore \qquad B_{cu} = \mu_0 (1 - 0.5 \times 10^{-5}) \times 10^6 \qquad \ldots (1)$

Similarly, $B_{fe2O3} = \mu_0 (1 + 1.4 \times 10^{-3}) \times 10^6 \qquad \ldots (2)$

From equations (1) and (2),

$$\therefore \dfrac{B_{cu}}{B_{fe2O3}} = \dfrac{\mu_0 (1 - 0.5 \times 10^{-5}) \times 10^6}{\mu_0 (1 + 1.4 \times 10^{-3}) \times 10^6}$$

$$= \dfrac{1 - 0.5 \times 10^{-5}}{1 + 1.4 \times 10^{-3}}$$

$$= \frac{0.9999}{1.0014}$$

$$\therefore \quad \frac{B_{cu}}{B_{fe2O3}} = 0.9985$$

Also, $M_{cu} = \chi_{mcu} \cdot H_{cu} = -0.5 \times 10^{-5} \times 10^6$

$$M_{cu} = -5 \quad \ldots (3)$$
$$M_{fe2O3} = 1.4 \times 10^{-3} \times 10^6$$
$$M_{fe2O3} = 1.4 \times 10^3 \quad \ldots (4)$$

From equations (3) and (4),

$$\frac{M_{cu}}{M_{fe2O3}} = \frac{-5}{1.4 \times 10^3}$$

$$\therefore \quad \frac{M_{cu}}{M_{fe2O3}} = 3.5714 \times 10^{-3}$$

Example 5.6 : In a certain transformer the hysteresis loss was 160 W when maximum flux density was 1.1 Wb/m² and the supply frequency 60 Hz. What will be the hysteresis loss of the transformer when maximum flux density is reduced to 1.05 Wb/m² and supply frequency as 50 Hz. Assume hysteresis loss is given by $W_h \propto f \cdot B^{1.6}_m$ where f is supply frequency and B_{max} is maximum flux density. **(May 08)**

Solution : Given : $B_{m(60)} = 1.1$, $W_{h(60)} = 160$, $B_{m(50)} = 1.05$, $W_{h(50)} = ?$

At 60 Hz, hysteresis loss is,
$$W_{h(60)} \propto 60\,(1.1)^{1.6} \quad \ldots (1)$$

At 50 Hz, hysteresis loss is,
$$W_{h(50)} \propto 50\,(1.05)^{1.6} \quad \ldots (2)$$

From (1),
$$\therefore \quad W_{h(60)} = K \cdot 60\,(1.1)^{1.6}$$
$$\therefore \quad 160 = K \cdot 60\,(1.1)^{1.6}$$
$$K = 2.29$$

∴ From (2),
$$W_{h(50)} = K \times 50\,(1.05)^{1.6}$$
$$= 2.29 \times 50\,(1.05)^{1.6}$$
$$\therefore \quad W_{h(50)} = 123.77 \text{ Watts}$$

Example 5.7 : In a material an application of magnetic field of 1.75×10^5 A/m causes a magnetic flux density of 0.2182 Wb/m². Calculate its permeability and susceptibility. Also find magnetization. **(Dec. 08)**

Soution : **Given** $B = 0.2182$ Wb/m², $H = 1.75 \times 10^5$ A/m

$$B = \mu_0 \mu_r H$$

$$0.2182 = 4\pi \times 10^{-7} \times \mu_r \times 1.75 \times 10^5$$

$$\therefore \quad \mu_r = \frac{0.2182}{4\pi \times 1.75 \times 10^{-2}}$$

$$\therefore \quad \mu_r = 0.9922$$

Now,
$$\mu = \mu_0 \mu_r$$
$$= 4\pi \times 10^{-7} \times 0.9922$$

$$\therefore \quad \mu = 12.468 \times 10^{-7}$$

$$\because \quad \chi_m = \mu_r - 1$$
$$= 0.9922 - 1$$

$$\therefore \quad \chi_m = -7.8 \times 10^{-3}$$

Now,
$$M = \chi_m \cdot H$$
$$= -7.8 \times 10^{-3} \times 1.75 \times 10^5$$

$$\therefore \quad M = -13.65 \times 10^2$$

$$\therefore \quad M = -1365 \text{ A/m}$$

Example 5.8 : The total loss in a sample of sheet steel to be used for transformer core at 50 Hz and 75 Hz are 20 watts and 35 watts respectively both having been measured at the same peak flux density. Separate the losses at 50 Hz into its hysteresis and eddy current components. **(Dec. 08)**

Solution : We have,
$$P_i = Af + Bf^2$$

∴ Total loss at 50 Hz,
$$20 = Af + B \cdot f^2$$
$$= A \times 50 + B \times (50)^2$$
$$20 = 50A + 2500B$$

$$\therefore \quad A + 50B = 0.4 \qquad \ldots (1)$$

Total loss at 75 Hz,

$$\therefore \quad 35 = Af + Bf^2$$
$$35 = 75A + B \cdot (75)^2$$

$$\therefore \quad A + 75B = 0.47 \qquad \ldots (2)$$

Solving equations (1) and (2), we get,
$$25B = 0.07$$

$$\therefore \quad \boxed{B = 0.0028}$$

Putting this in equation (1),

$$\therefore \quad A + 50 \times 0.0028 = 0.4$$

$$\therefore \quad \boxed{A = 0.26}$$

$$\therefore \quad \text{Hysteresis loss} = Af$$

$$= 0.26 \times 50 = 13 \text{ Watts}$$

∴ Eddy current loss $= Bf^2$

$$= 0.0028 \times (50)^2 = 7 \text{ Watts}$$

Example 5.9 : Calculate hysteresis loss is a specimen of iron subjected to magnetization of 50 Hz. The weight of specimen is 40 kg and its density is 7680 kg/m³. The hysteresis loop area is equivalent to 198 J/m³. **(Dec. 06, Dec.09)**

Solution : Given : $w_t = 40$ kg, density = 7680 kg/m², f = 50 Hz

$$\text{Volume of specimen} = \frac{40}{7680} \text{ m}^3$$

$$= 5.2083 \times 10^{-3} \text{ m}^3$$

∴ Hysteresis loss at 50 Hz = Volume × Loop area = $\left[\frac{40}{7680}\right] \times 198 = 1.03$ Joules

Example 5.10 : Give expression for hysteresis loss. The hysteresis loss for a given material is 1.55 watts per kg at 50 Hz, with maximum flux density of 1 Wb/m². Its specific gravity is 7.75. A core of this material is to be used, which will be subjected to 60 Hz and maximum flux density of 7.9 Wb/m². The volume of core is 980 cm³. Determine :

(i) The value of hysteresis loss constant in the above expression.

(ii) The hysteresis loss in the core at 60 Hz.

Assume that the hysteresis loss is proportional to $B_{max}^{1.6}$ where, B_{max} is maximum flux density in the core. **(May 07)**

Solution : Hysteresis loss, $W_h = K \cdot B_{max}^{1.6} \cdot f$

Hysteresis loss at 50 Hz,

$$W_h = 1.55 \text{ Watts/kg}$$

∴ $\text{Mass} = \frac{\text{Volume of core} \times \text{Specific gravity}}{1000}$ kg

$$= \frac{980 \times 7.75}{1000} \text{ kg}$$

Mass = 7.595 kg

∴ Total hysteresis loss W_h at 50 Hz

$$W_h = 1.55 \times 7.595$$

∴ $W_h = 11.772$ watts

Also, $W_h = K \cdot B_{max}^{1.6} \cdot f$ ... at 50 Hz

∴ $11.772 = K (1)^{1.6} \times 50$

∴ $K = 0.2354$

Now, Hysteresis loss, W_h at 60 Hz is

$$W_{h(60)} = K \cdot B_{max}^{1.6} \cdot f$$
$$= (0.2354) \cdot (7.9)^{1.6} \times 60$$
$$W_{h(60)} = 385.58 \text{ Watts}$$

Example 5.11 : In a magnetic material the field strength was found to be 10^6 Amp/m. If the magnetic susceptibility of the material is -0.5×10^{-5}. Calculate magnetization and flux density in the material.

(Dec. 04)

Solution : Given : $H = 10^6$ Amp/m, $\chi_m = -0.5 \times 10^{-5}$, $M = ?$, $B = ?$

$$M = \chi_m \times H$$
$$= -0.5 \times 10^{-5} \times 10^6$$
∴ $$M = -0.5 \times 10$$
∴ $$M = -5$$

Also, $$\chi_m = \mu_r - 1$$
∴ $$\mu_r = \chi_m + 1$$
$$= (-0.5 \times 10^{-5}) + 1$$
∴ $$\mu_r = 0.9999$$

Now, $$B = \mu_0 \mu_r H$$
$$= 4\pi \times 10^{-7} \times 0.9999 \times 10^6$$
∴ $$B = 1.2566 \text{ Wb/m}^2$$

Example 5.12 : In a certain transformer the hysteresis loss was formed to be 160 watt when maximum flux density was 1.1 Wb/m² and supply frequency 60 Hz. What will be the hysteresis loss of the transformer when the maximum flux density is reduced to 0.9 Wb/m² and the supply frequency to 50 Hz? Assume hysteresis loss is given by $W_h \propto f B_{max}^{1.6}$ where, f is frequency in Hz and B_{max} is maximum flux density.

(Dec. 04)

Solution : Given : $P_h = 160$ W, $B_m = 1.1$ T, $f = 60$ Hz, $P_{h(new)} = ?$, $B_{m(new)} = 0.9$ T, $f_{new} = 50$ Hz

Since hysteresis loss, $P_h \propto f B_m^{1.6}$

∴ At 60 Hz hysteresis loss is $160 \propto 60 \times (1.1)^{1.6}$ ... (1)

At 50 Hz hysteresis loss is $P_{h(new)} \propto 50(0.9)^{1.6}$ ... (2)

From equation (1),
$$160 = K \, 60 \times (1.1)^{1.6}$$
∴ $$K = \frac{160}{60 \times (1.1)^{1.6}}$$
∴ $$K = 2.2894$$

Putting this value of K in equation (2),

$$\therefore \quad P_{h(new)} = K \cdot 50 \times (0.9)^{1.6}$$
$$= (2.2894) \times 50 \times (0.9)^{1.6}$$
$$\therefore \quad P_{h(new)} = 96.71 \text{ watts}$$

Example 5.13: In a certain transformer the hysteresis loss is 300 watts when the maximum flux density is 0.9 Wb/m² and the frequency 50 Hz. What would be the hysteresis loss if the maximum flux density were increased to 1.1 Wb/m² and the frequency 40 Hz. Assume the hysteresis loss over this range to be proportional to $B_{max}^{1.7}$. **(May 06)**

Solution: Given: P_h = 300 W, B_{max} = 0.9 T, f = 50 Hz, $P_{h\,(new)}$ = ?, $B_{m\,(new)}$ = 1.1 T, $f_{(new)}$ = 40 Hz.

Since $\quad P_h \propto f B_m^{1.7}$

At 50 Hz, $\quad 300 \propto 50 \times (0.9)^{1.7}$ ... (1)

At 40 Hz, $\quad P_{n\,(new)} \propto 40 \times (1.1)^{1.7}$ ... (2)

From equation (1)

$$300 = K \cdot 50 \times (0.9)^{1.7}$$

$$\therefore \quad K = \frac{300}{50 \times (0.9)^{1.7}}$$

$$K = 7.1769$$

Putting this value of K in Equation (2), we get;

$$P_{h\,(new)} = K \cdot 40 \times (1.1)^{1.7}$$
$$= (7.1769) \times 40 \times (1.1)^{1.7}$$
$$P_{h\,(new)} = 337.57 \text{ Watts}$$

Example 5.14 Calculate hysteresis loss in iron specimen subjected to magnetization of 50 Hz. The weight of specimen is 50 kg and density is 8000 kg/m³. The hysteresis loop area is equivalent to 250 J/m³.

Solution Given: w_t = 40 kg, density = 8000 kg/m², f = 50 Hz

$$\text{Volume} = \frac{\text{Weight}}{\text{Density}}$$

$$= \frac{50 \text{ kg}}{8000 \text{ kg/m}^3}$$

$$= 6.25 \times 10^{-3} \text{ m}^3$$

$\therefore \quad$ Hysteresis loss = Volume × Area of hysteresis loop

$$= \left(\frac{50}{8000}\right) \times 250 = 1.5625 \text{ Joules}$$

Example 5.15 : Calculate loss of energy caused by hysteresis in one hour in 50 kg of iron, if peak flux density is 1.3 T and frequency is 25 Hz. Assume Stenmetz coefficient 628 J/m^3 and density of iron 7.5×10^3 kg/m^3.

Solution :

$$\text{Volume of iron} = \frac{\text{Weight}}{\text{Density}}$$

$$= \frac{50}{7.5 \times 10^3}$$

$$= 6.6 \times 10^{-3} \text{ m}^3$$

Hysteresis loss, $P_h = K_h \cdot B_m^{1.6} \cdot fv$

$$= 628 \times (1.3)^{1.6} \times 25 \times 6.6 \times 10^{-3}$$

∴ Loss of energy due to hysteresis in 1 hr. is

$$= 159.26 \times 60 \times 60 \text{ watt sec.}$$

$$= 573.33 \times 10^3 \text{ watt sec. or Joules.}$$

Example 5.16 : A magnetic field strength of Fe_2O_3 is 10^6 Amp/m. Given that magnetic susceptibility of Fe_2O_3 at room temperature is 1.25×10^{-3}. Calculate induced magnetization, flux density and permeability. **(Dec. 09)**

Solution : Given $\chi_m = 1.25 \times 10^{-3}$, $H = 10^6$ Amp/m

$$\chi_m = \frac{M}{H}$$

∴ $M = \chi_m \cdot H$

$$= 1.25 \times 10^{-3} \times 10^6$$

∴ $M = 1.25 \times 10^3$

Also, $\chi_m = \mu_r - 1$

∴ $\mu_r = \chi_m + 1$

$$= (1.25 \times 10^{-3}) + 1$$

∴ $\mu_r = 1.00125$

Since, $B = \mu_0 \mu_r H$

$$= 4\pi \times 10^{-7} \times 1.00125 \times 10^6$$

∴ $B = 1.2582 \text{ Wb/m}^2$

∴ Permeability, $\mu = B/H$

$$= \frac{1.2582}{10^6}$$

$$= 1.2582 \times 10^{-6}$$

Example 5.17 : In a certain transformer the hysteresis loss is 400 W when maximum flux density is 0.85 Wb/m^2 and frequency of 50 Hz. What would be the hysteresis loss if maximum flux density is increased to 1.4 Wb/m² and frequency to 60 Hz. Assume hysteresis loss over this range is to be proportional to $B_m^{1.7}$. **(Dec. 09)**

Solution : Given : P_h = 400 W, B_m = 0.85 T, f = 50 Hz, $P_{h(new)}$ = ?, $B_{m(new)}$ = 1.4 T, $f_{(new)}$ = 60 Hz.

Since hysteresis loss, $\quad P_h \propto B_m^{1.7} f$

∴ At 50 Hz, $\quad P_h \propto (0.85)^{1.7} \times 50$

∴ $\quad 400 = K \cdot (0.85)^{1.7} \times 50$

∴ $\quad K = \dfrac{400}{(0.85)^{1.7} \times 50}$

∴ $\quad K = 10.5457$

Now, at 60 Hz,

$\quad P_{h(new)} \propto (1.4)^{1.7} \times 60$

∴ $\quad P_{h(new)} = K \cdot (1.4)^{1.7} \times 60$

∴ $\quad P_{h(new)} = (10.5457)(1.4)^{1.7} \times 60$

∴ $\quad P_{h(new)} = 1121.09$ watts

Example 5.18 : Find the power loss in watts due to hysteresis only for an iron core of volume 100 cm³ which is subjected to 50 cycles of magnetization per sec. The hysteresis loop for the core has an area of 150 cm² when plotted to scales of 1 cm = 0.2 T and 1 cm = 500 A/m. **(Dec. 09)**

Solution :Given a=150 cm², f=50Hz

Hysteresis loop area $\quad = 150$ cm²

∴ $\quad$ Loss $= xy$ J/m³/cycle

$\quad = 0.2 \times 500$

$\quad = 100$ J/m³/cycle

∴ $\quad W_h = $ Hysteresis loss

$\quad = 100 \times 100 \times 10^{-4} \times 50$

∴ $\quad W_h = 50$ watts

Example 5.19 : Calculate hysteresis loss in a specimen of iron subjected to a magnetization of 60 Hz. The weight of specimen is 50 kg and its density is 8000 kg/m³. Hysteresis loop area is equivalent to 250 J/m³. What will be the hysteresis loss of specimen at 40 Hz? **(May 10)**

Solution : Given : w_t = 50 kg, density = 8000 kg/m², f = 60 Hz

Volume of specimen $\quad = \dfrac{560}{8000} = 6.25 \times 10^{-3}$ m³

Hysteresis loss, $\quad W_h = 250 \times 6.25 \times 10^{-3}$

$\quad = 1.5625$ Joules $\hfill ...(1)$

Also, $\quad W_h = A \cdot f = A \times 60 \hfill ...(2)$

From equations (1) and (2),

$$60 A = 1.5625$$
$$\therefore \quad A = 0.02604$$

At 40 Hz,

$$W_{h(40)} = A \cdot f$$
$$= (0.02604) \times 40$$
$$W_{h(40)} = 1.04166 \, J$$

Example 5.20 : In a material, an application of magnetic field of 2.75×10^6 A/m causes a magnetic flux density of 0.2485 Wb/m². Calculate its permeability, susceptibility and magnetization. **(May 10)**

Solution :

$$B = \mu_0 \mu_r H$$

$$\mu_r = \frac{B}{\mu_0 H} = \frac{0.2485}{4\pi \times 10^{-7} \times 2.75 \times 10^6}$$

$$\mu_r = 0.07190$$

$$\mu = \mu_0 \mu_r = 4\pi \times 10^{-7} \times 0.07190$$

$$\mu = 0.9036 \times 10^{-7}$$

Now,
$$\chi_m = \mu_r - 1$$
$$= 0.0719 - 1$$
$$\chi_m = -0.9281$$

Now,
$$M = \chi_m \cdot H$$
$$= (-0.9281) \times 2.75 \times 10^6$$
$$\therefore \quad M = -2552275 \, A/m$$

Example 5.21 : The total loss in a silicon sheet used for transformer core at 50 Hz and 75 Hz are 20 watts and 35 watts respectively, both being measured at same peak flux density. Calculate its hysteresis loss and eddy current loss at 75 Hz. **(May 11)**

Solution :

$$P_i = Af + Bf^2$$

At 50 Hz,
$$20 = 50 A + 2500 B$$
$$A + 50 B = 0.4 \quad \ldots (1)$$

At 75 Hz,
$$A + 75 B = 0.47 \quad \ldots (2)$$

Solving equations (1) and (2),

$$A = 0.26$$

At 75 Hz,

$$\therefore \quad P_h = Af$$
$$= 0.26 \times 75$$
$$= 19.5 \, watt$$

$$P_e = Bf^2$$

$$= 0.0028 \times (75)^2$$
$$= 15.75 \text{ watt}$$

Example 5.22 : Calculate loss of energy caused by hysteresis in two hours in 50 kg of iron if peak flux density is 1.3 T and frequency is 75 Hz. Assume the Stenmetz coefficient 628 J/m³ and density of iron as 7.5×10^3 kg/m³. **(May 11)**

Solution : Given : w_t = 50 kg, density = 7500 kg/m², f = 75 Hz

Volume of iron $= \dfrac{\text{Weight}}{\text{Density}}$

$$= \dfrac{50}{7.5 \times 10^3}$$

$$= 6.6 \times 10^{-3}$$

Hysteresis loss $= P_h = K_h B_m^{1.6} fv$

$P_h = 477.78$ watt

Loss and energy due to P_h in 2 hours $= 477.78 \times 2 \times 60 \times 60$

$$= 3440016 \text{ watt-sec. or Joules}$$

Example 5.23 : In a certain transformer the hysteresis loss is 500 W when the maximum flux density is 0.78 tesla and frequency is 40 Hz. What would be the hysteresis loss if maximum flux density is increased to 1.6 tesla and frequency is 70 Hz? Assume hysteresis loss over this range is to be proportional to $B_m^{1.7}$. **(May 12)**

Solution : Hysteresis loss $P_h \propto (B_m)^{1.7} \cdot f$

At 40 Hz, $P_{h(40)} \propto (0.78)^{1.7} \times 40$ ... (1)

At 70 Hz, $P_{h(70)} \propto (1.6)^{1.7} \times 70$ ... (2)

From equations (1) and (2),

$$\dfrac{P_{h(40)}}{P_{h(70)}} = \left(\dfrac{0.78}{1.6}\right)^{1.7} \times \dfrac{40}{70}$$

$$\dfrac{500}{P_{h(70)}} = 0.5714$$

∴ $P_{h(70)} = \dfrac{500}{0.1684}$

∴ $P_{h(70)} = 2969.12$ Watts

Example 5.24 : Calculate hysteresis loss in a specimen of iron subjected to magnetization at 50 Hz. The weight of the specimen is 70 kg and its density is 7680 kg/m³. The hysteresis loop area is equivalent to 300 J/m³. **(May 12)**

Solution : Given : w_t = 70 kg, density = 7680 kg/m², f = 50 Hz

Volume of specimen $= \dfrac{70}{7680}$ m³

$= 9.1146 \times 10^{-3}$ m³

Hysteresis loss at 50 Hz = Volume × Loop area

$= 9.1146 \times 10^{-3} \times 300$

= 2.734 Joules

Example 5.25 : Calculate Hysteresis loss in a specimen of iron subjected to a magnetization of 60 Hz. The weight of specimen is 50 kg and its density is 8000 kg/m³. Hysteresis loop area is equivalent 250 J/m³. What will be hysteresis loss of specimen of 40 Hz? **(Dec. 12)**

Solution : Given : w_t = 50 kg, density = 8000 kg/m², f = 60 Hz

Volume of specimen $= \dfrac{\text{Weight}}{\text{Density}}$

$= \dfrac{50}{8000}$

$= 6.25 \times 10^{-3}$ m³

Hysteresis loss $(W_h) = 250 \times 6.25 \times 10^{-3}$

W_h = 1.56 Joules

Now, $W_h = A \cdot f$

$= A \times 60$

1.56 = 60 A

A = 1/60

At 40 Hz, hysteresis loss is given by,

$W_h = A \times f$

$W_h = \dfrac{1}{60} \times 40$

W_h = 0.66 Joules

REVIEW QUESTIONS

1. Short note on :
   (i) Diamagnetism
   (ii) Paramagnetism
   (iii) Ferromagnetism
   (iv) Anti-Ferromagnetism
   (v) Ferrimagnetism
2. Explain application of magnetic materials.

3. Explain magnetic dipole moment.
4. What is relative permeability and magnetic susceptibility ?
5. Give classification of magnetic materials.

UNIVERSITY QUESTIONS

May 2008

1. What magnetic properties are required for the magnetic materials used in :
   (a) Power transformer
   (b) Memory disc of a computer **(4 Marks)**
2. What is ferrites name some ferrites and give their applications. **(4 Marks)**
3. What are ferrites? Name some ferrites and give their applications. **(4 Marks)**
4. Explain the terms : **(8 Marks)**
   (a) Permeability
   (b) Magnetic susceptibility
   (c) Magnetization
   (d) Magnetic dipole

Dec. 2008

5. Differentiate between : **(6 Marks)**
   (a) Soft and hard magnetic material.
   (b) Ferromagnetism and ferrimagnetism.
6. Explain : **(4 Marks)**
   (a) Magnetization
   (b) Susceptibility
7. List the properties and type of magnetic materials required for : **(4 Marks)**
   (a) Power transformer
   (b) D.C. shunt generator
8. Explain : **(6 Marks)**
   (a) Ferromagnetic domain
   (b) Spontaneous magnetization
9. From the basics' prove that $B = \mu_o (H + M)$ **(2 Marks)**

May 2009

10. Explain : **(8 Marks)**
    (a) Magnetic dipole moment

(b) Magnetic susceptibility
(c) Permeability
(d) Flux density

11. Draw the hysteresis loop of ferromagnetic material and explain the following :
    (8 Marks)
    (a) Coersive force
    (b) Residual magnetism

12. Classify magnetic material explain each class with respect to its properties and applications. **(8 Marks)**

13. What are ferrites? Give their properties and applications. **(8 Marks)**

Dec. 2009

14. Define relative permeability. Show that the relative permeability $\mu_r = 1 + x_m$ where, x_m is magnetic susceptibility. **(6 Marks)**

15. Explain classification of magnetic material on the basis of distribution of dipole moment. **(8 Marks)**

16. What is Curie temperature for ferromagnetic material? Describe Curie Weiss law.
    (6 Marks)

17. Differentiate between : **(6 Marks)**
    (a) Soft and hard magnetic material.
    (b) Ferromagnetism of antiferromagnetism.

May 2010

18. Define the following : **(4 Marks)**
    (a) Permeability
    (b) Magnetic dipole moment
    (c) Magnetic susceptibility
    (d) Magnetization

19. What are soft and hard magnetic materials? Give their characteristics and applications?
    (8 Marks)

20. Differentiate between : **(4 Marks)**
    (a) Magnetic dipole moment and electric dipole moment.
    (b) Ferromagnetism and antiferromagnetism.

21. Classify the magnetic material and explain each class with respect to its properties and applications. **(8 Marks)**

22. Calculate hysteresis loss in a specimen of iron subjected to a magnetisation of 60 Hz. The weight of specimen is 50 kg and its density is 8000 kg/m³. Hysteresis loop area is equivalent to 250 J/m³. What will be the hysteresis loss of specimen at 40 Hz?

(6 Marks)

23. In a material an application of magnetic field of 2.75×10^6 A/m causes a magnetic flux density of 0.2485 Wb/m². Calculate its permeability, susceptibility and magnetization.

(6 Marks)

Dec. 2010

24. Explain spontaneous magnetization and Curie Weiss law. **(9 Marks)**
25. Write a short note on magnetic recording materials and compact discs. **(9 Marks)**
26. Describe properties and applications of paramagnetic materials. **(9 Marks)**
27. Differentiate between :
    (a) Permeability and magnetic susceptibility. **(4 Marks)**
    (b) Soft and hard magnetic materials. **(5 Marks)**
28. Explain the terms : **(8 Marks)**
    (i) Permeability
    (ii) Magnetisation
    (iii) Curie temperature
    (iv) Magnetic susceptibility
29. State properties and applications of Hard magnetic materials. **(4 Marks)**
30. Classify magnetic materials based on dipole moment. Explain each class with respect to its properties and applications. **(8 marks)**
31. Write a note on behavior of ferromagnetic materials below critical temperature.

(6 Marks)

32. The total loss in a silicon sheet used for transformer core at 50 Hz and 75 Hz are 20 watts and 35 watts respectively, both being measured at same peak flux density. Calculate its hysteresis loss and eddy current loss at 75 Hz. **(6 Marks)**
33. Calculate loss of energy caused by hysteresis in two hours in 50 kg of iron if peak flux density is 1.3 T and frequency is 75 Hz. Assume the Stenmetz coefficient 628 J/m³ and density of iron as 7.5×10^3 kg/m³. **(4 Marks)**

Dec. 2011

34. Explain classification of magnetic materials on the basis of distribution of dipole components. Give applications of each class. **(8 Marks)**
35. Differentiate between :
    (i) Soft and hard magnetic materials. **(5 Marks)**

(ii) Permeability and magnetic susceptibility. **(5 Marks)**

36. What is Currie temperature for ferromagnetic material? Explain spontaneous magnetization and Curie-Weiss law. **(9 Marks)**

37. Write short notes on :
    (i) Magnetic recording materials. **(5 Marks)**
    (ii) Compact discs. **(4 Marks)**

May 2012

38. Explain Curie-Weiss law for ferromagnetic materials. Is this law application for spontaneous magnetization? Hence explain spontaneous magnetization. **(8 Marks)**

39. What are Ferrites? Give properties and applications of ferrites. **(6 Marks)**

40. Explain classification of magnetic materials on the basis of distribution of magnetic dipole moments. **(6 Marks)**

41. Write short notes on :
    (i) Compact Disc
    (ii) Magnetic Recording Materials

42. In a certain transformer the hysteresis loss is 500 W when the maximum flux density is 0.78 tesla and frequency is 40 Hz. What would be the hysteresis loss if maximum flux density is increased to 1.6 tesla and frequency is 70 Hz? Assume hysteresis loss over this range is to be proportional to $B_m^{1.7}$. **(4 Marks)**

43. Calculate hysteresis loss in a specimen of iron subjected to magnetization of 50 Hz. The weight of the specimen is 70 kg and its density is 7680 kg/m³. The hysteresis loop area is equivalent to 300 J/m³. **(4 Marks)**

Dec. 2012

44. Differentiate between Soft Magnetic Materials and Hard Magnetic Materials. **(8 Marks)**

45. Explain the properties and applications Diamagnetism, Para-magnetism, Ferro magnetism and Ferrimagnetism. **(16 Marks)**

46. Calculate hysteresis loss in a specimen of iron subjected to a magnetization of 60 Hz. The weight of specimen is 50 kg and its density is 8000 kg/m³. Hysteresis loop area is equivalent 250 J/m³. What will be hysteresis loss of specimen of 40 Hz? **(8 Marks)**

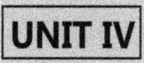

Chapter 6

CONDUCTING MATERIALS

6.1 INTRODUCTION TO ELECTRICAL CONDUCTING MATERIALS

Q. Give the properties of conductors.

Depending on current carrying ability of materials they are classified into three general types :
- Conductors
- Insulators
- Semiconductors

There are various conducting materials used in electrical engineering. Some of them along with their properties and applications are discussed below.

Properties of conductors

Electrical properties :
- Resistivity is low.
- Temperature resistance ratio is low.
- Energy dissipated in the form of heat is low.
- Conductivity is good.

Mechanical properties :
- Easy to fabricate.
- Withstand stress and strain.
- Elasticity should be high.
- It must be have high resistance to corrosion.
- It must have solder ability.
- It has good ductility property.

Economical factors :
- Easily available.
- Easy to manufacture.
- Low cost.

6.1.1 Copper

It is reddish brown in colour having the following properties :
- High electrical and thermal conductivity. It is highly sensitive towards impurities.

- Its resistance changes with temperature i.e. temperature coefficient of resistance is large.
- As compared to aluminium, copper is having superior heat dissipation capacity.
- Excellent soldering and welding property.
- High tensile strength varies from 3 – 4.8 tonnes/cm^2.
- Its melting point is near about 1100°C.
- Specific gravity is 8.9.
- Its electrical resistivity is 1.682 μΩ cm at 20°C.
- Boiling point is nearly 2600°C.
- It easily forms alloys like bronze, brass etc.
- Temperature coefficient of resistance is 0.00412 per degree centigrade.
- It is malleable and ductile.
- It has high current density.
- Moderate to high strength and hardness.
- Internal conductivity is 397.

Applications :
- As its resistance is low, it is more suitable for making electrical wires, cables, making windings of machines and transformer etc.
- It is used for making electromagnets and printed circuit boards.
- It is used for making electrical relays, bus bars and switches.

6.1.2 Aluminium

It is having the following properties :
- Poor soldering and welding ability.
- Specific gravity is 2.669
- Its melting point is 660°C.
- Its electrical resistivity is 2.669 μΩ cm at 20°C.
- Boiling point is nearly 1820°C.
- Temperature coefficient of resistance is 0.00412.
- Due to brittleness it can not be twisted.
- Aluminium has most excellent corrosion resistance ability.
- Its resistance is less but large than copper.
- Aluminium is a good electrical and thermal conductor but mechanical strength is less.
- It offers high resistance to corrosion.
- It is ductile and malleable.
- Tensile strength is 9 tones/in^2.
- Easily rolled drawn and forged and it is very soft.
- Welding of aluminium is much more difficult than that of other materials.

Applications :

- Powdered aluminium is used in paints, solid rocket fuels.
- It is used for street lighting poles.
- Super purity aluminium can be used in CDS, electronic kits, transistors.
- Used in over head transmission and distribution lines, for bus-bars, for ACSR conductors.
- Aluminium alloys can be used in as an additive to jet fuels, for laser production.
- Wide range household items.
- Used as wires for motors and electrolytic capacitors.

6.1.3 Constantan/Eureka

It is an alloy of copper and nickel. In which 60% copper and 40% nickel is present. It is silver white in appearance. Constantan is having good fatigue life and relatively high elongation capability.

Properties :

- It does not rust due to high working temperature.
- Very stable at high working temperature.
- It is having large temperature coefficient of resistance.
- Tensile strength is nearly 52 kg/mm^2.
- Specific weight is 8.92 g/cm^2.
- It possess high melting point near about 1300°C
- Maximum operating temperature is nearly 500°C.
- Its resistivity remains constant for wide range of temperatures.
- Resistivity is 0.48 – 0.52 Ω-mm^2/m.
- Temperature resistances coefficient 5.25×10^{-6} °C
- Tensile strength is 40 – 50 kg/mm^2.

Applications :

- It is used for making rheostat coil and similar control devices.
- Constantan used to form thermocouples with wires made of iron, copper.

6.1.4 Nichrome

Nichrome is an alloy of nickel (75% – 80%), chromium (20 – 25%), manganin (1.5%) and a small amount of Ferrous. It is silver in appearance. It tends to be expensive due to high nickel content.

Properties :

- High resistivity near about $1 – 1.11 \times 10^{-6}$ Ωm.
- Very high melting point (1350°C).
- Tensile strength is nearly equal to 75 kg/mm^2.

- Temperature coefficient of resistance is low.
- It with stand high temperature for longme without oxidising.
- High corrosion resistant property.
- Tensile strength is 65 – 70 kg/mm^2.

Applications :
- It can be used as internal support structure in ceramics.
- Nichrome is widely used in explosives as a bridge wire in electric ignition system.
- It is used as heating element in electric heaters, furnaces and electric iron etc.

6.1.5 Tungsten

It is a steel grey colour metal which is brittle in nature.

Properties :
- High melting point (3450°C).
- Boiling point is nearly 5950°C.
- Temperature coefficient of resistance is 0.00511.
- It is having high tensile strength.
- It is ductile in nature (can be drawn into very thick wires).
- Tungsten has lower coefficient of thermal expansion.
- Tungsten is chemically inert to acids and alkalis but oxidised in the presence of oxygen.
- Specific weight is 20 g/cm^3.
- Resistivity is 0.055 Ω-mm^2/m.
- Density is 19.3 g/cm^2.

Applications :
- Tungsten is used in many high temperature applications such as light bulb, cathode ray tube and vacuum tube as filaments, heating elements and nozzles of rocket engines.
- Vibrators.
- It is used in battery ignition system, X-ray tubes, Magneto ignition systems.
- It is used for making glass to metal seals.

6.2 MATERIAL USED FOR FILAMENTS

Q. Explain various materials use for filaments.
Q. Explain properties of materials use for filaments.

A material used for making filaments must have the following properties :
- High melting point.
- High mechanical strength.
- No tendency for oxidation.

- Ductility.
- Low resistance temperature coefficients.

Mostly Carbon, Tantalum and Tungsten are used as a filament material due to their following properties.

(a) Carbon :
- High commercial efficiency about 3.8 to 4.6.
- Prevent blackening of the bulb.

(b) Tantalum
- Commercial efficiency about 3.5.
- High melting point near about 2800°C.
- Low resistivity and low temperature coefficient of resistance.

(c) Tangsten
- Melting point near about 3450°C
- Lumen efficiency is large.

Fig. 6.1 showing different shapes of filaments used in bulbs.

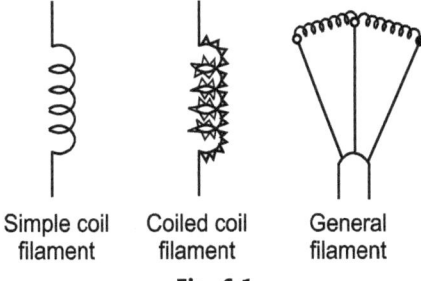

Simple coil filament   Coiled coil filament   General filament

Fig. 6.1

6.2.1 Materials used for making solders and contacts

Solder is an alloy used to join two or more metals pieces. Melting point of solders is lower than materials to be joint. This process of joining pieces of metals is known as soldering. There are two types of solders.

(a) Hard Solders : It is normally alloy of Cu and Zn. It melt at very high temperature nearly higher than 400°C. It is mainly use for joining brass copper iron and steel.

(b) Soft Solders : Soft solder is an alloy of tin and lead. The most popular composition is 50% tin and 50% lead. This is use for working temperature lower than 400°C. It is used to join copper, bronze, brass, lead, tinned, iron, zinc etc.

6.2.2 Rewireable fuse

Rewireable fuse has 3 parts :

1. **Base :** It consist of porcelain materials with fixed contacts which connected to live or phase wires.

2. **Fuse carrier :** It is part which can be separate or taken out or insert in base with out any risk when switch is off.

3. **Fuse wire :**
- Fuse wire is used depending on current ratting of the system.
- Standard rating are 6, 16, 32, 63 and 100 A. It may use materials like lead, tinned, copper, aluminium or alloy of tin lead.

Advantages :
- Easy to operate.
- Replacement is easy.
- Reusable.

Mechanical Properties :
- High resistance against corrosion.
- It should possess high mechanical strength.
- It should be able to draw into thin wires i.e. it should be ductile.
- It should be drawn into thin sheets i.e. it should be malleable.
- Easy to fabricate.
- Soldering welding of joints should have minimum contact resistance.
- Durability and low cost.

6.2.3 Kanthal

It is an alloy of iron, chromium and aluminium.

Properties :
- Low temperature coefficient of resistance.
- It withstands high temperature without oxidising.
- It has high melting point (1200°C).

Application :

It is used in electric furnaces as a heating element.

6.2.4 Manganin

It is an alloy of Cu, manganese and nickel. It has the following properties.

Properties :
- Its resistance is stable for long time.
- It has low temperature coefficient of resistance i.e. (0.00015/°C).
- It has high melting point (1020°C).
- Its resistivity is high 4.8×10^{-6} Ω-cm at 20°C.
- It is alloy of Cu – 80%, Mn – 17 to 18% and Ni – 1.5 to 2%.

Applications :

It is used in standard resistance coil for instrument shunts, precision instruments, resistance boxes and bridge potentiometers etc.

6.2.5 Silver

Silver is having symbol Ag. It is having highest electrical conductivity of all elements.

Properties :
- It absorbs free electrons.
- It is having low contact resistance.
- It is having highest electrical conductivity even greater than copper.
- High thermal conductivity.
- Ductile and malleable in nature.
  Its resistivity is 1.59×10^{-6} Ω-cm at 20°C.

Applications :
- Silver oxide batteries are used due to longer life and high energy / weight ratio.
- It is used in electrical contacts and conductors.
- It is used to make ornaments, jewellery, utensils and coins.
- As silver absorbs free electrons it is sometimes used as a control rods to regulate fission reaction.

6.3 COPPER ALLOYS

6.3.1 Brass

Brass is an alloy of copper and zinc. It is having bright gold like appearance.

Properties :
- It is having 900 – 950°C melting point.
- It has high soldering and welding property.
- It has very good resistance to corrosion.
- Brass has low conductivity.
- It has greater mechanical strength and bearing resistance than copper.
- Brass has higher malleability than copper or zinc.

. It's electrical resistivity is 9.1×10^{-6} Ω-cm at 20°C.

Applications
- Used for resistance welding.
- Brass can be used for making fan blades, fan cages and motor bearing.

- It is widely used in manufacture of electrical apparatus and current caring instruments.
- Brass can also be used for fixing for use in cryogenic systems.

6.3.2 Bronze

It is an alloy of copper and tin. It typically have 88% copper and 12% tin. It is hard and brittle material.

Properties :
- Bronze is less brittle than iron.
- Bronzes are softer but heavier and have high mechanical strength.
- Metal to metal friction is less.
- Bronze containing copper, 0.9% cadmium have 85 to 95% conductivity to copper.
- Bronze containing copper, 0.8% cadmium, 0.6% tin has 50 to 80% conductivity as compared to copper.
- It is having high resistance to salt water corrosion.
- They are better conductor of heat and electricity.

Applications :
- Bronze used as a heating element.
- It is used for making sliding contacts, current caring holders knife switch blades.
- It is used for making contact wires, commutator segments.

6.4 ELECTRIC FIELD AND SEMICONDUCTORS

> **Q.** Explain P.N. Junction and electric field inside it.

Semiconductors are a group of materials having electrical conductivities intermediate between conductors and insulators. All the properties of conductors under static electric field hold for semiconductors, only they have less carriers inside them.

A perfect semiconductor crystal with no impurities or lattice defects is called an intrinsic semiconductor. In such materials there are no charge carriers at 0 K, so we will raise the temperature in order to create electron-hole pairs of such materials. In addition to that it is possible to create carriers in semiconductors by purposely introducing impurities into the crystal which is called doping. There are two types of doped semiconductors, n-type mostly electrons doped and p-type mostly holes doped. If we combine an n-type material and p-type material we will build a p-n junction.

P-N Junction and the Electric Field Inside

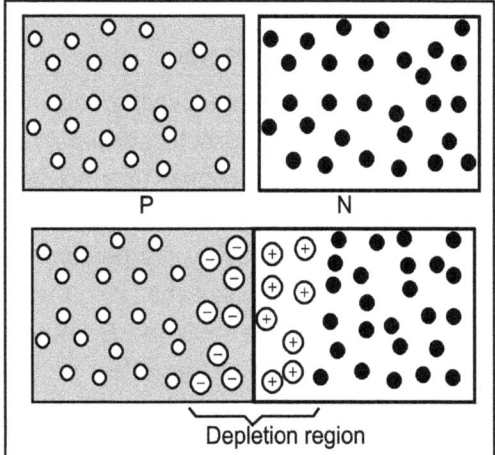

Fig. 6.2

In the above figure shows when we combine the two materials electrons start diffusing from the n-type leaving positively charged ions to p-type and the opposite from p-type to n-type. But this situation does not last long as the increasing potential difference in the depletion region causes an electric field from the n-type material to the p-type material as shown below

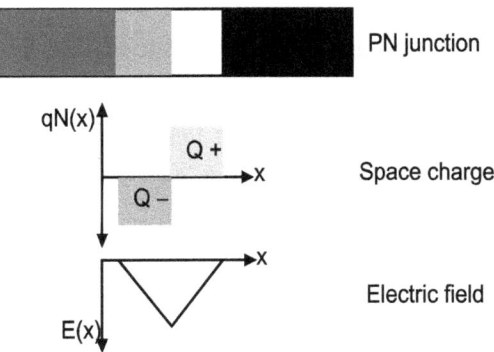

Fig. 6.3

The current due to diffusion of the charges is called the diffusion current which is from the p-type material to the n-type material. The current due to the electric field because the electric field pushes the positive charges to the p-type material and the negative charges to the n-type material is called the drift current. After a certain time these currents equal to each other in magnitude but in the opposite directions, however in the depletion region there is always carriers passing from one side to another.

There is current in the depletion region because of the carriers moving from one material to another, but there is no current outside this are so there is no electric field.

6.5 SUPERCONDUCTORS AND MAGNETIC FIELDS

Q. What is super conductors.
Q. Write short note on superconductor and its types.

In 1908 Heike Kammerlingh Onne succeeded in liquefying helium, which provided and ideal cold bath for experiments at temperatures close to absolute zero. In 1911 he made the discovery that when certain substances were cooled they act as superconductors. In 1933 Walter Meissner and Robert Ochsenfeld revealed that a superconducting material will repel a magnetic field. The reason behind this is that in a superconductor the induced currents exactly mirror the field that would have otherwise penetrated the superconducting material - causing the magnet to be repulsed. This phenomenon is known as diamagnetism and is often referred as the "Meissner effect". The Meissner effect is so strong that a magnet can actually be levitated over a superconductive material. In 1962 scientists at Westinghouse developed the first commercial superconducting wire, an alloy of Niobium and Titanium. The first use of this wire in high-energy, particle-accelerator electromagnets, on the other hand, did not use until 1987 when it was used at the Fermilab Tevatron.

Superconductors are substances that conduct electricity without any resistance, when they are sufficiently cooled. Also, since there is no resistance in a super conductor, there is no heat dissipated by the super conductor. While there is no heat dissipated, there must not be any energy loss. This can be seen from the fact that V/I is proportional to the volume integral of J.E. (energy), where J and E are the conduction current density and the electromotive intensity. The conductance in a super conductor goes to infinity, because of the fact that G = 1/R where G is the conductance and R is the resistance.

A superconductor will not allow any magnetic field to freely enter in it. This is because microscopic magnetic dipoles are induced in the superconductor that opposes the applied field.

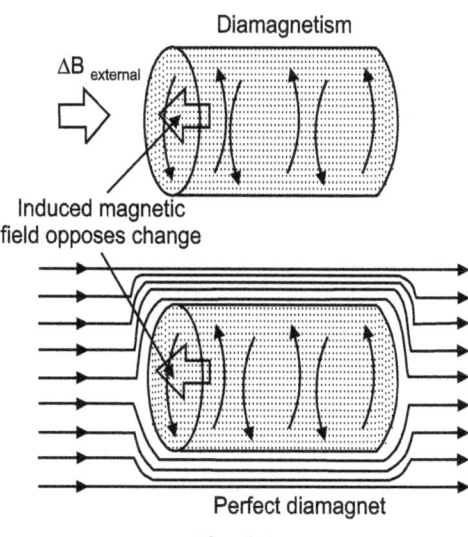

Fig. 6.4

This induced field then repels the source of the applied field, and will consequently drive back the magnet associated with that field. This implies that if a magnet was placed on top of the superconductor when the superconductor was above its Critical Temperature (Tc), and then it was cooled down to below Tc, the superconductor would then exclude the magnetic field of the magnet. This can be seen quite clearly since a magnet itself is repelled, and thus is levitated above the superconductor.

6.5.1 Type I Superconductors

There are two types of Superconductors Type I & Type II. The Type I category of superconductors is mainly comprised of metals and metalloids that show some conductivity at room temperature. Type 1 superconductors are characterized as the "soft" super-conductors and show a very sharp transition to a superconducting state.

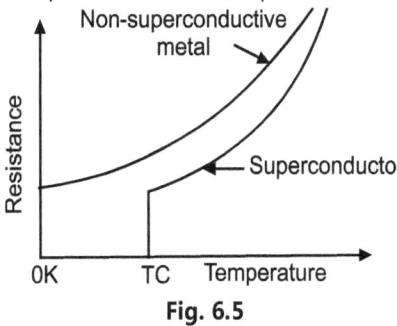

Fig. 6.5

They require the coldest temperatures to become superconductive and to slow down molecular vibrations sufficiently to facilitate unimpeded electron flow in accordance with it as per BCS theory. BCS theory suggests that electrons team up in Cooper pairs in order to help each other overcome molecular obstacles.

This process is called as phonon-mediated coupling. Type I super conductors have one critical magnetic field for any given temperature. If they are in a magnetic field that is weaker than the critical magnetic field, they have zero resistance and show ideal diamagnetism. If the magnetic field is stronger than the critical magnetic field, resistance is greater than zero, and there is flux penetration. below table give list of Type I super conductors and their critical temperature.

followin graph is showing a Type I superconductor and the measured µoM where M = Magnetization versus an applied magnetic field.

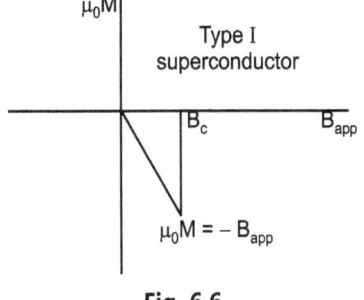

Fig. 6.6

Table 6.1

material	Tc
Carbon (C)	15 K
Lead (Pb)	7.196 K
Tantalum (Ta)	4.47 K
Mercury (Hg)	4.15 K
Tin (Sn)	3.72 K
Indium (In)	3.41 K
Thallium (Tl)	2.38 K
Rhenium (Re)	1.697 K
Protactinium (Pa)	1.40 K
Gallium (Ga)	1.083 K
Molybdenum (Mo)	0.915 K
Thorium (Th)	1.38 K
Aluminum (Al)	1.175 K
Zinc (Zn)	0.85 K
Osmium (Os)	0.66 K
Zirconium (Zr)	0.61 K
Americium (Am)	0.60 K
Cadmium (Cd)	0.517 K
Ruthenium (Ru)	0.49 K
Titanium (Ti)	0.40 K
Uranium (U)	0.20 K
Hafnium (Hf)	0.128 K
Iridium (Ir)	0.1125 K
Lutetium (Lu)	0.100 K
Beryllium (Be)	0.026 K
Tungsten (W)	0.0154 K
Platinum (Pt)	0.0019 K

6.5.2 Type II Superconductors

Except for the elements vanadium, technetium and niobium, the Type 2 category of superconductors is comprised of metallic compounds and alloys. The recently-discovered superconducting "perovskites" metal-oxide ceramics that normally have a ratio of 2 metal atoms to every 3 oxygen atoms fit in to this Type 2 group. They achieve higher Tc's than Type 1 superconductors by a mechanism that is still not completely understood. Conventional wisdom holds that it relates to the planar layering within the crystalline structure. The superconducting cuprates (copper-oxides) have achieved astonishingly high Tc's when consider at 1985 known Tc's had only reached 23 K. now, the highest Tc attained at ambient pressure has been 138K. One theory predicts an upper limit of about 200 K for the layered cuprates. Others assert there is no limit. moreover, it is almost certain that other more-synergistic compounds still look forward to discovery among the high-temperature superconductors. Type 2 superconductors - also known as the "hard" superconductors - differ from Type 1 in that their transition from a normal to a superconducting state is gradual across a region of "mixed state". A Type 2 will also permit some penetration by an external magnetic field into its surface. Type II superconductors have two critical magnetic fields, Bc1<Bc2. For a magnetic field B less than Bc1, the superconductor acts like a type I, and for a magnetic field B greater than Bc2, the substance behaves as a normal material. A unique phenomenon occurs when the magnetic field is between Bc1 and Bc2. In this case, the superconductor has zero resistance but allows partial flux penetration. This is supposed to be the vortex state. In the vortex state there are cores of normal material, surrounded by material in the superconducting state. As the magnetic field increases, the number of normal cores increases until eventually, the material becomes non-superconducting. below table give list of some Type II super conductors.

COMPOUND	Tc
$HgBa_2Ca_2Cu_3O_8$	133K
$HgBa_2Ca_3Cu_4O_{10}$	127K
$SmBaSrCu_3O_7$	86K
$HgBa_2CuO_4$	94K
$Tl_2Ba_2Ca_3Cu_4O_{10}$	128K
$Tl_2Ba_2CaCu_3O^8$	119K
$TlBa_2Ca_2Cu_3O_8$	110K
$TlBa_2CaCu_2O_7$	92K
$Bi_2CaSr_2Cu_2O_8$	92K
$Bi_2Ca_2Sr_2Cu_3O_{10}$	110K
$YBa_2Cu_3O_7$	93K

figure is showing a Type II superconductor and the measured μoM (M = Magnetization) versus an applied magnetic field

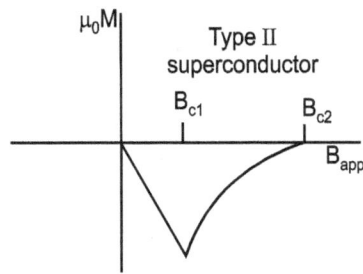

Fig. 6.7

6.5.3 Applications of Superconductors

Electric Power

High Temperature superconductors can be used in the production of more cost effective motors and generators. Also High temperature superconductor power cables can carry 2 to 10 times more power in equally or smaller sized cables, since the fact that with zero resistance there is no heat loss during the transmission of current over the transmission lines. A superconductivity technology depends on whether wires can be prepared from the brittle ceramics that retain their superconductivity at 77 K while supporting large current densities.

Cutaway of HTS Power Transmission Cable

Following figure Shows how Liquid nitrogen circulates through the hollow core of an High temperature Superconductor assembly, which is enclosed by layers of thermal and electrical insulation encapsulated in an outer steel jacket. Cable cross-section

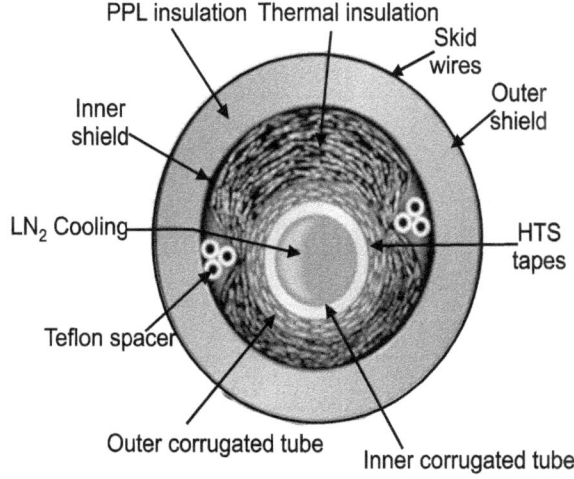

Fig. 6.8

Transportation

The use of superconductors for transportation has already been established using liquid helium as a refrigerant. Prototype levitated trains have been constructed in Japan by using superconducting magnets. High temperature superconductor coils create strong magnetic fields that produce the effect of levitation by repulsion or attraction. This is the principle underlying magnetically levitated or maglev trains. Maglev trains hover above a magnetic field without any physical contact with a track during operation. As a result, high speeds of up to 500 miles per hour are possible with only a small consumption of energy.

Medical Industry

Magnetic resonance imaging (MRI) is playing an ever growing role in diagnostic medicine. Superconductive magnetic coils are an important portion of this whole-body scanner. Since these coils are capable of producing very stable, large magnetic field strengths, they generate high quality images. Currently, low temperature superconductors are employed in these coils, but the ultimate use of High Temperature Superconductor materials will significantly enhance the cost-benefit aspect of the application.

6.6 BIMETALLIC STRIPS

Bonding two metals with different thermal expansion coefficients can produce useful devices for detecting and measuring temperature changes. A typical pair is brass and steel with typical expansion coefficients of 19 and 13 parts per million per degree Celsius respectively.

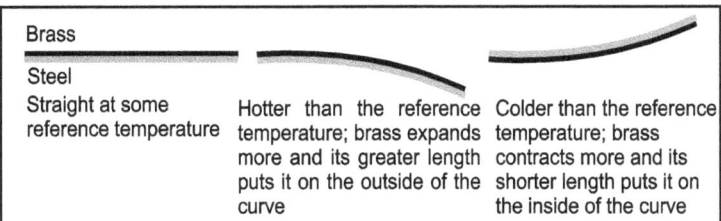

Fig. 6.9

The examples shown are straight strips, but bimetallic strips are made in coils to increase their sensitivity used in thermostats. One of the many uses for bimetallic strips is in electrical breakers where excessive current through the strip heats it and bends it to trip the switch to interrupt the current.

6.7 THERMOCOUPLE

Q. Short note on thermocouple
Q. Explain working principle of thermocouple and its types.

A thermocouple is a device used widely for measuring temperature. A thermocouple is comprised of at least two metals joined together to form two junctions. One is connected to the body whose temperature is to be measured; this is called hot or measuring junction. The other junction is connected to a body of known temperature; this is called cold or reference junction. as a result the thermocouple measures unknown temperature of the body with reference to the known temperature of the other body.

Working Principle

The working principle of thermocouple is based on three effects, revealed by Seebeck, Peltier and Thomson. They are as follows:

1) Seebeck effect: The Seebeck effect states that when two different or unlike metals are joined together at two junctions, an electromotive force is generated at the two junctions. The amount of emf generated is different for different combinations of the metals.

2) Peltier effect: As per the Peltier effect, when two different or unlike metals are joined together to form two junctions, emf is generated within the circuit due to the different temperatures of the two junctions of the circuit.

3) Thomson effect: As per the Thomson effect, when two different or unlike metals are joined together forming two junctions, the potential exists within the circuit due to temperature gradient along the entire length of the conductors within the circuit.

In most of the cases the emf suggested by the Thomson effect is very small and it can be neglected by making proper selection of the metals. The Peltier effect plays a important role in the working principle of the thermocouple.

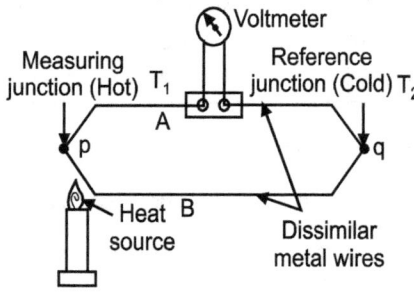

Fig. 6.10

Working

The general circuit for the working of thermocouple is shown in the figure 1 above. It consist of two dissimilar metals, A and B. These are joined together to form two junctions, p and q, which are maintained at the temperatures T1and T2 respectively. keep in mind that the thermocouple cannot be formed if there are not two junctions. Since the two junctions are maintained at different temperatures. the Peltier emf is generated within the circuit . it is the function of the temperatures of two junctions.

If the temperature of both the junctions is same, equal and opposite emf will be generated at both junctions and the net current flowing through the junction is zero. If the junctions are maintained at different temperatures, the emf's will not become zero and there will be a net current flowing through the circuit. The total emf flowing through this circuit depends on the metals used within the circuit as well as the temperature of the two junctions. The total emf or the current flowing through the circuit can be measured easily.

The device for measuring the current or emf is connected within the circuit of the thermocouple. It measures the amount of emf flowing through the circuit due to the two junctions of the two dissimilar metals maintained at different temperatures. Now, the temperature of the reference junctions is already known, while the temperature of measuring junction is unknown. The output obtained from the thermocouple circuit is calibrated against the unknown temperature. Thus the voltage or current output obtained from thermocouple circuit gives the value of unknown temperature directly.

Types of thermocouple

    J type - 0°C to 750°C
    K type - −200°C to 1250°C
    E type - −200°C to 900°C
    T type - 250°C to 350°C

SOLVED EXAMPLES

Example 6.1: A filament of 230V, 100w lamp is to be constructed. The temperature of filament is to be 2460°C at 100 w dissipation. Rasistivity of the filament material at 20°C is 4.3 × 10^{-6} Ω cm and temperature coefficient is 0.005/°C calculate the length of the filament at 20°C if its diameter at 20°C is 0.026mm.   **(PU. Dec. 08, May 07, May 09, May 12.)**

Solution : Given : V = 230 V, W_{diss} = 100 W, $α_{20}$ = 0.005/°C, $ρ_{20}$ = 4.3 × 10^{-6} Ω-cm, d = 0.026 mm.

∴   r = 0.013 mm

Power dissipated = W = $I^2 R$

∴ $100 = \left(\frac{V}{R}\right)^2 R = \frac{V^2}{R} = \frac{(230)^2}{R_{2460}}$

∴ R_{2460} = 529 Ω

$R_{2460} = R_{20} [1 + α_{20} \cdot (T_2 - T_1)]$

∴   529 = R_{20} [1 + 0.005 × (2460 − 20)]

∴ $R_{20} = \frac{529}{13.2}$ = 40.075 Ω

At 20°C,

∴ $R_{20} = ρ_{20} \left(\frac{l_{20}}{A_{20}}\right)$

∴ $40.075 = 4.3 \times 10^{-6} \left(\frac{l_{20}}{π \cdot (0.013 \times 10^{-3})^2}\right)$

$$\therefore \quad 40.075 = \frac{4.3 \times 10^{-6}}{5.309 \times 10^{-9}} \times l_{20}$$

$$\therefore \quad l_{20} = \frac{40.075 \times 5.309}{4.3}$$

$$\therefore \quad l_{20} = 49.48 \text{ cm}$$

$$\therefore \quad l_{20} = 0.4958 \text{ m}$$

Example 6.2 : Annealed copper has resistivity of 1.56×10^{-8} Ω-m at 300°K. With 2 atomic percent Nickel, the resistivity of alloy of copper and Nickel becomes 4.06×10^{-8} Ω-m. With the addition of 3 atomic percent silver, the resistivity of copper and silver alloy is found to be 1.98×10^{-8} Ω-m. What will be the resistivity of copper alloy for 0.5 atomic percent of nickel and 1.2 atomic percent of silver at 300°K. **(PU-Dec. 05, 06, 07, 08)**

Solution : Given :

$$\rho_{Cu} = 1.56 \times 10^{-8} \text{ Ω-m}$$

$$\rho_{Cu-Ni} = 4.06 \times 10^{-8} \text{ Ω-m}$$

$$= 1.56 \times 10^{-8} + 2 \times \rho_{\text{increase per atomic percent}}$$

$$\rho_{\text{increase per atomic percent Ni}} = \frac{(4.06 - 1.56) \times 10^{-8}}{2}$$

$$= 1.25 \times 10^{-8} \text{ Ω-m}$$

$$\rho_{Cu-Ag} = 1.98 \times 10^{-8} + 3 \times \rho_{\text{increase per atomic percent}}$$

$$\rho_{\text{increase per atomic percent of Ag}} = \frac{(1.98 \times 1.56) \times 10^{-8}}{3}$$

$$= 0.14 \times 10^{-8} \text{ Ω-m}$$

$$\rho_{Cu-Ni-Ag} = 1.56 \times 10^{-8} + 0.5 \times 1.25 \times 10^{-8} + 1.2 \times 0.14 \times 10^{-8}$$

$$= 2.353 \times 10^{-8} \text{ Ω-m}$$

Example 6.3 : The filament of a 230 V incandescent lamp is to be drawn from a wire having a diameter of 0.025 mm and resistivity at 20°C of 4.3×10^{-6} Ω-cm. If co-efficient of temperature $\alpha = 0.05/°C$. Calculate the length of filament to dissipate 100 W at filament temperature of 2600°C. **(PU-Dec. 05)**

Solution : Solution of this problem is same as numarical no. 1.

$$R_{2600°C} = 529 \text{ Ω,}$$

$$\rho_{2600} = 59.77 \times 10^{-6} \text{ Ω-cm}$$

$$l = 43.45 \text{ cm}$$

Example 6.4 : A specimen of copper wire has resistivity of 1.6×10^{-6} Ω-cm at 0°C and a temperature coefficient of $\frac{1}{254.5}$ at 20°C. Find the resistivity and temperature co-efficient of the wire at 50°C. **(PU-May 08)**

Solution : Given : $\alpha_{20} = 1/254.5$ per degree, $\rho_0 = 1.6 \times 10^{-6}$, T = 50.

$$\alpha_{20} = \frac{1}{\frac{1}{\alpha_0} + 20} = \frac{1}{254.5}$$

∴ Resisvitity at 50°C,

$$\rho_t = \rho_0 [1 + \alpha_0 t]$$

∴ $$\rho_{50} = \rho_0 (1 + \alpha_0 \, 50)$$

$$= 1.6 \times 10^{-6} \left(1 + \frac{1}{234.5} \times 50\right)$$

$$\rho_{50} = 1.941 \times 10^{-6} \, \Omega\text{-cm}$$

∴ $$\alpha_{50} = \frac{\alpha_0}{1 + \alpha_0 (50)}$$

$$= \frac{1/234.5}{1 + \frac{1}{234.5}(50)}$$

∴ $$\alpha_{50} = 3.515 \times 10^{-3}$$

Example 6.5 : Calculate the resistance of a wire at 50°C which is 300 m long and has an area of cross-section of 25 mm². The wire is made of aluminium. Resistivity of aluminium at 15°C is 2.7 Ω-m, temperature coefficient of aluminium is 0.004°C at 0°C. **(PU-Dec.06)**

Solution : Given : l = 300 m, a = 25 mm² = 25×10^{-6} m², $T_2 = 50$, $T_1 = 15$, ρ at 15°C = 2.7 Ω-m = ρ_{15}, $\alpha_0 = 0.004$

∴ $$R_{15} = \rho_{15} \times \frac{l}{a}$$

$$= 2.7 \times \frac{300}{25 \times 10^{-6}}$$

$$= 32.4 \times 10^{-6} \, \Omega$$

$$R_{50} = R_{15} [1 + \alpha_{15} (T_2 - T_1)]$$

$$= 32.4 \times 10^6 \left[1 + \left(\frac{\alpha_0}{1 + \alpha_0 t}\right)(T_2 - T_1)\right]$$

$$= 32.4 \times 10^6 \left[1 + \left(\frac{0.004}{1 + 0.004 \times 15}\right)(50 - 15)\right]$$

$$= 32.4 \times 10^6 \left[1 + \frac{0.004 \times 35}{1 + 0.006}\right]$$

$$= 32.4 \times 10^6 \left[1 + \frac{0.14}{1.06}\right]$$

$$= 32.4 \times 10^6 [1 + 0.132]$$
$$= 32.4 \times 10^6 \times 1.132$$
$$\therefore \quad R_{50} = 36.22 \times 10^6 \ \Omega$$

Example 6.6 : A 60 W, 230V filament bulb operates at 2000°C. Room temperature is 25°C. Temperature coefficient of filament material is 4.44×10^{-3} /°C. Determine the length of filament at room temperature if diameter of the filament wire at room temperature is 2.546 mm. Given resistivity of filament material at 25°C is 459.55×10^{-6} Ω-m. Also find currents drawn by the bulb during switching and during operation at 2000°C. **(PU-Dec. 06)**

Solution : Given : V = 230 V, P = 60 W, $\alpha_{25} = 4.44 \times 10^{-3}$, T_2 = 2000°C, T_1 = 25°C, $\rho_{25} = 459.55 \times 10^{-6}$ Ω-m, d = 2.546 mm

$$R_{2000} = \frac{(230)^2}{60} = \frac{V^2}{P}$$

$$R_{2000} = 881.67 \ \Omega$$

$$R_{2000} = R_{25} [1 + \alpha_{25} (T_2 - T_1)]$$

$$\therefore \quad 881.67 = R_{25} [1 + 4.44 \times 10^{-3} (1975)]$$

$$\therefore \quad R_{25} = 90.25 \ \Omega$$

Area of cross-section $= a = \frac{\pi}{4} (d)^2$

$$= \frac{\pi}{4} (2.546 \times 10^{-3})^2$$

$$\therefore \quad a = 5.092 \times 10^{-6} \ m^2$$

$$R_{25} = \rho_{25} \times \frac{l}{a}$$

$$90.25 = 459.55 \times 10^{-6} \cdot \frac{l}{5.092 \times 10^{-6}}$$

$$\therefore \quad l = \frac{459.55 \times 10^{-6}}{459.55 \times 10^{-6}} = 1 \ m$$

Current at switching (at 25°C) $= I_{25} = \frac{V}{R_{25}}$

$$I_{25} = \frac{230}{90.25} = 2.548 \ A$$

Current at operation at 2000°C $= I_{2000} = \frac{V}{R_{2000}}$

$$I_{2000} = \frac{230}{881.67} = 0.26 \ A$$

Example 6.7 : A copper conductor of resistance 80Ω at 40°C is heated upto 100°C. The temperature coefficient of resistance at 0°C is 0.00531 per degree. Calculate the resistance when the conductor is at 100°C. **(PU-May 12)**

Solution : Given : $T_2 = 100°C$, $T_1 = 40°C$, $R_{Cu40} = 80Ω$

And temperature coefficient of resistance at 0°C.

$$(\alpha_0) = 0.00531 \text{ per degree}$$

$$\therefore \quad \alpha_{40} = \frac{\alpha_0}{(1 + 40\,\alpha_0)}$$

$$\alpha_{40} = \frac{0.00531}{1 + 40 \times 0.00531}$$

$$= 0.00437947$$

$$= 0.00438$$

$$R_{100} = R_{40}\,[1 + \alpha_{40}\,(100 - 40)]$$

$$= 80\,[1 + 0.00438 \times 60]$$

$$= 80 \times 1.2628$$

$$\therefore \quad R_{100} = 101.024 \;Ω$$

Example 6.8 : A 230 V filament lamp dissipate 60 watt at 2700°C. The resistivity of filament material at 20°C is 4.3×10^{-6} Ω-cm and its temperature coefficient at 20°C is 0.005/°C. Calculate the length of filament at 20°C is 20°C if its diameter at 20°C is 0.028 mm. **(PU-Dec. 09)**

Solution : Given : $V = 230$ V, $W_{diss} = 60$ W, $\alpha_{20} = 0.005/°C$, $\rho_{20} = 4.3 \times 10^{-6}$ Ω-cm, $d = 0.028$ mm.

$$\therefore \quad 100 = \left(\frac{V}{R}\right)^2 R = \frac{V^2}{4} = \frac{(230)^2}{R_{2700}}$$

$$\therefore \quad R_{2700} = 882\;Ω$$

$$R_{2700} = R_{20}\,[1 + \alpha_{20} \cdot (T_2 - T_1)]$$

$$\therefore \quad 882 = R_{20}\,[1 + 0.005 \times (2700 - 20)]$$

$$\therefore \quad R_{20} = \frac{882}{14.4} = 61.25\;Ω$$

At 20°C,

$$\therefore \quad R_{20} = \rho_{20}\left(\frac{l_{20}}{A_{20}}\right)$$

$$\therefore \quad 61.25 = 4.3 \times 10^{-6}\left[\frac{l_{20}}{\pi \cdot (0.014 \times 10^{-3})^2}\right]$$

$$\therefore \quad 61.25 = \frac{4.3 \times 10^{-6}}{6.168 \times 10^{-9}} \times l_{20}$$

$$\therefore \quad l_{20} = \frac{61.25 \times 6.168 \times 10^{-9}}{4.3 \times 10^{-6}}$$

$$\therefore \quad l_{20} = 87.859 \text{ cm}$$

$$\therefore \quad l_{20} = 0.87859 \text{ m}$$

Example 6.9 : Annealed copper has resistivity 17.2×10^{-9} Ωm at 20°C with 2 atomic percentage of nickel the resistivity of alloy of copper and nickel becomes 4.06×10^{-8} Ωm. With the addition of 3 percent atomic silver the resistivity of alloy of copper and silver becomes 1.98×10^{-8} Ωm. What will be the resistivity of copper alloy for addition of 0.3 atomic percent of nickel and 0.2 atomic percent of silver at 20°C. **(PU-Dec. 09)**

Solution : Given :

$$\rho_{cu} = 17.2 \times 10^{-9} = 1.72 \times 10^{-8} \text{ } \Omega\text{m}$$

$$\rho_{cu\text{-}Ni} = 4.06 \times 10^{-8}$$

$$= 1.72 \times 10^{-8} + 2 \times \rho_{increase}$$

$$\therefore \quad \rho_{increase/atomic\ percent\ Ni} = (4.06 - 1.72) \times 10^{-8}$$

$$= 2.34 \times 10^{-8} \text{ } \Omega\text{m}$$

$$\rho_{cu\text{-}Ag} = 1.98 \times 10^{-8}$$

$$= 1.72 \times 10^{-8} + 3 \times \rho_{increase}$$

$$\therefore \quad \rho_{increase/atomic\ percent\ Ag} = \frac{(1.98 - 1.72) \times 10^{-8}}{3}$$

$$= 0.087 \times 10^{-8} \text{ } \Omega\text{m}$$

$$\therefore \quad \rho_{cu\text{-}Ni\text{-}Ag} = 1.72 \times 10^{-8} + 2 \times 2.34 \times 10^{-8} + 0.087 \times 10^{-8} \times 0.2$$

$$= (1.72 + 4.68 + 0.0174) \times 10^{-8}$$

$$= 6.4174 \times 10^{-8} \text{ } \Omega\text{m}$$

Example 6.10 : Annealed copper has resistivity of 1.56×10^{-8} Ωm at 300°K with 2 atomic percent nickel, the resistivity of alloy of copper and nickel becomes 4.06×10^{-8} Ωm. With the addition of 3 atomic percent silver the resistivity of copper and silver alloy as found to be 1.98×10^{-8} Ωm. What will be the resistivity of copper alloy for 0.2 atomic percent of nickel and 0.4 atomic percent of silver at 300°K. **(PU-Dec. 06)**

Solution : Given :

$$\rho_{cu} = 1.56 \times 10^{-8} \, \Omega m$$

$$\rho_{cu-Ni} = 4.06 \times 10^{-8}$$

$$= 1.56 \times 10^{-8} + 2 \times \rho_{increase}$$

$$\therefore \rho_{increase/atomic\ percent\ Ni} = (4.06 - 1.56) \times 10^{-8}$$

$$= 1.25 \times 10^{-8} \, \Omega m$$

$$\rho_{cu-Ag} = 1.98 \times 10^{-8}$$

$$= 1.56 \times 10^{-8} + 3 \times \rho_{increase}$$

$$\therefore \rho_{increase/atomic\ percent\ Ag} = \frac{(1.98 - 1.56) \times 10^{-8}}{3}$$

$$= 0.14 \times 10^{-8} \, \Omega m$$

$$\therefore \rho_{cu-Ni-Ag} = 1.56 \times 10^{-8} + 2 \times 1.25 \times 10^{-8} + 0.14 \times 10^{-8} \times 0.4$$

$$= 1.866 \times 10^{-8} \, \Omega m$$

Example 6.11 : The resistivity of copper at 300°K is 1.56×10^{-8} Ωm. With 2 atomic percent Nickel, the resistivity of copper and nickel becomes 4.06×10^{-8} Ωm at 300°K with 0.2 atomic percent of Nickel and 0.4 at atomic percent of silver at 300°K the resistivity becomes 1.866×10^{-8} Ωm. What will be the resistivity of Cu-silver alloy at 300°K with 3 atomic percent of silver? **(PU-Dec. 05)**

Solution : Given :

$$\rho_{cu} = 1.56 \times 10^{-8} \, \Omega m$$

$$\rho_{cu-Ni} = 4.06 \times 10^{-8} \, \Omega m$$

$$= 1.56 \times 10^{-8} + 2 \, \rho_{increase}$$

$$\therefore \rho_{increase/atomic\ percent\ Ni} = (4.06 - 1.56) \times 10^{-8}$$

$$= 1.25 \times 10^{-8} \, \Omega m$$

$$\rho_{cu-Ag} = 1.866 \times 10^{-8}$$

$$= 1.56 \times 10^{-8} + 4 \times \rho_{increase}$$

$$\therefore \rho_{increase/atomic\ percent\ Ag} = \frac{(1.866 - 1.56) \times 10^{-8}}{3}$$

$$= 0.306 \times 10^{-8} \, \Omega m$$

$$\therefore \quad \rho_{cu\text{-}Ni\text{-}Ag} = 1.56 \times 10^{-8} + 2 \times 1.25 \times 10^{-8} + 0.306 \times 10^{-8} \times 0.4$$

$$= (1.56 + 2.5 + 0.1224) \times 10^{-8}$$

$$= 4.1824 \times 10^{-8} \, \Omega m$$

Example 6.12 : Calculate the length of heater element having 0.4 mm diameter to get a resistance of 40Ω and 1000 watts if :

(a) Nichrome wire having resistivity 100×10^{-8} Ωm is used.

(b) Copper wire having resistivity 1.72 10^{-8} Ωm is used. Which wire will you prefer for heater element? **(PU-May 10)**

Solution : Given : $R_{cu} = 40\Omega, d = 0.4$ mm

$$a = \frac{\pi}{4} d^2$$

$$= \frac{\pi}{4} \times (0.4 \times 10^{-3})^2$$

$$= 1.2566 \times 10^{-7}$$

$$R_{cu} = \frac{\rho \, l_{cu}}{a}$$

$$l_{cu} = \frac{R_{cu} \cdot a}{\rho}$$

$$= \frac{40 \times 1.2566 \times 10^{-7}}{1.72 \times 10^{-8}}$$

$$\therefore \quad l_{cu} = 292.24 \text{ m}$$

So length of copper heater element required is 292.24 m

$$R_{Ni} = \frac{\rho \, l_{Ni}}{a}$$

$$\therefore \quad l_{Ni} = \frac{R_{Ni} \cdot a}{\rho}$$

$$= \frac{40 \times 1.2566 \times 10^{-7}}{100 \times 10^{-8}}$$

$$\therefore \quad l_{Ni} = 5.0264 \text{ m}$$

So, length of nichrome heater element required is 5.0264 m. Hence, nichrome heater element is preferred than copper element.

Example 6.13 : Annealed copper has resistivity of 1.56×10^{-8} Ωm at 300°K. With 4 atomic percent nickel, the resistivity of copper and nickel becomes 4.06×10^{-8} Ωm. With the addition of 3 atomic percent silver the resistivity of copper and silver alloy is found to be 2.10×10^{-8} Ωm. What will be resistivity of copper alloy for 0.8 atomic percent of nickel and 1.5 atomic percent of silver at 300°K? **(PU-May 11)**

Solution : Given :

$$\rho_{cu} = 1.56 \times 10^8 \text{ Ωm}$$

$$\rho_{cu \cdot Ni} = 4.06 \times 10^{-8}$$

$$= 1.56 \times 10^{-8} + 4 \cdot \rho_{increase}$$

$$\rho_{increase} / \text{atomic \% age of Ni} = \frac{(4.06 - 1.56) \times 10^{-8}}{4}$$

$$= 0.625 \times 10^{-8} \text{ Ωm}$$

$$\rho_{cu \cdot Ag} = 2.10 \times 10^{-8} + 3 \times \rho_{increase} \text{ per atomic percentage}$$

$$\therefore \rho_{increase} \text{ per atomic percentage of Ag} = \frac{(2.10 - 1.56) \times 10^{-8}}{3}$$

$$= 0.18 \times 10^{-8} \text{ Ωm}$$

$$\rho_{cu \cdot Ni-Ag} = 1.56 \times 10^{-8} + 0.8 \times 0.625 \times 10^{-8} + 1.5 \times 0.18 \times 10^{-8}$$

$$= 2.33 \times 10^{-8} \text{ Ωm}$$

Example 6.14 : A copper conductor has resistance of 80Ω at 40°C. It is heated to 100°C. Calculate its resistance and temperature coefficient of resistance at 100°C. Given α_0 = 0.00531 per degree centigrade. **(PU-May 11)**

Solution :

$$\alpha_{40} = \frac{\alpha_0}{1 + 40 \alpha_0}$$

$$\alpha_{40} = 0.00438 \text{ /°C}$$

$$R_{100} = R_{40} [1 + \alpha_{40} (100 - 40)]$$

$$\therefore R_{100} = 101.024 \text{ Ω}$$

$$\alpha_{100} = \frac{\alpha_0}{1 + 100 (\alpha_0)}$$

$$\alpha_{100} = 0.00346 \text{ /°C}$$

Example 6.15 : A filament of a 230V, 60 W lamp is to be constructed. The temperature of the filament is to be 1500°C at 60 W. Resistivity of the filament material at 30°C is 5.3×10^{-6} Ω-cm and temperature co-efficient $\alpha_{30} = 0.005/°C$. Calculate the length of the filament at 30°C if its diameter at 30°C is 0.025 mm. **(PU-Dec. 12)**

Solution : Given : $V = 230$, $W_{diss} = 60$ W, $\alpha_{30} = 0.005/°C$, $\rho_{30} = 5.3 \times 10^{-6}$, $d = 0.025$ mm, $r = 0.0125$ mm

$$\text{Power dissipated} = W = I^2 R$$

$$60 = \left(\frac{V}{R}\right)^2 R$$

$$= \frac{V^2}{R}$$

$$= \frac{(230)^2}{R_{1500}}$$

$$\therefore R_{1500} = 881.7 \, \Omega$$

$$\therefore R_{1500} = R_{30}[1 + \alpha_{30}(T_2 - T_1)]$$

$$\therefore 881.7 = R_{30}[1 + 0.005(1500 - 30)]$$

$$\therefore 881.7 = R_{30}[1 + 7.35]$$

$$R_{30} = \frac{881.7}{8.35} = 105.6 \, \Omega$$

At 30°C,

$$R_{30} = \rho_{30}\left(\frac{l_{30}}{A_{30}}\right)$$

$$105.6 = 5.3 \times 10^{-6} \left(\frac{l_{30}}{r(0.0125 \times 10^{-3})^2}\right)$$

$$105.6 = \frac{5.3 \times 10^{-6}}{1.5625 \times 10^{-10} \times l_{30}}$$

$$105.6 = 3.392 \times 10^{-4} \times l_{30}$$

$$\therefore l_{30} = \frac{105.6}{3.392 \times 10^4}$$

$$= 31.132 \times 10^{-4}$$

$$= 3.1132 \times 10^{-3}$$

$$\therefore l_{30} = 3.1132 \text{ mm}$$

REVIEW QUESTIONS

1. Explain properties of conducting materials.
2. Explain classification of thermocouples.
3. Explain materials use for element filament lamp.
4. What is bi-metal?
5. Short note on :
   (i) Silver alloys
   (ii) Eureka
   (iii) Bronze
   (iv) Constantan

UNIVERSITY QUESTIONS

May 2008

1. Explain the factors which affect the resistivity of conducting material. Give examples in support of your answer. (6 Marks)
2. What is thermal bimetal? Name some bimetals and their applications. (5 Marks)
3. Give the electrical properties and applications of the following materials : (8 Marks)
   (i) Aluminium
   (ii) Carbon
   (iii) Nichrome
   (iv) Eureka
4. Give the salient properties and applications of high conductive and high resistivity materials. (8 Marks)

Dec. 2008

5. Why is carbon preferred for brushes in electric machines? (4 Marks)
6. State properties and application of : (6 Marks)
   (i) Eureka
   (ii) Tungsten
7. What properties of conductors are required for electric machines? Discuss the conductors required for D.C. machines. (6 Marks)
8. Explain the factors which affect the resistivity of conducting material. Give examples in support of your answer. (6 Marks)
9. Describe the properties and applications of the following materials : (8 Marks)
   (i) Constantan
   (ii) Nichrome
   (iii) Canthal
   (iv) Bronze

10. What are thermocouples? Name some thermocouples and their applications.
(4 Marks)

May 2009

11. Describe the groups into which the materials as electric conductors are divided.
(6 Marks)

12. Why is carbon preferred for brushes in electric machines? (4 Marks)

13. List the properties of a conductive material. Describe in brief the properties, characteristics and application of aluminum as a conductive material. **(8 Marks)**

Dec. 2009

14. State the properties and application of : **(12 Marks)**
    (a) Eureka
    (b) Tungsten
    (c) Kanthal

15. Why is carbon preferred for brushes in electric machines? **(4 Marks)**

16. What are the groups into which solders are grouped? Give their applications. **(4 Marks)**

17. A 230 V filament lamp dissipates 60 Watt at 2700°C. Resistivity of filament material at 20°C is 4.3×10^{-6} Ω-cm and its temperature coefficient at 20°C is 0.005/°C. Calculate the length of filament at 20°C if its diameter at 20°C if its diameter at 20°C is 0.028 mm.
(8 Marks)

18. Annealed copper has resistivity 17.2×10^{-9} Ωm at 20°C. With 2 atomic percent of nickel, the resistivity of alloy of copper and nickel becomes 4.06×10^{-8} Ωm. With the addition of 3 percent atomic silver, the resistivity of alloy of copper and silver becomes 1.98×10^{-8} Ωm. What will be the resistivity of copper alloy for addition of 0.3 atomic percent of nickel and 0.2 atomic percent of silver at 20°C? **(4 Marks)**

May 2010

19. What is a bi-metal? Give two applications of bi-metals. **(4 Marks)**

20. State properties and applications of :
    (a) Nichrome
    (b) Constantan

21. Describe the groups into which the materials as electric conductors are divided?
(6 Marks)

22. Name the materials used in the following cases with reasons. **(6 Marks)**
    (a) Element in filament lamp.
    (b) Resistance in loading rheostat.

23. Calculate the length of heater element having 0.4 mm diameter to get a resistance of 40 Ω and 1000 Watts if : **(6 Marks)**
    (a) Nichrome wire having resistivity 100×10^{-8} Ωm is used.
    (b) Copper wire having resistivity 1.72×10^{-8} Ωm is used. Which wire will you prefer for heater element? **(6 Marks)**

Dec. 2010

24. Write down properties and applications of constantan, nickel-chromium alloy, tungsten, Kanthal, silver, copper alloy and carbon. **(16 Marks)**
25. Describe lamp filament, solders, thermal bi-metal and thermocouple. **(16 Marks)**

May 2011

26. State the properties and applications of : **(12 Marks)**
    1. Nichrome
    2. Manganin
    3. Tungsten
27. Explain the factors which affect resistivity of conducting materials. **(6 Marks)**
28. What are thermocouples? Name some thermocouples. Give their applications. **(4 Marks)**
29. Annealed copper has resistivity of 1.56×10^{-8} Ωm at 300°K. With 4 atomic percent nickel, the resistivity of copper and nickel becomes 4.06×10^{-8} Ωm. With the addition of 3 atomic percent silver the resistivity of copper the silver alloy is found to be 2.10×10^{-8} Ωm. What will be resistivity of copper alloy for 0.8 atomic percent of nickel and 1.5 atomic percent of silver at 300°K? **(4 Marks)**
30. A copper conductor has resistance of 80 Ω at 40°C. It is heated to 100°C. Calculate its resistance and temperature coefficient of resistance at 100°C. Given $\alpha_0 = 0.00531$ per degree centigrade. **(6 Marks)**

Dec. 2011

31. State the properties and applications of : **(16 Marks)**
    (i) Tungsten
    (ii) Eureka
    (iii) Kanthal
    (iv) Nichrome
32. Why is carbon preferred for brushes in electric machines? **(4 Marks)**
33. What are the groups into which solders are grouped? Give their applications. **(4 Marks)**
34. Describe in brief the properties and applications of aluminium as conductive material. **(4 Marks)**
35. Write a short note on "Thermocouples". **(4 Marks)**

May 2012

36. State properties and applications of : **(12 Marks)**
    - (i) Eureka
    - (ii) Nichrome
    - (iii) ACSR
    - (iv) Carbon

37. A copper conductor of resistance 80 Ω at 40°C is heated upto 100°C. The temperature coefficient of resistance at 0°C is 0.00531 per degree. Calculate the resistance when the conductor is at 100°C. **(4 Marks)**

38. Why is carbon preferred for brushes in electric machines? **(4 Marks)**

39. What are thermocouple? Name some thermocouples and their applications. **(4 Marks)**

40. A filament of a 230 V, 100 W lamp is to be constructed. The temperature of the filament is to be 2460°C at 100 W dissipation. Resistivity of the filament material at 20°C is 4.3×10^{-6} Ωcm and temperature coefficient ρ_{20} = 0.005/°C. Calculate the length of the filament at 20°C. If its diameter at 20°C is 0.026 mm. **(8 Marks)**

Dec. 2012

41. Write a short note on thermocouple. **(4 Marks)**

42. What is a bi-metal? Give two applications of bimetal. **(4 Marks)**

43. Write a short note on superconductivity. **(6 Marks)**

44. Give the electrical properties and applications of Nichrome and Tungsten. **(4 Marks)**

45. A filament of a 230 V, 60 W lamp is to be constructed. The temperature of the filament is to be 1500°C at 60 W. Resistivity of the filament material at 30°C is 5.3×10^{-6} Ω-cm and temperature co-efficient α_{30} = 0.005/°C. Calculate the length of the filament at 30°C if its diameter at 30°C is 0.025 mm. **(8 Marks)**

46. Describe the groups into which the materials as electric conductors are divided. **(6 Marks)**

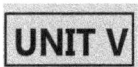

Chapter 7

NANOTECHNOLOGY

INTRODUCTION

Nano technology basically deals with the material having nano particals. Nano is 10^{-9} dimension of the order of a billionth of mater. The materials like carbon or gold changes their properties on nano scale. Therefore the study of these properties is very important in this technology. In this chapter study of various sectors of nano technology is included.

7.1 ENERGY BAND THEORY OF SOLIDS

> **Q.** Explain what is valence band, and conduction band.
> **Q.** Write short note on fermilevel.

A simplest way to visualize the difference between conductors, insulators and semiconductors is to plot the available energies for electrons in the materials. Instead of having discrete energies as in the case of free atoms, the available energy states form bands. The conduction band is the range of electron energies sufficient to free an electron from binding with its atom to move freely within the atomic lattice of the material as a delocalized electron.

Various materials may be classified by their band gap

Band gap is defined as the difference between the valence and conduction bands. In insulators, the conduction band is higher than that of the valence band, so it takes high energies to delocalize their valence electrons. They have a non-zero band gap. In semiconductors, the band gap is small. Due to this it takes a little energy (in the form of heat or light) to make semiconductors' electrons delocalize and conduct electricity, hence the name, semiconductor. In metals, the Fermi level is inside at least one band. Electrons within the conduction band are mobile charge carriers in metals, responsible for conduction of electric currents in metals and other good electrical conductors.

Valence Band

This is the band of energy where all of the valence electrons reside and are involved in the highest energy molecular orbital.

Conduction Band

This is the band energy where positive or negative mobile charge carriers exist. Negative mobile charge carriers are simply electrons that had enough energy to escape the valence band and jump to the conduction band. They move freely throughout the crystal lattice and are directly involved in the conductivity of semiconductors. Positive mobile charge carriers are also referred as holes. Holes refer to the lack of an electron in the conduction band. In other words, a hole refers to the fact that within the band there is a place where an electron can exist.

Fermi Level

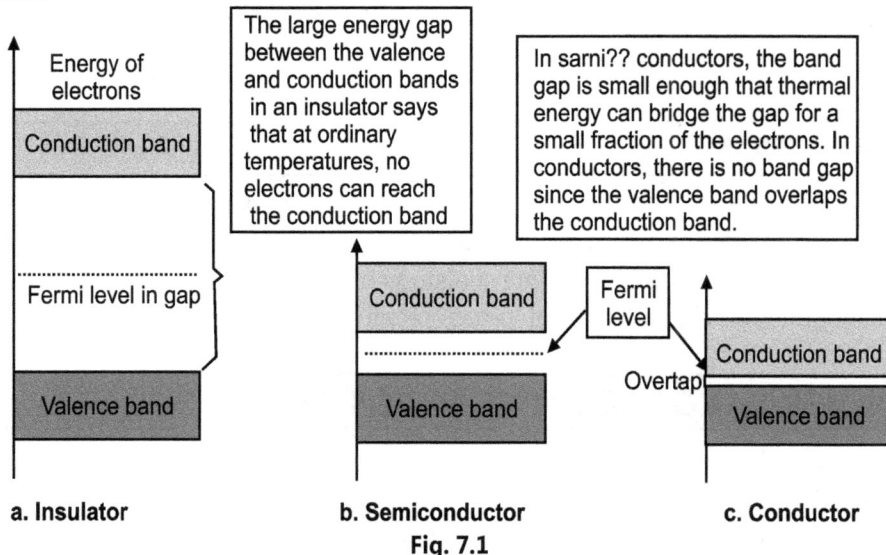

a. Insulator b. Semiconductor c. Conductor
Fig. 7.1

This level refers to the highest occupied molecular orbital at absolute zero. It is usually found at the center between the valence and conduction bands. The particles in this state have their own quantum states and generally do not interact with each other. When the temperature rise above absolute zero, these particles will begin to occupy states above the Fermi level and states below the Fermi level become unoccupied. The position of the Fermi level with the relation to the conduction band is a crucial factor in determining electrical properties. In insulators the electrons in the valence band are separated by a large gap from the conduction band. In conductors like metals the valence band overlaps the conduction band, and in semiconductors there is a small enough gap between the valence and conduction bands. With such a small gap, the presence of a small percentage of a doping material can increase conductivity of semiconductors dramatically.

Insulator Energy Bands

Most solid substances are insulators, and in terms of the band theory of solids this implies that there is a large forbidden gap between the energies of the valence electrons and the energy at which the electrons can move freely through the material that is conduction band. Glass is an insulating material which may be transparent to visible light for reasons closely correlated with its nature as an electrical insulator. The visible light photons do not have enough quantum energy to bridge the band gap and get the electrons up to an available energy level in the conduction band. A very small percentage of impurity atoms in the glass can give it color by providing specific available energy levels which absorb certain colors of visible light. The ruby mineral (corundum) is aluminum oxide with a small amount (about 0.05%) of chromium which gives it its characteristic pink or red color by absorbing green and blue light.

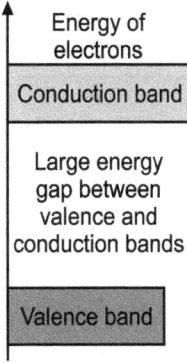

Fig. 7.2

This shows the doping of insulators can dramatically change their optical properties, but it is not enough to overcome the large band gap to make them good conductors of electricity. However, the doping of semiconductors has a much more dramatic effect on their electrical conductivity and is the basis for solid state electronics.

Semiconductor Energy Bands

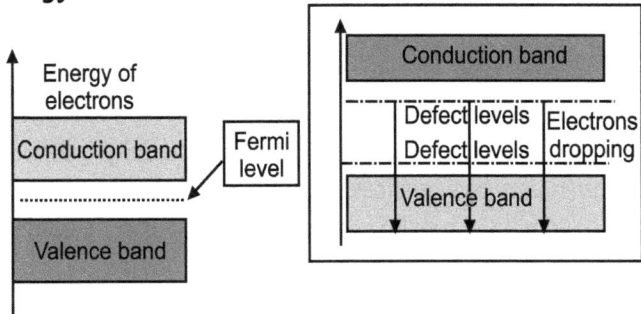

Fig. 7.3

For intrinsic semiconductors like silicon and germanium, the Fermi level is essentially halfway between the valence and conduction bands. Although no conduction occurs at 0 K, at higher temperatures a finite number of electrons can reach the conduction band and provide current. In doped semiconductors, extra energy levels are added. The increase in conductivity with temperature can be modeled in terms of the Fermi function.

Conductor Energy Bands

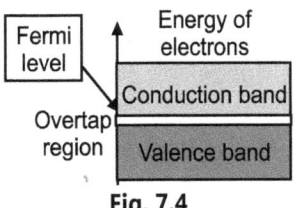

Fig. 7.4

In terms of the band theory of solids, metals are good conductors of electricity. This can be seen to be a result of their valence electrons being essentially free. In the band theory, this is depicted as an overlap of the valence band and the conduction band so that at least a fraction of the valence electrons can move through the material.

7.2 NANOSTRUCTURES

Q. Explain what is nano structures.

Nanoscience : Nanoscience is the branch of science concerned with the development and production and uses of materials whose basic components are of nanoscale size, i.e. ~1 - 100 nm in size.

Nanotechnology

Nanotechnology involves methods for transforming matter, energy and information based on nanometer scale components with particular defined molecular features and prescribed physical and chemical properties. It involves techniques that produce materials with characteristic features with particle sizes of ~1 - 100 nm. The manufacturing processes of Nanotechnology is based on the use typical chemical and mechanical principles but in novel and unfamiliar situations. The use of the scanning tunneling microscope allows us to 'see' individual atoms in an atomic or molecular lattice. consequently, it is now possible to see and investigate nanoscale structures at the atomic-molecular level and this 'feedback' enables to compare the actual structure with the desired designed structure which eventually would hope to have the prescribed desirable properties. The many applications of nanotechnology include the use of semi-conductors that only conduct electricity in specific conditions and allows the design of much very tiny 'devices' normal scale conductors, at the molecular level. It is possible to make very tiny mechanical devices to perform some task in otherwise inaccessible situations.

Nanostructures

Nanostructures are material structures assembled from layers or clusters of atoms of nanoscale size. By controlling the size and assembling of nanoscale constituents it is possible to alter and control the structure and properties of the final nanostructure. A good example is the ongoing development in the design and use carbon nanotubes. Nanostructures may consist of over 1000 atoms but it can be quite variable within the 1-100 nm range. The wide application of nanostructures includes semi-conductor devices, strained-layer lattices, magnetic multilayers. Nanostructures are built up from processed via chemical deposition or physical vapour deposition, gas condensation, chemical precipitation, aerosol reactions and biological templating - a wide range of methods of assembling arrays of atoms.

Nanomaterials

Nanomaterials is any material that has a composition based on nanoparticle units e.g. nanoparticles of silver, carbon nanotubes, inorganic ceramic materials etc. Some nanoparticles are created naturally e.g. very finely suspended mineral particles in water - the tiniest of colloidal particles act as nanoparticles. During inefficient combustion of organic molecules e.g. fossil fuels or plastics, nanosized particles of soot (mainly carbon) are formed. Evaporated sea spray can produce nanoscale salt particles.

7.3 CARBON

Q. write short note on carbon-important in nano technology.

Carbon is found in many different compounds. It is in the food you eat, the clothes you wear, the cosmetics you use and the gasoline. Carbon is the sixth most abundant element in the universe. Carbon discovered in prehistory and was known to the ancients, who manufactured it by burning organic material making charcoal. There are four known form of carbon : (a) amorphous, (b) graphite, (c) diamond and (d) fullerene. A new allotrope of carbon was recently found. It is a spongy solid that is extremely lightweight and unusually attracted to magnets. The inventors of this new form of carbon - a magnetic carbon nanofoam .

Physical Properties of the Carbon Atom
Atomic Number :- 6
Atomic Mass Average:- 12.011
Melting Point:- 3823 K (3550°C or 6422°F)
Boiling Point:- 4098 K (3825°C or 6917°F)
Density:- 2.267g/cu.cm.
Velocity of sound [/m s-1]:- 18350
Hardness Scale Mohs:- 0.5
Stable Isomers:-2

Atomic Structure
The Carbon atom has six electrons, 4 of the electrons are in its valence shell .The circles in the diagram show energy levels - representing increasing distances from the nucleus.

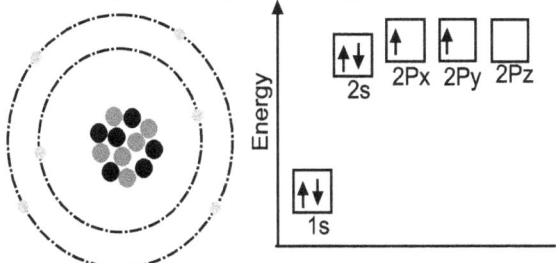

Fig. 7.5

Two electrons are found in the 1s orbital close to the nucleus. The next two will go into the 2s orbital. The remaining ones will be in two separate 2p orbital. This is because the p orbital have the same energy and the electrons would rather be in separate orbital. The actual location of electrons in a carbon atom cannot be determined with certainty.

7.4 ISOTOPES

Q. What is carbon cluster?
Q. Write short note on C-60.

Isotopes are atoms which have the same atomic number but different mass numbers. They have the same number of protons but different numbers of neutrons. The number of neutrons in an atom can vary within small limits. For example, there are three kinds of carbon atom 12C, 13C and 14C. They all have the same number of protons, but the number of neutrons varies.

	Protons	**Neutrons**	**Mass number**
carbon 12	6	6	12
carbon 13	6	7	13
carbon 14	6	8	14

These different types of carbon atoms are called isotopes. The fact that they have varying numbers of neutrons makes no difference to the chemical reactions of the carbon atom.

Uses of Carbon

Carbon added to iron makes steel. Carbon is used for control rods in nuclear reactors. Graphite combined with clays form the 'lead' used in pencils. Diamond is used for decorative purposes, and also as drill bits. Graphite carbon in a powdered, caked form is used as charcoal for cooking, artwork and other uses. Charcoal pills are used in medicine in pill or powder form to adsorb toxins or poisons from the digestive system.

Carbon cluster

Carbon is forming many allotropes. Well known forms of carbon include diamond and graphite. In recent decades many more allotropes and forms of carbon have been discovered. It including ball shapes such as buckminster fullerene and sheets such as graphene which is also known as carbon cluster.

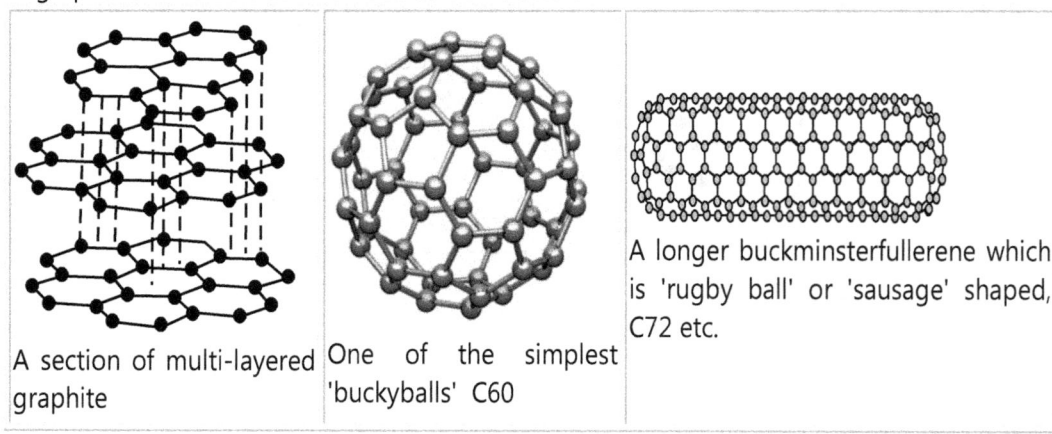

A section of multi-layered graphite | One of the simplest 'buckyballs' C60 | A longer buckminsterfullerene which is 'rugby ball' or 'sausage' shaped, C72 etc.

Fig. 7.6

Graphite :

Soft and slippery : Strong covalent bonds holding the structure together but only in 2 dimension. The layers are free to slide easily over one another. Graphite powder is used as a lubricant.

Graphite Brittle is Material : All of the bonds are directional within a layer and stress across a layer will tend to break them. Graphite rods used for electrolysis easily break when dropped.

Electrical conductor : Only three of the valence (outer shell) electrons are used in sigma bonding. The other electron is in a 'p' orbital which can overlap laterally.

Insoluble in water : There are only very weak Van der Wall's attractions between the carbon atoms and the water molecules whereas the carbon atoms are bonded very tightly to one another.

Very high meltting point : Many strong covalent bonds holding the layers together it requires massive amounts of energy to pull it apart.

Diamond :

Hard : Many strong covalent bonds holding the structure together.

Brittle : All of the bonds are directional and stress will tend to break the structure.

Insulator : All of the valence (other shell) electrons are used in bonding. The bonds are sigma and the electrons are located between the two carbon nuclei being bonded together. None of the electrons are free to move.

It is Insoluble in water. It has very melting point.

7.4.1 Fullerenes

> Q. Give the types of fullerenes?
> Q. Write short notes on Fullerenes.

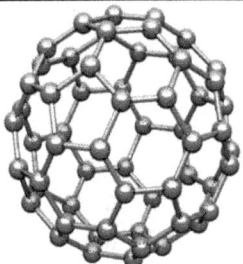

Fig. 7.7

Types of fullerene

After discovery of fullerenes in 1985, structural variations on fullerenes have evolved well beyond the individual clusters themselves as follows :

Buckyball clusters : smallest member is C20 and the most common is C60.

polymers : chain, two-dimensional and three-dimensional polymers are formed under high-pressure high-temperature conditions; single-strand polymers are formed using the Atom Transfer Radical Addition Polymerization (ATRAP) route.

nano"onions" : spherical particles based on multiple carbon layers surrounding a buckyball core; proposed for lubricants.

Linked "ball-and-chain" dimers : two buckyballs linked by a carbon chain, fullerene rings.

Nanotubes : hollow tubes of very small dimensions, having single or multiple walls; potential applications in electronics industry.

Megatubes : larger in diameter than nanotubes and prepared with walls of different thickness; potentially used for the transport of a variety of molecules of different sizes.

Buckyballs

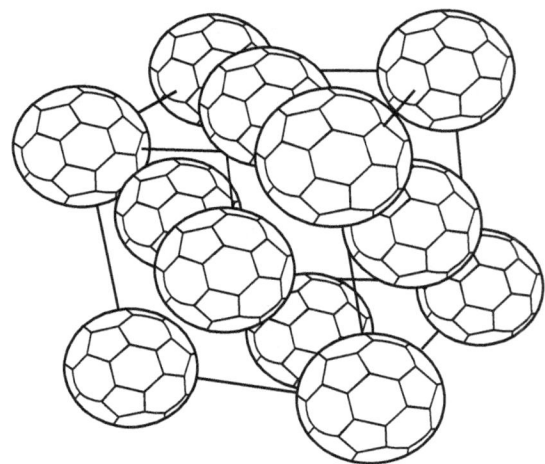

Fig. 7.8

Buckminsterfullerene is the smallest fullerene molecule having pentagonal and hexagonal rings in which no two pentagons share an edge. It is also the most common in terms of natural occurrence, as it can often be found in soot. The structure of C60 is a truncated icosahedron, which resembles an association of football ball of the type made of twenty hexagons and twelve pentagons, with a carbon atom at the vertices of each polygon and a bond along each polygon edge. The nucleus to nucleus diameter of a C60 molecule is about 0.71 nm. The van der Waals diameter of a C60 molecule is about 1.1 nanometers (nm). The C60 molecule has two bond lengths. The bonds between two hexagons can be considered "double bonds". Its average bond length is 1.4 angstroms.

Boron buckyball

In this type of buckyball in which boron atoms use instead of the usual carbon. This was predicted and described in 2007. The B80 structure, with each atom forming 5 or 6 bonds, and is predicted to be more stable than the C60 buckyball. Because that the B-80 is actually more like the original geodesic dome structure, which uses triangles rather than hexagons. The number of six-member rings in this molecule is 20 and number of five-member rings is 12. There is an additional atom in the center of each six-member ring, bonded to each atom surrounding it. By employing a systematic global search algorithm, later it was found that the previously proposed B80 fullerene is not global minimum for 80 atom boron clusters and hence can not be found in nature

Other buckyballs

Another fairly common fullerene is C70, but fullerenes with 72, 76, 84 and even up to 100 carbon atoms are commonly obtained. In mathematical terms, the structure of a fullerene is a trivalent convex polyhedron with pentagonal and hexagonal faces. In graph theory, the term fullerene refers to any 3-regular, planar graph with all faces of size 5 or 6 which also including the external face. It follows from Euler's formula, $V - E + F = 2$ (where V, E, F are the numbers of vertices, edges, and faces), that there are exactly 12 pentagons in a fullerene and $V/2 - 10$ hexagons.

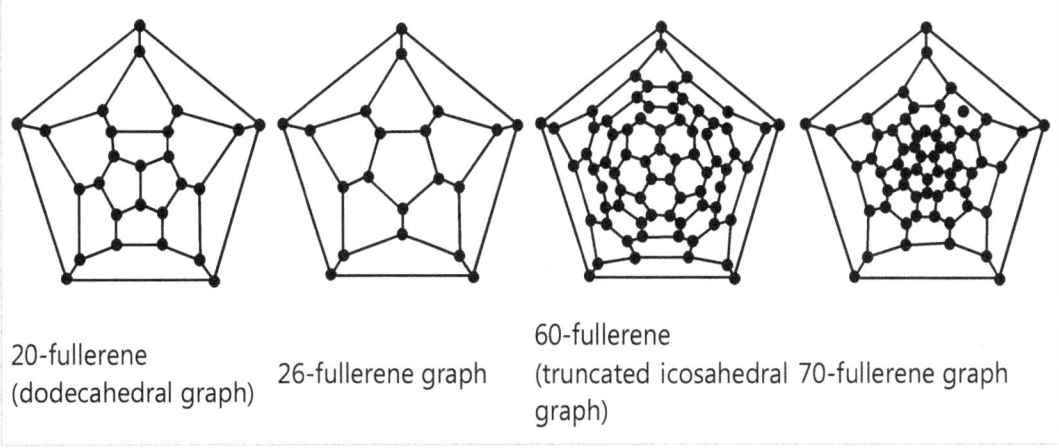

20-fullerene (dodecahedral graph)   26-fullerene graph   60-fullerene (truncated icosahedral graph)   70-fullerene graph

Fig. 7.9

The smallest fullerene available is the dodecahedral C20. There are no fullerenes with 22 vertices. The number of fullerenes C2n grows with increasing $n = 12, 13, 14,...$ roughly in proportion to n^9 For example, there are 1812 non-isomorphic fullerenes C60. Note that only one form of C60, the buckminsterfullerene aliastruncated icosahedron, has no pair of adjacent pentagons (the smallest such fullerene). To further illustrate the growth, there are 214,127,713 non-isomorphic fullerenes C200, 15,655,672 of which have no adjacent pentagons.

7.5 CARBON NANO TUBES (CNT)

Q. Explain carbon nano tubes.
Q. Write applications of carbon nano tubes.
Q. Explain various types of carbon nano tubes.

Carbon nanotubes (CNTs) are made of carbon with a cylindrical nanostructure. These cylindrical carbon molecules have unusual properties, which are valuable for electronics, optics and other fields of materials science and technology. This have extraordinary thermal conductivity and mechanical and electrical properties. Carbon nanotube name is derived from their long, hollow structure with the walls formed by one-atom-thick sheets of carbon. These sheets are rolled at specific and discrete angles, and the combination of the rolling angle and radius decides the nanotube properties. Depending on this Nanotubes are categorized as :

1. single-walled nanotubes(SWNTs)
2. multi-walled nanotubes (MWNTs).
3. torus
4. nanobud

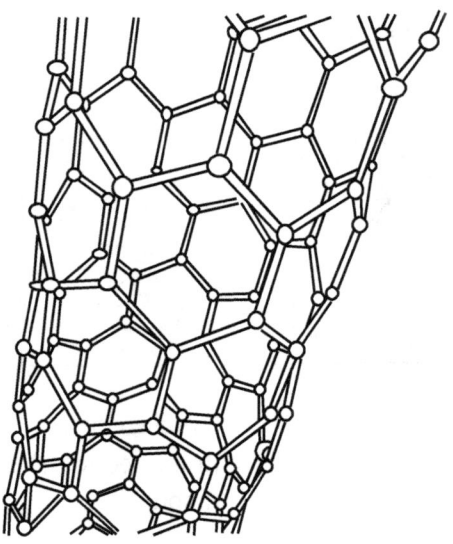

Fig. 7.10

Individual nanotubes naturally align themselves into "ropes" held together by vander Waal's forces. This chemical bonding of nanotubes is composed entirely of sp2 bonds, similar to those of graphite. These bonds, provide nanotubes with their unique strength.

Single-Walled Carbon Nanotubes

SWCNTs are produced through the Arc- discharge process. They have a purity of about 95 to 98% and include roughly 92 to 95% of carbon nano particles. SWCNT has a diameter of about 0.7 to 2nm and forms a bundle measuring 8nm. It does not require any separate refinery process.

Characteristics and Applications of Single-walled Carbon Nanotubes

SWCNTs have excellent mechanical strength with superior heat and electric conductivity. They have high crystallinity and aspect ratio together with excellent Arc- discharge element characteristics.

SWCNTs are used in chemical sensors, nano biomaterial, conductive heating film, conductive transparent electrode, conductive nanoink, nano device, and display, flat lamp and field emitter.

Double-walled carbon nanotubes (DWNT) is a special class of nanotubes because their properties are similar to those of SWNT but their resistance to chemicals is significantly improved. This is especially important when functionalization is required (this means grafting of chemical functions at the surface of the nanotubes) to add new properties to the CNT. In the case of SWNT, covalent functionalization will break some C=C double bonds, leaving "holes" in the structure on the nanotube and, thus, modifying both its mechanical and electrical properties. In the case of DWNT, only the outer wall is modified.

2 multi-walled nanotubes (MWNTs)
Multi-walled nanotubes (MWNT) consist of multiple rolled layers (concentric tubes). There are two models that can be used to describe the structures of multi-walled nanotubes.

MWCNT is produced by means of thermal CVD process and does not need a separate refinery process. Its diameter ranges from 10 to 30nm and has a purity of at least 95%. MWCNT are suitable for polymer and CNT-metal composites.

Characteristics and Applications of Multi-Walled Carbon Nanotubes
Similar to SWCNTs, MWCNTs have excellent mechanical strength with superior heat and electric cond1uctivity. They also have high specific surface area, high crystallinity, and high length-to-diameter ratio.

3 torus

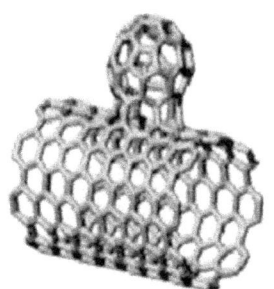

Fig. 7.11

Nanotori are predicted to have many unique properties, such as magnetic moments 1000 times larger than previously expected for certain specific radii. In theory, a nanotorus is a carbon nanotube bent into a torus (doughnut shape). Properties such as magnetic moment, thermal stability, etc. vary widely depending on radius of the torus and radius of the tube.

4 nanobud
Carbon nanobuds are material combined two previously discovered allotropes of carbon: carbon nanotubes and fullerenes. In this new material, fullerene-like "buds" are bonded to the outer sidewalls of the carbon nanotube. This hybrid material has useful properties of both fullerenes and carbon nanotubes. In particular, they have been found to be exceptionally good field emitters. In composite materials, the attached fullerene molecules may function as molecular anchors preventing slipping of the nanotubes, thus improving the composite's mechanical properties.

7.5.1 Properties of CNT

Mechanical properties of carbon nanotubes :

Strength
Carbon nanotubes are one of the strongest and stiffest materials. This strength results from the covalent sp^2 bonds formed between the individual carbon atoms. In 2000, a multi-walled carbon nanotube was tested to have a tensile strength of 63 GPa nearly. Although the

strength of individual CNT shells is extremely high, weak shear interactions between adjacent shells and tubes leads to significant reductions in the effective strength of multi-walled carbon nanotubes and carbon nanotube bundles down to only a few GPa's. This limitation has been recently addressed by applying high-energy electron irradiation, which crosslinks inner shells and tubes, and effectively increases the strength of these materials to ~60 GPa for multi-walled carbon nanotubes. CNTs are not nearly as strong under compression. Because of their hollow structure and high aspect ratio, they tend to undergo buckling when placed under compressive, torsional, or bending stress.

Hardness

Standard single-walled carbon nanotubes can withstand a pressure up to 25 GPa without deformation. They then undergo a transformation to superhard phase nanotubes.

Kinetic properties

Multi-walled nanotubes are multiple concentric nanotubes precisely nested within one another. These exhibit a striking telescoping property whereby an inner nanotube core may slide, almost without friction, within its outer nanotube shell, thus creating an atomically perfect linear or rotational bearing.

Electrical Properties

Because of the symmetry and unique electronic structure of graphene, the structure of a nanotube strongly affects its electrical properties. for a given (n,m) nanotube, if n = m, the nanotube is metallic; if n − m is a multiple of 3, then the nanotube is semiconducting with a very small band gap, otherwise the nanotube is a moderate semiconductor. Thus all (n = m) nanotubes are metallic, and nanotubes (6,4), (9,1), etc. are semiconducting.

However, this rule has exceptions, because curvature effects in small diameter carbon nanotubes can strongly influence electrical properties. In theory, metallic nanotubes can carry an electric current density of 4×10^9 A/cm^2, which is more than 1,000 times greater than those of metals such as copper.

Optical Properties

Thermal Properties

All nanotubes are expected to be very good thermal conductors along the tube. Measurements show that a SWNT has a room-temperature thermal conductivity along its axis of about 3500 W·m^{-1}·K^{-1}. Where as copper, a metal well known for its good thermal conductivity, which transmits 385 W·m^{-1}·K^{-1}. The temperature stability of carbon nanotubes is estimated to be up to 2800 °C in vacuum and about 750 °C in air.

Defects

As with any material, the existence of a crystallographic defect affects the material properties. Defects can occur in the form of atomic vacancies. High levels of such defects can lower the tensile strength by up to 85%. An important example is the Stone Wales defect, which creates a pentagon and heptagon pair by rearrangement of the bonds. Because of the very small structure of CNTs, the tensile strength of the tube is dependent on its weakest segment in a similar manner to a chain, where the strength of the weakest link becomes the maximum strength of the chain.

Crystallographic defects also affect the tube's electrical properties. A common result is lowered conductivity through the defective region of the tube. A defect in armchair-type tubes (which can conduct electricity) can cause the surrounding region to become semiconducting, and single monatomic vacancies induce magnetic properties.

Crystallographic defects strongly affect the tube's thermal properties. Such defects lead to phonon scattering, which in turn increases the relaxation rate of the phonons. This reduces thermal conductivity of nanotube structures.

Toxicity

The toxicity of carbon nanotubes has been an important question in nanotechnology. Parameters such as structure, size distribution, surface area, surface chemistry, surface charge, and agglomeration state as well as purity of the samples, have considerable impact on the reactivity of carbon nanotubes. if raw materials reach the organs, they can induce harmful effects such as inflammatory and fibrotic reactions.

Although further research is required, the available data suggests that under certain conditions, especially those involving chronic exposure, carbon nanotubes can pose a serious risk to human health.

Synthesis

techniques have been developed to produce nanotubes in sizable quantities, including arc discharge, laser ablation, high-pressure carbon monoxide disproportionation, and chemical vapor deposition (cvd). most of these processes take place in vacuum or with process gases. cvd growth of CNTs can occur in vacuum or at atmospheric pressure. large quantities of nanotubes can be synthesized by these methods; advances in catalysis and continuous growth are making cnts more commercially viable.

Methods of Synthesis

Arc discharge

Nanotubes were observed in 1991 in the carbon soot of graphite electrodes during an arc discharge, by using a current of 100 amps, that was intended to produce fullerenes. However the first macroscopic production of carbon nanotubes was made in 1992 by two researchers at NEC's Fundamental Research Laboratory. The method used was the same as in 1991. During this process, the carbon contained in the negative electrode sublimates because of the high-discharge temperatures. Because nanotubes were initially discovered using this technique, it has been the most widely used method of nanotube synthesis.

Laser ablation

In laser ablation, a pulsed laser vaporizes a graphite target in a high-temperature reactor while an inert gas is bled into the chamber. Nanotubes develop on the cooler surfaces of the reactor as the vaporized carbon condenses. A water-cooled surface may be included in the system to collect the nanotubes.

The laser ablation method yields around 70% and produces primarily single-walled carbon nanotubes with a controllable diameter determined by the reaction temperature. However, it is more expensive than either arc discharge or chemical vapor deposition.

Plasma torch

Single-walled carbon nanotubes can also be synthesized by a thermal plasma method. It was first invented in 2000 at INRS (Institut National de la Recherche Scientifique in Varennes, Canada).In this method, the to reproduce the conditions prevailing in the arc discharge and laser ablation approaches, but a carbon-containing gas is used instead of graphite vapors to supply the carbon necessary for the production of SWNT. For the growth of SWNT is more efficient .It is also continuous and occurs at low cost. To produce a continuous process, a gas mixture composed of argon, ethylene and ferrocene is introduced into a microwave plasma torch, where it is atomized by the atmospheric pressure plasma, which has the form of an intense 'flame'. The fumes created by the flame are found to contain SWNT, metallic and carbon nanoparticles and amorphous carbon.

Another way to produce single-walled carbon nanotubes with a plasma torch, is to use the induction thermal plasma method, implemented in 2005 by groups from the University of Sherbrooke and the National Research Council of Canada. The method is similar to arc-discharge in that both use ionized gas to reach the high temperature necessary to vaporize carbon-containing substances and the metal catalysts necessary for the ensuing nanotube growth. The thermal plasma is induced by high frequency oscillating currents in a coil, and is maintained in flowing inert gas. Typically, a feedstock of carbon black and metal catalyst particles is fed into the plasma, and then cooled down to form single-walled carbon nanotubes. Different single-wall carbon nanotube diameter distributions can be synthesized.

Chemical Vapor Deposition (CVD)

the catalytic vapor phase deposition of carbon was reported in 1952. it was not until 1993 that carbon nanotubes were formed by this process. In 2007, researchers at the University of Cincinnati (UC) developed a process to grow aligned carbon nanotube arrays of 18 mm length on a FirstNano ET3000 carbon nanotube growth system.

During CVD, a substrate is prepared with a layer of metal catalyst particles, most commonly nickel, cobalt, iron, or a combination. The metal nanoparticles can also be produced by other ways, including reduction of oxides or oxides solid solutions. The diameters of the nanotubes that are to be grown are related to the size of the metal particles. This can be controlled by patterned deposition of the metal, annealing, or by plasma etching of a metal layer. The substrate is heated to approximately 700°C. To initiate the growth of nanotubes, two gases are bled into the reactor: a process gas and a carbon-containing gas. Nanotubes grow at the sites of the metal catalyst; the carbon-containing gas is broken apart at the surface of the catalyst particle, and the carbon is transported to the edges of the particle, where it forms the nanotubes. The catalyst particles can stay at the tips of the growing nanotube during growth, or remain at the nanotube base, depending on the adhesion between the catalyst particle and the substrate. Thermal catalytic decomposition of hydrocarbon has become an active area of research and can be a promising route for the bulk production of CNTs. Fluidised bed reactor is the most widely used reactor for CNT preparation.

CVD is a common method for the commercial production of carbon nanotubes. For this purpose, the metal nanoparticles are mixed with a catalyst support such as MgO or Al2O3 to increase the surface area for higher yield of the catalytic reaction of the carbon feedstock with the metal particles. One issue in this synthesis route is the removal of the catalyst support via an acid treatment, which sometimes could destroy the original structure of the carbon nanotubes. However, alternative catalyst supports that are soluble in water have proven effective for nanotube growth.

7.5.2 Application of nanotube

Q. Give the applications of Nano tube.

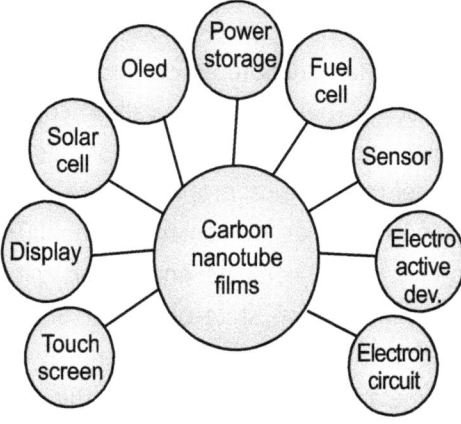

Fig. 7.12

Current applications

Current use and application of nanotubes has mostly been limited to the use of bulk nanotubes, which is a mass of rather unorganized fragments of nanotubes. Bulk nanotube materials may never achieve a tensile strength similar to that of individual tubes, but such composites may, nevertheless, yield strengths sufficient for many applications. Bulk carbon nanotubes have already been used as composite fibers in polymers to improve the mechanical, thermal and electrical properties of the bulk product.

Other current applications include :

Tips for atomic force microscope probes in tissue engineering, carbon nanotubes can act as scaffolding for bone growth It has been used for wind turbines, marine paints and variety of sports gear such as skis, ice hockey sticks, baseball bats, hunting arrows, and surfboards

Structural

Because of the carbon nanotube's superior mechanical properties, many structures have been proposed ranging from everyday items like clothes and sports gear to combat jackets and space elevators. single and multi-walled nanotubes can produce materials with toughness unmatched in the man-made and natural worlds.

Carbon nanotubes are also a promising material as building blocks in bio-mimetic hierarchical composite materials given their exceptional mechanical properties. Initial attempts to incorporate CNTs into hierarchical structures led to mechanical properties that were considerably lower than these achievable limits. Because of the high mechanical strength of carbon nanotubes, research is being made into weaving them into clothes to create stab-proof and bulletproof clothing. The nanotubes would effectively stop the bullet from penetrating the body, although the bullet's kinetic energy would likely cause broken bones and internal bleeding.

Electrical circuits

Nanotube-based transistors, also known as carbon nanotube field-effect transistors (CNTFETs), have been made that operate at room temperature and that are capable of digital switching using a single electron. However, one major obstacle to realization of nanotubes has been the lack of technology for mass production. In 2001 IBM researchers demonstrated how metallic nanotubes can be destroyed, leaving semiconducting ones behind for use as transistors. Their process is called "constructive destruction," which includes the automatic destruction of defective nanotubes on the wafer. This process, however, only gives control over the electrical properties on a statistical scale.

The potential of carbon nanotubes was demonstrated in 2003 when room-temperature ballistic transistors with ohmic metal contacts and high-k gate dielectric were reported, showing 20–30x higher ON current than state-of-the-art Si MOSFETs. This presented an important advance in the field as CNT was shown to potentially outperform Si. At the time, a major challenge was ohmic metal contact formation. In this regard, palladium, which is a high-work function metal was shown to exhibit Schottky barrier-free contacts to semiconducting nanotubes. Large structures of carbon nanotubes can be used for thermal management of electronic circuits.

7.6 BORON NITRIDE NANOTUBE

Q. Explain what is Boronnitride nanotube.
Q. What is difference between carbon nanotube and Boronnitride nanotube.
Q. What are the application of Boronnitride nanotube.

Boron nitride has the formula $(BN)_n$, (n is a very large number, but the empirical formula is BN). It forms cubic and hexagonal structures which correspond (analogous) to carbon in the form of diamond and graphite respectively.

Nanotechnology research scientists have discovered that all boron-nitride nanotubes have semiconductor properties, making this nano-material very useful in electronics. Additionally, nanotechnologists are working to create composites to make very strong, but light-weight, materials. Boron-nitride nanotubes were discovered in 1995. Research into applications for carbon nanotubes is much further along than for boron-nitride nanotubes; but researchers are working on taking advantage of the benefits that boron-nitrite nanotubes offer.

Boron-nitride nanotubes are similar to carbon nanotubes, in that they are hollow cylinders formed by atoms connected together in hexagonal shapes. However, boron-nitride nanotubes, instead of being composed of carbon atoms, are composed of boron atoms covalently bonded to nitrogen atoms to form hexagons.

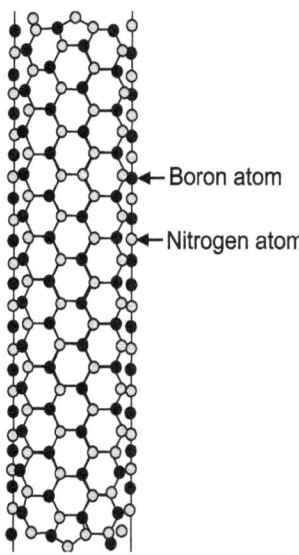

Fig. 7.13

The bonding structure between boron and nitrogen in a boron-nitride nanotube. boron-nitride nanotubes have more consistent electrical properties than carbon nanotubes. unlike carbon nanotubes, only some of which have the electrical properties of semiconductors, all boron-nitride nanotubes have those properties. for that reason, using boron-nitride nanotubes as the transistor channel in place of carbon nanotubes ensures that you have a nanotube with semiconductor properties.

Researchers are also looking at the possibility of using boron-nitride nanotubes, which are almost as strong as carbon nanotubes, in composites to create strong lightweight materials. Such composites may be particularly useful for spacecraft. In a hull built using a composite material containing boron-nitride nanotubes, the boron atoms can absorb neutrons from the solar wind and protect the crew and electronics.

7.7 SINGLE ELECTRON TRANSISTOR

Q. Write short note on single electron transistor.

A transistor is a solid state semiconductor device which can be used for numerous purposes including signal modulation, amplification, voltage stabilization, and many others.

Transistors act like a variable valve which, based on its input current (BJT) or input voltage (FET), allow a precise amount of current to flow through it from the circuit's voltage supply.

The single electron transistor is a new type of switching device that uses controlled electron tunneling to amplify current.

SET is An ultra-small device, that transfers one electron at a time, based on Coulomb interaction. This occurs on a tiny conducting layer know as an island. This island's electrostatic potential increases significantly with the introduction of just one electron.

Single-electron transistors SET's are considered to be the elements of the future. In this future, integrated circuits will be highly dense and low powered. These ultra-low powered circuits will be of a nanometer scale electronic and they will be able to detect the motion of individual electrons. Problems, however, are that SET's have low voltage gain, high output impedances, and are sensitive to random background charges. Also, for SET's to be useful in practical applications they must be able to operate in room temperature. SETs are required to be no larger than ~10 nm. This is why its highly unlikely that single-electron transistors would ever replace field-effect transistors (FET's) which work better in applications where large voltage gain or low output impedance is necessary.

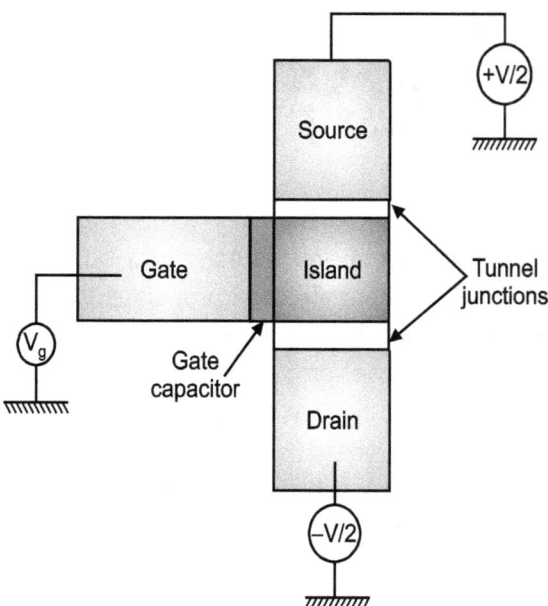

Fig 7.14 : Single Electron Transistor

Operation

The start of the SET transistor began in 1985 thanks to Dmitri Averin and Konstantin Likharev. They proposed the idea of a new three-terminal device called a single-electron tunneling (SET) transistor. Two years later Theodore Fulton and Gerald Dolan at Bell Labs in the US,

created such a device and demonstrated how it would operate. What are SET transistor made from :
Single-electron transistors have been made with just a few nanometers using;
1. Metals
2. Semiconductors
3. Carbon nanotubes
4. Individual molecules

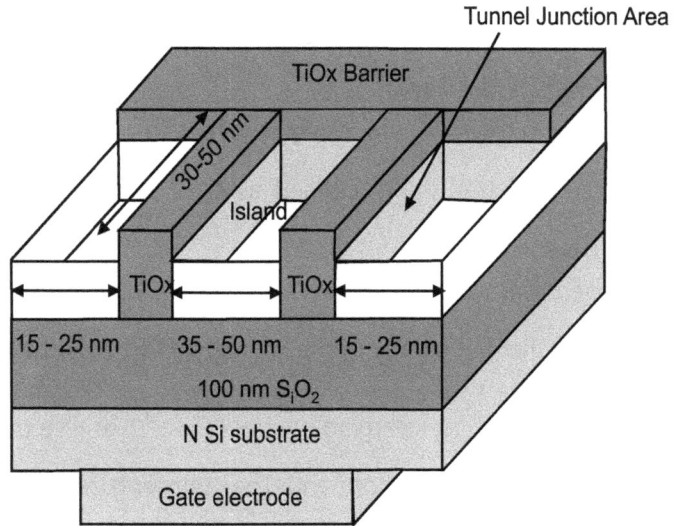

Fig. 7.15 : Schematic of a single electron transistor

The tunnel junction consists of two pieces of metal separated by a very thin (~1nm) insulator. The only way for electrons in one of the metal electrodes to travel to the other electrode is to tunnel through the insulator.

Since tunneling is a discrete process, the electric charge that flows through the tunnel junction flows in multiples of the charge of electrons e.

The charging of electrons for a tunnel junction with a Capacitance C and an Charge Q has been the bases for how SETs would function.

The electric current.

$I = \Delta Q / \Delta t$,

that is associated with tunneling of single electrons is

$I \approx e/\tau \geq e^3/2\pi hC$

A single-electron transistor consists of a small conducting island connected to an source and drain leads by tunnel junctions and connected to one or more gates.

Generally two gates are used, one used as an input for the SET while the second is used to tune the background charge, a common obstacle needed to be overcome.

It consists of two electrodes known as the drain and the source, connected through tunnel junctions to one common electrode with a low self-capacitance, known as the island. The electrical potential of the island can be tuned by a third electrode, known as the gate, capacitively coupled to the island.

In the blocking state no accessible energy levels are within tunneling range of the electron on the source contact. All energy levels on the island electrode with lower energies are occupied.

When a positive voltage is applied to the gate electrode the energy levels of the island electrode are lowered. The electron can tunnel onto the island occupying a previously vacant energy level. From there it can tunnel onto the drain electrode where it inelastically scatters and reaches the drain electrode Fermi level

The energy levels of the island electrode are evenly spaced with a separation of ΔE. This gives rise to a self-capacitance C of the island, defined as $C = \frac{e^2}{\Delta E}$. To achieve the Coulomb blockade, three criteria have to be met :

The bias voltage must be lower than the elementary charge divided by the self-capacitance of the island $V_{bias} < \frac{e}{C}$; The thermal energy in the source contact plus the thermal energy in the island, i.e. $k_B T$, must be below the charging energy $k_B T < \frac{e^2}{2C}$ or else the electron will be able to pass the QD via thermal excitation; and The tunneling resistance, R_t, should be greater than eq $\frac{h}{e^2}$, which is derived from Heisenberg's uncertainty principle.

Application of SETs
Quantum computers
 -1000x Faster
Microwave Detection
High Sensitivity Electrometer
Single-Electron MOS Memory (SEMM)
Miniature Flash Memory

7.8 MOLECULAR MACHINES

It has recently become possible to synthesize molecules that function like mechanical devices, for example switches, motors, brakes, and even small elevators. Such man-made molecular machines might be considered as nanoscale versions of their macroscopic analogues. on the other hand, many well-known macroscopic concepts no longer apply at a molecular level. For instance, the concept of viscous friction becomes meaningless: the friction that a molecular machine experiences is caused by molecules that have the roughly same size as the machine, and the time scale of the machine's motion is similar to that of the molecules causing the friction. Continuum mechanics clearly cannot be used to describe the dynamics of molecular machines, and new approaches have to be developed. To obtain a better understanding of the physics and chemistry of molecular machines, experiments that directly probe their motion are essential, and the insights obtained from such experiments should be important for potential applications.

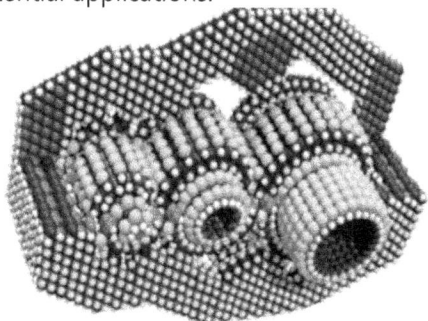

Fig. 7.16

A molecular machine, or nanomachine, is any discrete number of molecular components that produce quasi-mechanical movements (output) in response to specific stimuli (input). The expression is often more generally applied to molecules that simply mimic functions that occur at the macroscopic level. The term is also common in nanotechnology where a number of highly complex molecular machines have been proposed that are aimed at the goal of constructing a molecular assembler. Molecular machines can be divided into two broad categories; synthetic and biological.

Examples of Molecular Machines

From a synthetic perspective, there are two important types of molecular machines: molecular switches (or shuttles) and molecular motors. The major difference between the two systems is that a switch influences a system as a function of state, whereas a motor influences a system as function of trajectory. A switch may appear to undergo translational motion, but returning a switch to its original position undoes any mechanical effect and liberates energy to the system. Furthermore, switches cannot use chemical energy to repetitively and progressively drive a system away from equilibrium where a motor can.

Molecular motors are molecules that are capable of unidirectional rotation motion powered by external energy input. A number of molecular machines have been synthesized powered by light or reaction with other molecules.

A molecular propeller is a molecule that can propel fluids when rotated, due to its special shape that is designed in analogy to macroscopic propellers. It has several molecular-scale blades attached at a certain pitch angle around the circumference of a nanoscale shaft.

A molecular switch is a molecule that can be reversibly shifted between two or more stable states. The molecules may be shifted between the states in response to changes in e.g. pH, light, temperature, an electrical current, microenvironment, or the presence of a ligand.

A molecular shuttle is a molecule capable of shuttling molecules or ions from one location to another. A common molecular shuttle consists of a rotaxane where the macrocycle can move between two sites or stations along the dumbbell backbone.

A molecular sensor is a molecule that interacts with an analyte to produce a detectable change. Molecular sensors combine molecular recognition with some form of reporter, so the presence of the item can be observed.

A molecular logic gate is a molecule that performs a logical operation on one or more logic inputs and produces a single logic output. Unlike a molecular sensor, the molecular logic gate will only output when a particular combination of inputs are present.

7.9 NANO WIRES

> **Q.** Write short note on Nano wires.
> **Q.** Give the properties of Nano wires.
> **Q.** Give the application of Nano wires.

Nanowires are microscopic wires that have a width measured in nanometers. Typically their width ranges from forty to fifty nanometers, but their length is not so limited. Since they can be lengthened by simply attaching more wires end to end or just by growing them longer, they can be as long as desired.

Nanowires are metal just like other, regular wires. The only real difference in concept is their size. They also vary in complexity and uses. While they can do many of the same things, they have many other capabilities beyond those of regular wire.

There are varying methods used to create nanowires. The most common involve either growing them or using DNA as a template. For the latter method, a solution containing the desired metal is mixed with DNA and then exposed to UV light. When exposed, the metal in the mixture bonds to the DNA and forms a microscopic wire, a nanowire. It's width is dependent upon how concentrated the solution of the metal is. The more concentrated the metal solution, the wider the nanowire; likewise, the less concentrated, the thinner the wire will be.

The alternative method, growing the nanowire, uses drops of gold in precise locations on a sapphire wafer. At high temperatures the gold beads up in droplets only a few nanometers large. These droplets act as points on which zinc oxide can form crystals. The crystals grow from there and take the shape of a wire. With this method it is possible to control the direction in which the nanowire forms as well as its shape. This would make it easier to make a component such as a tiny circuit from nanowires by growing them in place instead of trying to position them in precise locations later.

Nanowire Properties are just some of the ways in which nanowires differ from their corresponding bulk materials.

Properties
Because of their unique density of electronic states, nanowires in the limit of small diameters are expected to exhibit significantly different optical, electrical, and magnetic properties from their bulk 3-D crystalline counterparts.

Increased surface area,
very high density of electronic states
enhanced exciton binding energy,
diameter-dependent bandgap,
increased surface scattering for electrons

Applications of nanowires
Data storage/transfer - transfer data up to 1,000 times faster, and store data for as long as 100,000 years without degradation

Batteries/generators - tiny, efficient solar panels, turning light into energy, able to hold 10 times the charge of existing batteries

Transistors

LED's

Optoelectronic devices

Biochemical sensors

Heat-pumping Thermoelectric devices

Electronic devices

Nanowires still belong to the experimental world of laboratories. However, they may complement or replace carbon nanotubes in some applications.

To create active electronic elements, the first key step was to chemically dope a semiconductor nanowire. This has already been done to individual nanowires to create p-type and n-type semiconductors.

The next step was to find a way to create a p–n junction, one of the simplest electronic devices. This was achieved in two ways. The first way was to physically cross a p-type wire over an n-type wire. The second method involved chemically doping a single wire with different dopants along the length. This method created a p-n junction with only one wire.

After p-n junctions were built with nanowires, the next logical step was to build logic gates. By connecting several p-n junctions together, researchers have been able to create the basis of all logic circuits: the AND, OR, and NOT gates have all been built from semiconductor nanowire crossings.

It is possible that semiconductor nanowire crossings will be important to the future of digital computing. Though there are other uses for nanowires beyond these, the only ones that actually take advantage of physics in the nanometer regime are electronic.

Nanowires are being studied for use as photon ballistic waveguides as interconnects in quantum dot/quantum effect well photon logic arrays. Photons travel inside the tube, electrons travel on the outside shell.

When two nanowires acting as photon waveguides cross each other the juncture acts as a quantum dot.

Conducting nanowires offer the possibility of connecting molecular-scale entities in a molecular computer. Dispersions of conducting nanowires in different polymers are being investigated for use as transparent electrodes for flexible flat-screen displays.

Because of their high Young's moduli, their use in mechanically enhancing composites is being investigated. Because nanowires appear in bundles, they may be used as tribological additives to improve friction characteristics and reliability of electronic transducers and actuators. Because of their high aspect ratio, nanowires are also uniquely suited to dielectrophoretic manipulation, which offers a low-cost, bottom-up approach to integrating suspended dielectric metal oxide nanowires in electronic devices such as UV, water vapor, and ethanol sensors.

Sensing of proteins and chemicals using semiconductor nanowires

In an analogous way to FET devices in which the modulation of conductance (flow of electrons/holes) in the semiconductor, between the input (source) and the output (drain) terminals, is controlled by electrostatic potential variation (gate-electrode) of the charge carriers in the device conduction channel, the methodology of a Bio/Chem-FET is based on the detection of the local change in charge density, or so-called "field effect", that characterizes the recognition event between a target molecule and the surface receptor.

The wire, which serves as a tunable conducting channel, is in close contact with the sensing environment of the target, leading to a short response time, along with orders of magnitude increase in the sensitivity of the device as a result of the huge S/V ratio of the nanowires.

Several examples of the use of silicon nanowire sensing devices include the ultra sensitive, real-time sensing of biomarker proteins for cancer, detection of single virus particles, and the detection of nitro-aromatic explosive materials such as 2,4,6 Tri-nitrotoluene (TNT) in sensitives superior to these of canines

REVIEW QUESTIONS

1. Explain nanotube.
2. Explain application of carbon nanotubes.
3. Short note on Nanowires.
4. Explain boron nitride nanotube.

UNIVERSITY QUESTIONS

Dec. 2009

1. Discuss in brief the concepts of energy bands in insulators, semiconductors and conductors.
2. What are Carbon Nano-tubes? Discuss their electrical, mechanical and vibrational properties.
3. Write a short note on Single Electron Transistor.
4. Write a short note on BN Nano-tubes.

May 2010

5. Write a short note on molecular machines which uses nanotechnology.
6. What are carbon clusters? Write short note on C_{60}.
7. Discuss in brief the electrical and mechanical properties of carbon nanotubes. State some applications of carbon nanotubes.

Dec 2010

8. With neat diagrams describe :
   (a) Carbon nanostructures and carbon molecules.
   (b) Carbon clusters.
   (c) Carbon nano-tubes.
   (d) Nano wires.
9. Write applications of carbon nano-tubes and BN nano-tubes.
10. What do you mean by single electron transistor and molecular machines?

May 2011

11. What are carbon nanotubes? Discuss briefly various types of carbon nanotubes. List some applications of carbon nanotubes.
12. Write a short note on 'Nano-wire'.
13. Discuss briefly the energy bands in conductors, insulators and semiconductors.
14. Write a short note on molecular machines.

Dec. 2011

15. What are carbon nanotubes? Discuss their electrical, mechanical and vibrational properties. Give some applications of carbon nanotubes.
16. Write a short note on 'BN nanotubes'.
17. Write short notes on :
    (i) Single electron transistor
    (ii) Molecular machine

  (iii) Nano wire
  (iv) Carbon clusters

May 2012

18. How are carbon nanotubes fabricated? Give two methods and draw sketches where necessary.
19. What do you mean by single electron transistor, molecular machines?
20. Write down application of carbon nanotubes and BN nanotubes?
21. Discuss briefly the energy bands in conductors, insulators and semiconductors.

Dec. 2012

22. What are carbon clusters? Write a short note on C60.
23. How are carbon nanotubes fabricated? Give two methods with sketches wherever necessary.
24. What are molecular machines? Why are molecular machines currently been extensively investigated? What are different possible applications of molecular machines?
25. Write a short note on different types of conduction mechanisms involved in nanomaterials.

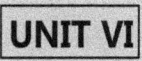

CHAPTER 8
TESTING OF MATERIALS

INTRODUCTION

In this chapter, the various test to be done on insulating material, their purpose and importance of various type of test is given. This familiarize with various standards IS its need and uses. This is chapter contain measurement of dielectric loss tangent (tan δ) for solid, liquid insulating material. This also includes measurement of dielectric strength of solid liquid and gaseous insulating material. Since it is containing experimentations so it is more important chapter.

8.1. MEASUREMENT OF DIELECTRIC LOSS TANGENT (TAN δ) BY SCHERING BRIDGE, IS 13585-1994

Objectives : To find out dissipation factor or tanδ of dielectric materials. This value gives idea of dielectric loss occurring in the capacitor dielectric material.

Equipments :

1. Unknown capacitor
2. Schering bridge
3. Standard capacitor C_n/C_3
4. High voltage testing set
5. Null detector
6. CRO.

Theory : Capacitor is static device which is nothing but the two conducting plates separated by the insulator or dielectric material. In ideal capacitor current I always lead the voltage by 90° but as we know in ideal insulator or dielectric material have free electron. But no insulator or dielectric material is perfect. So, when capacitor is connected across the e.m.f. source very small amount of current flow through dielectric material. Due to this dielectric loss, current through capacitor does not lead to voltage by 90° but the angle (90–δ) where δ is known as loss angle which shown in Fig. 8.1.

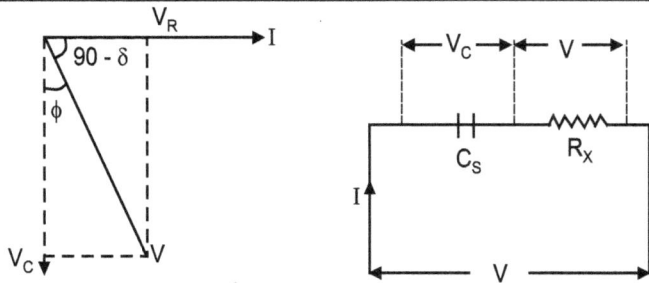

Fig. 8.1

Loss tangent : The fraction of the maximum energy lost each cycle, divided by 2π is termed the loss factor and its value is given by $\tan \delta$.

Test specification as per IS :

1. Test on the capacitor is done at ambient temperature i.e. between +10°C to +45°C.
2. Voltage applied should be between 0.9 to 1.1 rated voltage at standard rated frequency.
3. Value of dielectric loss should not be exceeding the value given by the manufacturer.

Connection diagram :

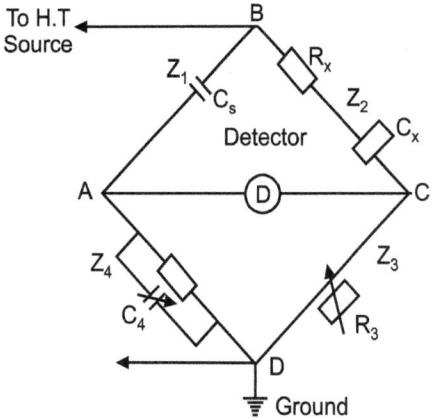

Connection diagram

Fig. 8.2

Description of connection diagram : In this between arm A and B standard capacitor C_s with negligible loss is connected between arm B and C, C_x and R_x represent capacitor which has to test. In arm C and D, R_3 is variable resistance connected and in between arm A and D combination of R_4 and variable capacitor C_4 is connected. In A and C detector is connected.

Procedure :

1. Connect single phase supply to control panel.
2. Do the high voltage connection and ground connection.
3. Put 'Mains ON' and HT OFF and set dimmer to zero position.

4. When test unit is ready. Make HT ON.
5. Increase voltage level by varying knob of dimmer.
6. Do not apply voltage more than withstanding voltage of capacitor.
7. Try to get zero reading of detector by varying C_4 and R_3.

Observation table :

Sr. No.	Value of C_4 at null deflection	Value of R_3 at null deflection
1.		
2.		
3.		

Derivation and formula for loss angle : At balanced condition i.e. at null deflection of detector.

$$Z_1 Z_3 = Z_2 Z_4$$

$$\frac{1}{j\omega C_5} \times R_3 = \left(R_x + \frac{1}{j\omega C_x}\right)\left(\frac{1}{1/R_4 + j\omega C_4}\right)$$

By rearranging this we get,

$$\left(R_x - \frac{j}{\omega C_x}\right) = \frac{-jR_3}{\omega C_5}\left(\frac{1}{R_4} + j\omega C_4\right)$$

$$R_x - \frac{j}{\omega C_x} = \frac{C_4 R_3}{C_5} - \frac{jR_3}{\omega R_4 C_5}$$

By separating real and imaginary part.

$$R_x = \frac{C_4}{C_5} \cdot R_3$$

and,

$$C_x = \frac{R_4}{R_3} \cdot C_5$$

Therefore, at low power factor $\tan \delta = \cos \delta$ = p.f.

$$\therefore \tan \delta = \frac{R_x}{XC_x} = \frac{R_x}{1/\omega C_x}$$

$$\therefore \boxed{\tan \delta = \omega C_x R_x}$$

Calculation :

1. $R_x = \dfrac{C_4}{C_5} \cdot R_3$

2. $C_x = \dfrac{R_4}{R_3} \cdot C_5$

3. $\tan \delta = \omega\, C_x R_x$

Conclusion :

The value of $\tan \delta$ is ...... and it is in acceptable / rejectable range.

8.2 MEASUIREMENT OF DIELECTRIC STRENGTH OF SOLID INSULATING MATERIALS IS 2584

Objectives : To determine the dielectric strength of various solid dielectrics.

Equipments :
1. Various solid dielectric materials
2. High voltage testing equipments
3. Flat electrodes set

Theory : All electrical apparatus are designed to operate at a particular voltage. If this voltage gradually increased then at some voltage the dielectric used in apparatus get ruptures or fails. This is called breakdown of dielectric.

Breakdown strength is defined as the minimum stress usually expressed in kV/mm which will cause the rapture of insulating material under specified condition of temperature, duration of applied voltage waveform of applied voltage, frequency and type of electrodes.

Breakdown voltage is the voltage below which the dielectric materials remains stable in its property but above which it results in distraction of insulating properties. Basic breakdown mechanism in solid dielectrics are observed as follows :

1. Thermal breakdown
2. Intrinsic breakdown
3. Electrochemical breakdown
4. Partial discharge breakdown
5. Treeing and tracking

Connection diagram

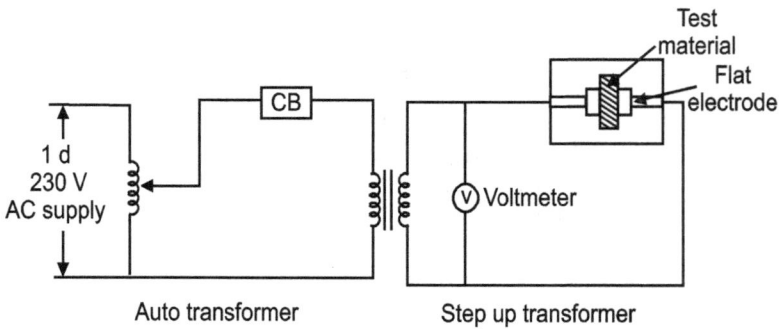

Fig. 8.3

1. Connect 1ϕ, 230 V A.C. supply to the autotransformer which is connected to step-up transformer.
2. Place test material in the flat plate electrodes.
3. Do proper connection of voltmeter.

Procedure :
1. Do proper connection and place test material in between electrodes.
2. Ensure all meters showing zero readings.
3. Switch A.C. mains after that HT supply.
4. Motor automatically raises the voltage.
5. Note the reading and repeat the test for same thickness of same material and take average value.

Observation table :

Sr. No.	Name of material	Thickness (mm)	Breakdown voltage (kV)
1.			
2.			
3.			

Calculation :

$$\text{Breakdown strength} = \frac{\text{Breakdown voltage}}{\text{Thickness of dielectric}}$$

Conclusion :

The ...... material is having ...... breakdown strength.

8.3. MEASUREMENT OF DIELECTRIC STRENGTH OF LIQUID DIELECTRIC MATERIAL

Objective : To measure dielectric strength of an insulating oil.

Equipments :
1. High voltage testing unit.
2. Insulating oil.
3. Semi-spherical electrodes.

Theory : In the liquid insulators/dielectrics insulating oil is very important material. In case of liquid dielectrics various theories are used to explain breakdown in liquids like :

(i) Colloidal theory.
(ii) Bubble theory.
(iii) Breakdown due to liquid globules.

These are observed in this experimentation. Another important property of liquid insulating material is specific resistance or resistivity and tan δ. There is relationship between tan δ and resistivity of insulating oil. If resistivity of the insulating oil is decreased, the value of tan δ increases and vice-versa. So resistivity test or tan δ test only one test is perform normally on bunch of insulating oil. This helps in measure of dielectric losses in an electrical insulating liquid when used across e.m.f. Breakdown strength of liquid dielectric depends on various factors such as :

1. Condition and nature of electrodes.
2. Purity of liquid.
3. Moisture content in liquid.

Experiment shows that breakdown strength of liquid dielectric is depend on gap distance between electrodes.

$$V_b = Ad^\eta$$

where,

A = constant

d = gap distance between electrodes

η = constant always less than 1

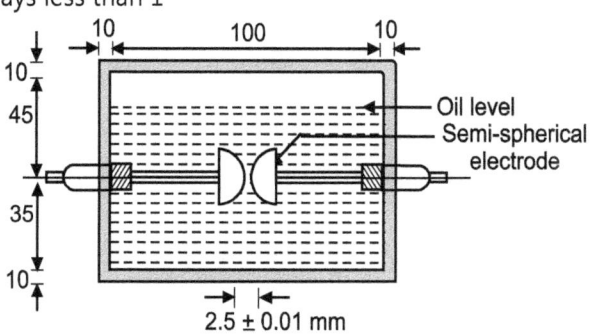

Fig. 8.4

Connection diagram :

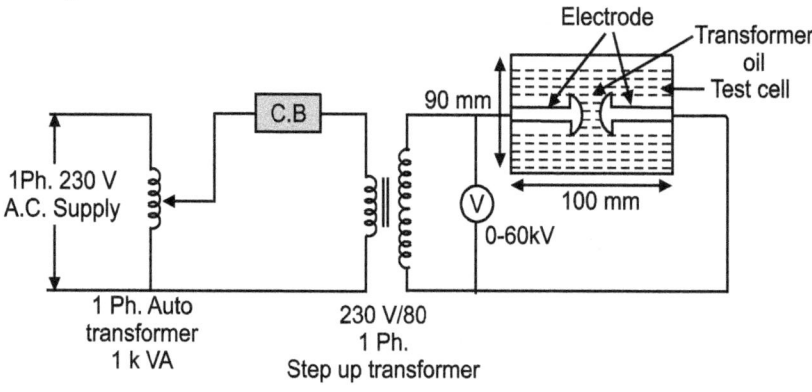

Fig. 8.5

1. Do a proper connection as shown in figure.
2. The semispherical electrodes are used in test cell. These are made up of either brass, bronze, copper or stainless steel material. Their diameter varies from 12.5 mm to 13 mm. These are mounted on horizontal axis in test cell.

3. Test cell is made up of glass or plastic which rigid oil resistant and transparent material. It consists of 350 ml to 500 ml of oil.
4. Electrode should be completely dipped in oil.
5. Oil is not filling full in test cell some gap is kept in oil level and top of cell as shown in Fig. 8.5.

Procedure :
1. Do the connection as per diagram.
2. Adjust the gap between electrodes to 2.5 mm in test cell.
3. Add oil in the test cell.
4. Apply voltage to the unit.
5. Increase voltage at the rate of 2 kV/sec manually or by help of automatic motorized system.
6. Note down the reading at breakdown take place.
7. If needed repeat the procedure by adding moisture content and impurities in oil.

Observation table :

For pure liquid

Gap distance = 2.5 mm.

Sr. No.	Breakdown voltage	Dielectric strength
1.		
2.		
3.		

For moisture content in liquid.

Sr. No.	Breakdown voltage	Dielectric strength
1.		
2.		
3.		

For impure liquid.

Sr. No.	Breakdown voltage	Dielectric strength
1.		
2.		
3.		

Calculation : Calculate mean breakdown voltage and mean dielectric strength for all three cases.

where, Breakdown strength = $\dfrac{\text{Breakdown voltage}}{\text{Distance between electrodes}}$

Conclusion :
1. Breakdown strength of oil is ......
2. Breakdown strength of oil is varies with moisture content and impurities.

8.4. MEASUREMENT OF RESISTIVITY OF LIQUID DIELECTRIC

Objective : To measure resistivity of liquid dielectric.

Equipments :
1. Insulating oil
2. Electrodes
3. Testing unit.

Theory :

Specific resistivity : Specific resistivity is define as ratio of D.C. potential gradient paralleling current flow with in the specimen to the current density at a given instant of time under prescribed condition. Resistivity of the insulating oil must be high at room temperature and also it should have good value at high temperature as well. Therefore the specific resistivity of insulating liquid is measured at high as well as ambient temperature.

Connection diagram

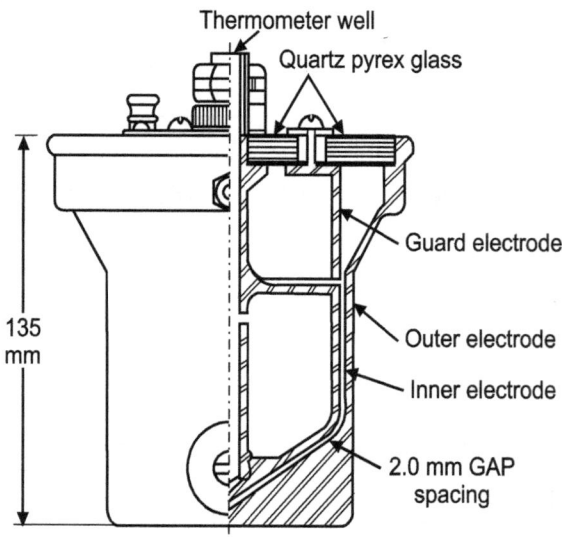

Fig. 8.6

Description of connection diagram :
1. Test cell is made of non-porous material. It also has facility to measure temperature of liquid under test.

2. The current and voltage measuring device should have high sensitivity and good accuracy.
3. Electrodes used in this are made up of platinum, stainless steel, nickel or monel material.
4. Electrodes should not be affected by higher temperature.

Procedure :
1. Apply D.C. voltage to specimen.
2. Note current and voltage after every one minute.
3. Short circuit the cell electrodes for five minutes.
4. Then change polarity of supply and repeat the procedure.

Observation :

Sr. No.	Voltage	Current	Galvanometer deflection
1.			
2.			
3.			

Calculation :

$$\text{Resistivity} = \frac{V \times K}{D \times G}$$

where,

V = Test voltage
K = Cell constant in cm
D = Galvanometer deflection in divisions
G = Galvanometer sensitivity in ampere per division
I = Current

Conclusion :
Specific resistivity of insulating oil is ......

8.5. MEASUREMENT OF DIELECTRIC STRENGTH OF GASES

Objective : To measure the breakdown strength of air.

Equipments required :
1. Sphere gap set-up.
2. High voltage transformer.
3. Voltmeters.

Theory : Air is very popular dielectric material and which is free. So most of the transmitter and distribution system are using air as insulator. Breakdown in gases are initiated by ionization. Ionization takes place by collision between electron and production of another electron by ion. This cumulative process results in to breakdown in to gas. This caused by field strength is increased high enough.

Breakdown in gases are described by two mechanisms.
1. Avalanche mechanism.
2. Streamer mechanism.

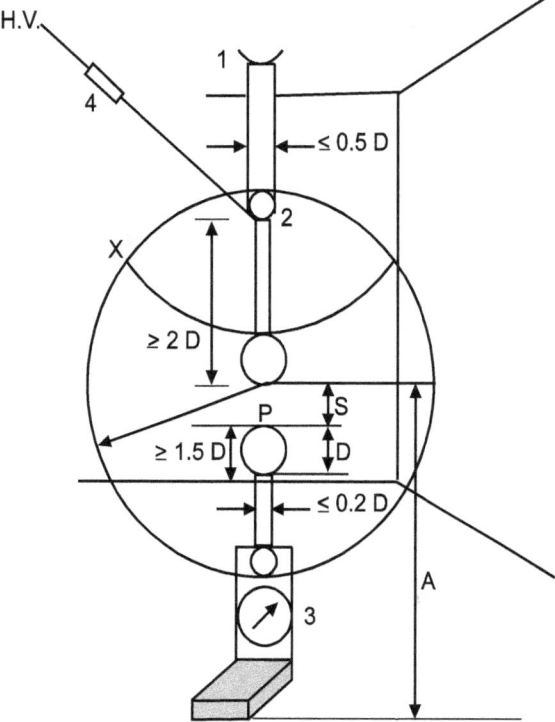

1 - Insulator support
2 - Sphere shrunk
3 - Operating motor and gear for Changing gap distance
4 - H.V. connection
P - Sparking point

S - Spacing
D - Diameter of sphere
A - Height of P above earth
B - Radius of the clearance from external structure
X - High voltage lead should not pass through this plane within a distance B from P

Fig. 8.7

Connection diagram :
1. Sphere shape electrodes are use for this experiment.
2. They are mounted vertically and the gap is adjusted by remote control.
3. Top sphere is connected to HT point which is fixed and lower sphere is at earth potential.
4. This arrangement is in the cage for the earthing and safety.

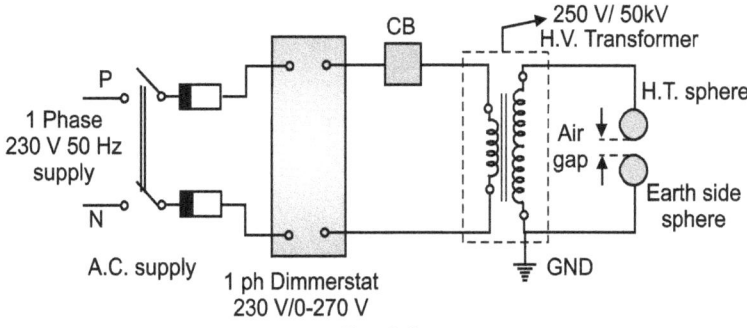

Fig. 8.8

Procedure :
1. Connect HV terminal of transformer to upper sphere.
2. Earth the sphere gap unit.
3. Adjust air gap.
4. Apply the high voltage and vary it till spark occurs.
5. Repeat this process for different air gaps and note down the voltages.

Observation :

Sr. No.	Breakdown voltage	Gap distance
1.		
2.		
3.		

Calculation :

$$\text{Dielectric strength} = \frac{\text{Breakdown voltage}}{\text{Gap distance}}$$

Conclusion :
1. Breakdown voltage of air is kV.
2. Breakdown strength of air is ...... kV/mm.
3. Breakdown voltage increases when gap between two sphere increases and vice-versa.

8.6. MEASUREMENT OF POWER FACTOR AND PARTIAL DISCHARGE OF HIGH VOLTAGE CABLES

Q. Explain general construction of cable.
Q. Explain procedure to measurement of tan δ in cable.

8.6.1 GENERAL CONSTRUCTION OF A CABLE

The general construction of the cable is shown in Fig. 8.9. The various parts in the cable are :
Core : All cables have one or more cores at the centre, depending upon the service requirement. The material used for the core conductor could be of aluminum or copper and is stranded in order to provide flexibility to the cable.

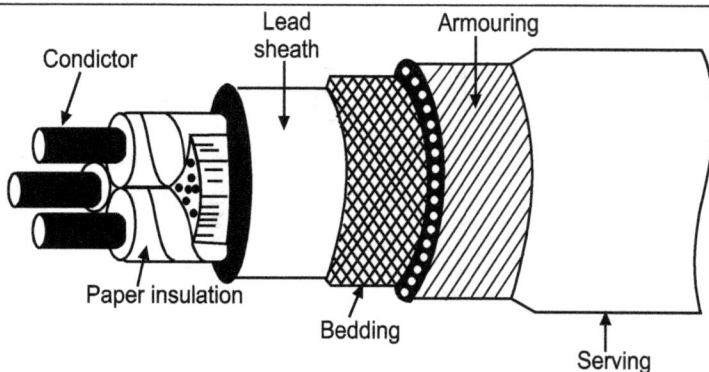

Fig. 8.9 : Construction of a cable

Insulation : The insulation over the core is generally provided with different layers. Thickness of each layer depends upon the operating voltage of cable. The different materials used for insulation of cable are paper, varnished cambric, vulcanized bitumen, Poly Vinyl Chloride (PVC), and cross-linked polyethylene (XLPE).

Metallic Sheath : For protecting the insulation material from moisture, gases and any other harmful liquids in the soil, a metallic sheath is provided over the insulation. It also protects the insulation from mechanical damage. The metallic sheath is usually of lead or lead alloy. Recently, aluminium is also being used as metallic sheath because it has greater mechanical strength, low weight and cost when compared to lead sheath.

Bedding : Bedding is provided to protect the metallic sheath from corrosion also from mechanical damage due to armoring. It is a fibrous material like jute or hessian tape.

CLSSIFICATION OF CABLES

Low tension (L.T.) – upto 1k V

High tension (H.T.) – upto 11k V

Super tension (S.T.) – from 22 KV to 33 kV

Extra high tension (E.H.T.) cables – from 33 kV to 66 kV

Extra super voltage cables – beyond 132 kV

8.6.2 Tan δ, Or Tan Delta

Q. Explain Tanδ and how it is measured.

Tan Delta, also called Loss Angle or Dissipation Factor. Tan δ testing, is a indicative method of testing cables to determine the quality of the cable insulation. This is done to predict the expected life of cable and in order to prioritize cable replacement.

If the insulation of a cable is free from defects, like water trees, electrical trees, moisture and air pockets, etc. the cable gives the properties of a perfect capacitor. It is similar to a parallel plate capacitor with the two plates separated by the insulation material. In capacitor, the voltage and current are phase shifted 90 degrees and the current through the insulation is capacitive. If there are impurities in the insulation, the resistance of the insulation decreases, resulting in an increase in resistive current through the insulation. It is no longer a perfect capacitor. The current and voltage will be shifted something less than 90 degrees. This angle is called as "Loss Angle" and it is measured and analyzed. The measured tangent of the angle δ is indicating the level of resistance in the insulation. By measuring IR/IC we can determine the quality of the cable insulation. In a perfect cable, the angle would be nearly zero. An increasing angle indicates an increase in the resistive current through the insulation, meaning contamination. The greater the angle, the worse the cable condition.

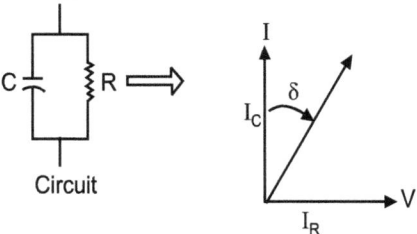

Fig. 8.10

Water Trees

Water trees are small tree shaped found within the insulation of a cable, caused by the presence of moisture. They are very common in service aged and other solid dielectric cables, like PE and EPR cables. These tree creat moisture channels, in the presence of an electrical field. It sooner or later lead to the inception of partial discharge (pd), which finally leads to the formation of electrical trees, which grow to a point where insulation failure occurs. The tan delta test shows the extent of water tree damage in a cable.

Necessary Hardware

The tan delta unit consists of a high voltage divider and a fibre optically linked measurement box. The high voltage divider measures the voltage and current input to the cable, sends this information to the controller, which analyzes the voltage and current waveforms and calculates the tan delta number. A voltage source is needed to energize the cable.

Frequency (VLF) AC Hipot :

The VLF here is a 40 kV unit that is capable of testing from 1.1 μF of cable load at 0.1 Hz, up to 5.5μF at 0.02 Hz. Other models offer an output frequency of 0.01 Hz, used to test very long cables. VLF hipots are also widely used for testing newly installed and/or repaired cable before reenergizing to insure the cable is sound and for testing critical cable runs.

Procedure:

The cable to be tested must be de-energized and each end must be isolated. Using a VLF AC Hipot, the test voltage is applied to the cable while the tan delta controller takes measurements. Typically, the applied test voltage is raised in steps, with measurements first taken up to 1 Unit, or normal line to ground operating voltage. If the tan delta numbers indicate good cable insulation, the test voltage is raised up to 1.5 – 2 Unit. The tan delta at the higher voltages are compared to those at lower voltages. The test itself can take less than twenty minutes, depending upon the settings of the instrument and the number of different test voltage levels used. It is only necessary to capture a few cycles of the voltage and current waveform to make the analysis. At 0.1 Hz, the period of the sine wave is 10 seconds, so it takes 20 – 30 seconds for a reading to be made. At 0.02 Hz, the period is 50 seconds, requiring perhaps 3 minutes of test time at each voltage setting.

The Test Results Interpretation

The very first test on a cable yields valuable information about the insulation. Also, most tan delta testing is performed on a comparative basis. If a cable's insulation is perfect, the loss factor (tan delta) will change little as the applied voltage is increased. The capacitance and loss will be similar with 1 kV or 10 kV applied to the cable. If the cable has water tree contamination, it will change the capacitive/resistive nature of the insulation. This lead to the higher tan delta numbers at higher voltages. Rather than a flat curve for the loss number versus voltage, the curve will be non linear. The Loss Angle increases with increasing voltage, indicating a high resistive current element to the insulation. These results can be compared to other cables tested to determine which cables are in need of immediate replacement and which can wait a bit longer. Also, many tests are measured on a comparative basis. Many of the same type of cables may be tested, with the results compared against each other. An average value for the tan delta can be calculated and possibly used as a future benchmark.

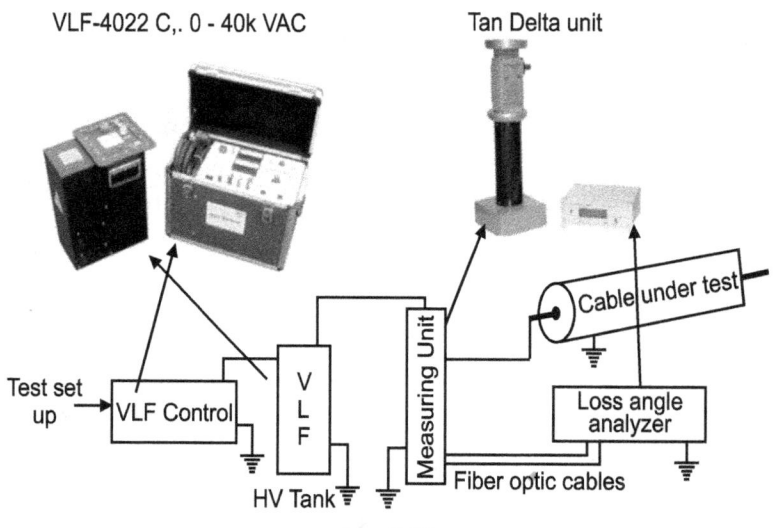

Fig. 8.11

Important note regarding partial discharge versus tan delta :

Accepting that there are not established, well proven standards for 'PD' or tan delta testing, and both are best used on a comparative study to help prioritize cable replacement. The VLF hipot is useful in its own right as the best method of AC cables to expose defects in insulation. With the VLF and tan delta bridge, you actually have two tools to use for cable testing, both of which can be operated with minimal training. That's not the case with a PD system, which requires a highly trained operator, and is very expensive.

Limitations To Using Tan Delta Testing

Since we are measuring the loss angle of an insulating material, and making an analysis about the test results possibly based on historical data, it is not advisable to test a cable length that contains more than one type of cable. Different cables have different loss characteristics. It is not a good practice to test a cable length of XLPE insulation spliced to an EPR or PILC cable. The only way in which this is meaningful is when many tests are done on the same cable length over time and the results are carefully trended.

8.6.3 Partial Discharge Testing for Cables

Q. Explain online and offline partial discharge methods.

- Performed online without disrupting plant or facilities, or offline when required
- Non-destructive, noninvasive predictive maintenance tool
- Optimizes capital expenditures and improves system reliability
- Helps eliminate unplanned outages and lost profit as a result of system downtime
- Identifes and prioritizes cable sections and terminations for replacement
- Focus on the right cables for targeted investment -minimizes unnecessary spending

Condition Assessment of Cables

Partial discharge can occur at voids, gaps and similar defects in medium and high voltage cable systems. If continue, partial discharge will erode the insulation. It usually forming a tree shaped pattern of deterioration (electrical tree) and eventually result in complete breakdown and failure of the cable or accessory. Such failures cause unplanned power outages, loss of plant production, equipment damage. Data obtained through Partial Discharge testing and monitoring can provide critical information regarding the quality of insulation and its impact on cable system health. By detecting and trending partial discharge, it is possible to observe its development over time. Problem identification using our integrated partial discharge testing and monitoring solutions can identify :

- Defective Cable Insulation
- Location of Defects
- Extent of Insulation Degradation
- Defective Splices
- Defective Terminations.

PD measurements are made using a range of calibrated sensors that are either inductively, capacitively or acoustically coupled to the cable. Signals are captured synchronously across the 50 Hz power cycle via our test application enabling to observe phase-related patterns of discharge, online and in real-time. Online Partial Discharge testing is a non-destructive, non-invasive predictive maintenance tool that assesses the condition of aging cable systems. It including splices and terminations accuracy is improved through the use of the cable. Another distinct advantage is its ability to test branched circuits on network feeders. And, the cost to perform online testing is relatively economical compared with offline testing that requires interruption of service and production. For critical facilities that operate 24 x 7, this is perhaps the single best option for

detecting insulation condition.

Offline Partial Discharge Testing

Offline Partial Discharge Testing offers a significant advantage over other technologies because of its ability to measure the cable system's response to a specific stress level and predict its future performance without creating a fault. Offline testing is also known for its ability to pinpoint the exact defect location on field aged cables, enabling to accurately plan for maintenance and/or repair. Offline testing is also commonly used in conducting acceptance testing on newly installed equipment. For systems already in service, the challenge is that the equipment must be taken out of service for the test to be performed.

8.7 FLUX DENSITY TEST (GAUSS METER)

Q. Explain Gauss meter.

Q. Short note on methods to measure flux density.

(1) The surface flux density or the flux density at a certain distance from the magnet can be obtained using a Gauss meter. The probes contain a Hall Effect device whose output voltage is proportional to the flux density. Fig. 8.13 (a) and 8.13 (b) show the placement and direction of prob while testing when using the two types of probes. Gauss meter measurements provide an accurate and easily calibrated value for flux density (Gauss or Tesla). However, the position of the probe in relation to the magnet must be in exactly the same place for each sample. Brass fixtures are commonly used for locating the probe to the sample being tested. Calibration is done for Gauss meter by using a Zero Gauss chamber or a magnet sample with a known flux density value.

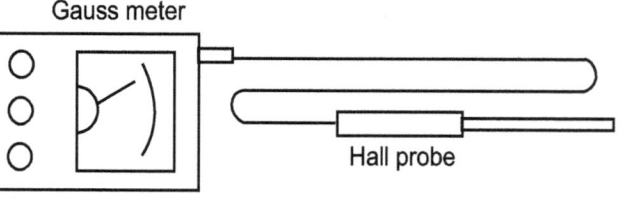

Fig. 8.12

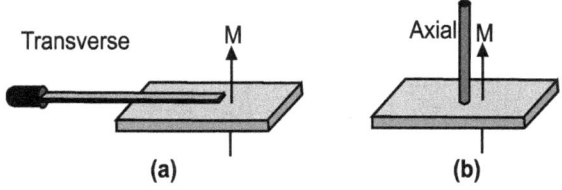

Fig. 8.13

(2) Measurement method of center flux density

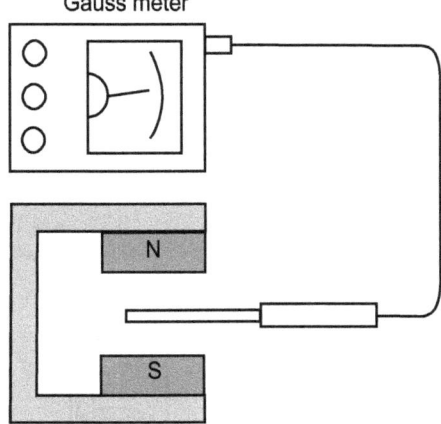

Fig. 8.14

(3) Measurement method at some distance from the magnet surface in an open circuit.

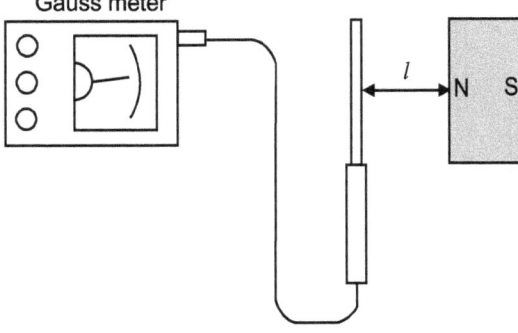

Fig. 8.15

Measurement method of flux

When measuring flux, flux-meter and search coils are regularly used.

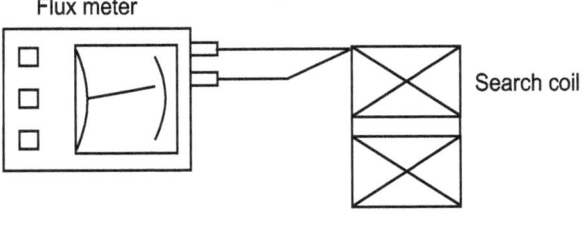

Fig. 8.16

(1) Open flux method

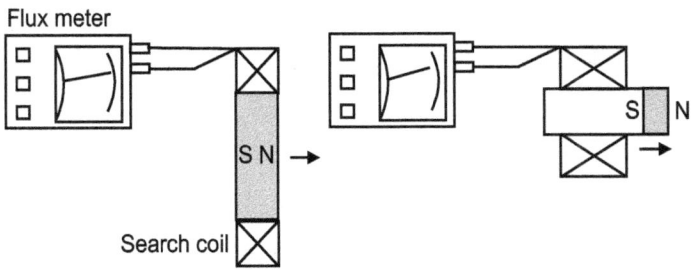

Fig. 8.17

(2) Measurement method used for magnetic circuits

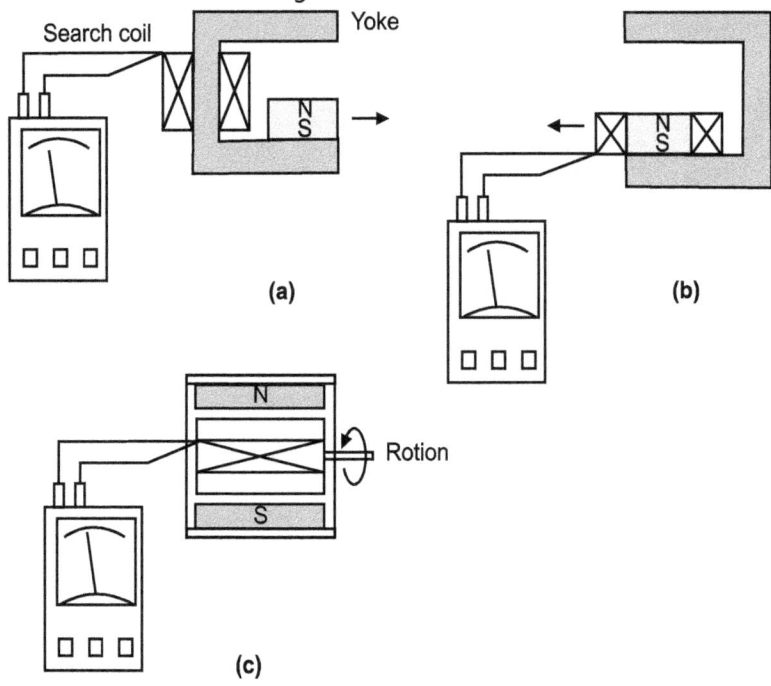

Fig. 8.18

8.7.1 Total Flux Test (Flux Meter)

Q. Explain how total flux out put of magnet is obtain.

The total flux output of a magnet can be measured using a Flux meter connected to a Helmholtz coil. As shown in Fig. 8.19, the coil is actually a pair of coils with a known number of turns and at a certain distance from each other. The resulting data (mVs, Weber, Maxwells) can be interpolated to obtain an approximate value for Br or Bdi. The coil diameter should be at least three times the largest dimension of the magnet and the spacing between the two coils should be equal to their radius. The test procedure is very simple. A magnet is placed mid-space inside the coils and is pulled out so that the lines of flux from the magnet perpendicularly cross through the plane of one coil. The connected Flux meter will measure the induced voltage and provide data in mVs, Webers, or Maxwells. Also some new Flux meters allow users to input the magnet volume and thus provide results in Tesla. Although the procedure is simple and results are highly repeatable, for this must undertake certain steps :

1. Flux meters must be de-drifted. Although this is done by simply activating the unit's de-drift feature, this process can take 10 to 30 minutes.
2. The magnet must be pulled out of the coil so that its magnetic orientation is perpendicular to the plane of the coil.
3. The Helmholtz Coil must be located for minimal outside magnetic interference. It is advisable to keep magnets at a proper distance from the coil and to avoid placing it on a metal surface.

Fig. 8.19

Fig. 8.20

8.7.2 Hysteresis Test

Hysteresis curves, also known as B-H curves, describe the intrinsic and normal magnetic properties of a material. This test can be performed at various temperatures. This equipment includes; a gauss meter, flux meter, X-Y recorder, electromagnet and a sample that allows no air gap in the circuit when it is inserted between the electromagnet pole-pieces. To remove the air gap, a small core sample is precisely machined. following simple methods are used to measure magnet properties

The equipment is comprised of a DC Magnetizer and a Flux meter connected to a search coil. Of the various tests for magnetic materials, this is one of the most expensive because the sample material must be machined to a precise dimension, usually a cube, and a search coil is then wound around the sample. The sample is then placed between two large pole pieces which create a closed loop system. A DC magnetizer cycles the sample from origin to saturation, to complete demagnetization, to saturation in the opposite direction, and finally back to the original saturation level. The fluxmeter continuously records B and H and, via some special software, provides a B-H or Hysteresis Curve. The test is normally performed by the magnet manufacturer during the initial stage of processing. Because of the lengthy process, it is not practical to perform the test on large numbers of finished parts. Instead, it is common to have one B-H curve supplied with each lot of parts.

(a)

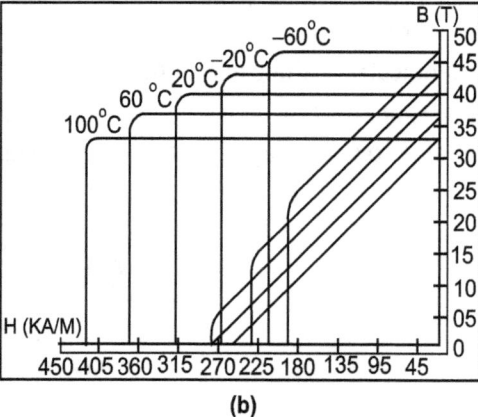
(b)

Fig. 8.21

8.8 RESINS

Q. What are the different use of resins.
Q. Explain types of resins.

Electrical and electronic resins are used in electrical, electronic, and semiconductor applications and include :

- Adhesives
- Greases
- Pads
- Stock shapes
- Tapes
- Encapsulants
- Potting compounds
- Thermal interface materials
- Electrically conductive substances

Applications :

1. Electrical and electronic resins are used in many industries and applications.
2. Some products are used in the manufacture of printed circuit boards (PCBs). Some are designed for electrical power and high voltage products such as generators, transformers, circuit breakers, and motor assemblies.

3. Specialized electrical and electronic resins meet military specifications (MIL-SPEC) and are suitable for many aerospace applications. Products for automotive and optoelectronic applications are also available.

Electrically conductive products provide low resistivity and are often used to prevent electrostatic discharge (ESD), electromagnetic interference (EMI), and radio frequency interference (RFI). Thermally conductive electrical and electronic resins are applied between a heat-generating electrical device and a heat sink in order to get better heat dissipation. These products form a thermally conductive layer, either between components or within a finished product.

8.8.1 Materials

Chemical Systems :

Chemical systems may contain :

- Acrylics
- Elastomers
- Natural or synthetic rubbers
- E-poxy resins
- Water-based resins
- Silicone compounds
- Volatile organic compounds (VOCs)
- Bismaleimide (BMI) resins
- Phenolics
- Formaldehyde resins
- Cellulosic thermoplastics
- Liquid crystal polymers (LCPs)
- Vinyl compounds
- Polyamide
- Polybutadiene
- Polycarbonate (PC)
- Polyolefin
- Polypropylene (PP)
- Polysulfide
- Polyurethane (PUR)

Filler Materials

In terms of filler materials, some electrical resins and electronic compounds include :
- Aramid fibre
- Chopped fibre
- Carbon powder
- Graphite powder
- Glass fillers
- Metal fillers
- Inorganic compounds
- Unfilled electrical and electronic resins are also available.

Curing Technologies :

Typically, thermoplastics and hot melt adhesives are cured using heat or heat and pressure combination. Vulcanization, a thermosetting reaction, uses heat and pressure in conjunction with a vulcanizing agent to produce materials with greatly increased strength, stability, and elasticity. Some products also vulcanize at room temperature. Some also cure with radiation, electron beam irradiation, visible light, or ultraviolet (UV) light.

Single curing systems consist of a resin that hardens through the application of heat or a reaction with surface moisture. Two-component and multi-component curing systems consist of two or more resins and a hardener.

8.8.2 Specifications

Selecting electrical and electronic resins requires an analysis of physical, mechanical, thermal, electrical, and optical properties.

Physical Properties :

most important physical property is Melt Flow Index. Melt flow index (MFI) is the output flow occurring in a 10 minutes period through a standard die while a fixed pressure is applied via a piston to a 190° C melt. Other physical properties are :

- Viscosity
- Gap fill
- Water absorption

Mechanical Properties :

- Tensile strength
- Tensile modulus
- Elongation

Thermal Properties :

- Temperature range
- Deflection temperature
- Thermal conductivity
- Coefficient of thermal expansion (CTE)

Electrical Properties :

- Resistivity
- Dielectric strength
- Dielectric constant

8.8.3 Dielectric Strength Of Resins

> **Q.** Explain how dielectric strength of resin is measured.

Scope:

Dielectric strength is a measure of the electrical strength of a material as an insulator. Dielectric strength is defined as the maximum voltage required producing a dielectric breakdown through the material and is expressed as volts per unit thickness. A higher dielectric strength represents a better quality of insulator.

Test Procedure:

There are three basic procedures that used to determine the dielectric strength of an insulator. These procedures are the short-time method, the slow rate-of-rise method and the step-by-step method. Each of these three methods has the same basic set-up, which consists of the test specimen placed between two electrodes in air or oil.

For the most common test, the short-time method, voltage is applied across the two electrodes and raised from zero to dielectric breakdown at a uniform rate. Breakdown is when an electrical burn through or decomposition occurs in the specimen. The rate of voltage rise is determined by the time it takes the sample to reach dielectric breakdown. The slow-rate-of rise method starts at 50% of the breakdown voltage as determined by the short-time-method and is increased at a uniform rate. The step-by-step method starts at 50% of the short-time-test then voltage is increased for a specified time period until breakdown. The test is sometimes performed in oil to prevent arcing from the electrode to the ground.

Specimen size :

The recommended specimen type for this test is a 4 inch plaque or larger. Any specimen thickness can be used; however the most common thickness is between 0.8 to 3.2 mm. Specimens over 2 mm thick are typically tested in oil to decrease the chance of flashover before breakdown.

Observations

Dielectric strength is calculated by dividing the breakdown voltage by the thickness of the sample. The data is expressed in Volts/mil. The location of the failure is also recorded. A higher dielectric strength represents a better quality of insulator.

SOLVED EXAMPLES

Example 8.1 : A Bakelite is tested by Schering bridge method having of 100 µF. The balance was obtained with a capacitance 0.65 µF in parallel with non-inductive resistance of 300 Ω the non-inductive resistance in the remaining arm of the bridge was 130 Ω. Test voltage 20 kV, 50 Hz. Find the capacitance the p.f. and equivalent series resistance of the specimen.

Solution.

Given
C_1 = 100 µF
C_4 = 0.65 µF
R_4 = 300 Ω
R_3 = 130 Ω
C_2 = ?
r = ?

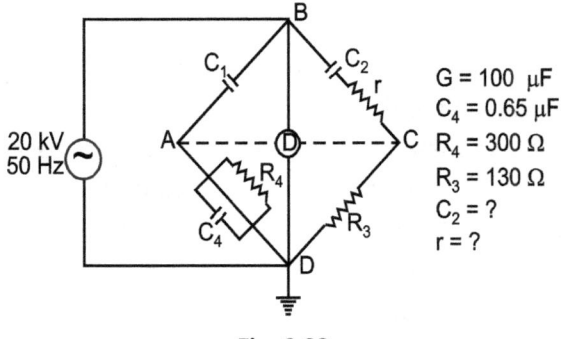

Fig. 8.22

From the derived ratio,

$$C_2 = C_1 (R_4/R_3)$$
$$= 100 \times \frac{300}{130}$$

$$\boxed{C_2 = 230.76 \ \mu F}$$

Series resistance,
$$r = R_3 (C_4/C_1)$$
$$= 130 \left(\frac{0.65 \times 10^{-6}}{100 \times 10^{-6}} \right)$$

$$\boxed{r = 0.845 \ \Omega}$$

Power factor $= \omega \cdot r \cdot C_2$
$$= (2\pi \times 50) \times (0.845) \times (230.76 \times 10^{-6})$$
$$= 0.0612 \text{ leading.}$$

Example 8.2 : Two parallel plates $0.2 \times 0.6 \ m^2$ in area are separated by dielectric of thickness 0.08 m dielectric constant $\varepsilon_r = 5$. The capacitor so formed is subjected to an alternating field of 50 kV/cm at frequency of 50 Hz. Calculate the dielectric loss of the capacitor if loss tangent is 0.001.

Solution :

Given
$$\varepsilon_r = 5$$
$$f = 50 \text{ Hz}$$
$$E = 50 \text{ kV/cm}$$
$$\omega = \text{Dielectric loss}$$
$$= \frac{E^2 f \varepsilon_r \tan \delta}{1.8 \times 10^{12}}$$
$$= \frac{(50)^2 \times (10)^6 \times 50 \times 5 \times 0.001}{1.8 \times 10^{12}}$$

$$= \frac{2500 \times 50 \times 5 \times 10^6 \times 10^{-3} \times 10^{-12}}{1.8}$$

$$= \frac{625000 \times 10^{-9}}{1.8}$$

$$= 347222.2 \times 10^{-9}$$

$$\boxed{\omega = 3.47 \times 10^{-4} \text{ }\omega/cm^3}$$

Example 8.3 : Two parallel plates 0.15×0.3 m² in area are separated by a dielectric of thickness 0.06 m dielectric constant $\varepsilon_r = 5.4$. The capacitor so formed is subjected to an alternating field of 60 kV/cm at a frequency of 50 Hz. Calculate the dielectric loss of the capacitor if loss tangent is 0.001.

Solution : Given :

$$E = 60 \text{ kV/cm}$$
$$f = 50 \text{ Hz}$$
$$\varepsilon_r = 5.4$$
$$\tan \delta = 0.001$$
$$\omega = \text{Dielectric loss}$$

$$\omega = \frac{E^2 f \varepsilon_r \tan \delta}{1.8 \times 10^{12}}$$

$$= \frac{60^2 \times 10^6 \times 50 \times 5.4 \times 0.001}{1.8 \times 10^{12}}$$

$$= \frac{3600 \times 50 \times 5.4 \times 10^6 \times 10^{-2}}{1.8 \times 10^{12}}$$

$$= \frac{972000 \times 10^4}{1.8 \times 10^{12}}$$

$$= 540000 \times 10^4 \times 10^{-12}$$

$$\boxed{\omega = 5.4 \times 10^{-4} \text{ }\omega/cm^3}$$

REVIEW QUESTIONS

1. What is dielectric loss and how it affects on the insulator?
2. What is breakdown strength and what is its importance in solid, liquid, gas insulator.
3. What is Gauss meter? How it works?
4. Explain the type tests and routine tests, performed.
5. Explain basic principle of measurement of flux density by Gauss meter.

UNIVERSITY QUESTIONS

May 2008

1. With a neat connection diagram, explain step by step a procedure to determine dielectric strength of transformer oil as per IS code of practice. What precautions are to be taken during the test? **(10 Marks)**
2. Describe in detail the procedure for measurement of dielectric strength of air as per relevant IS code practice. **(8 Marks)**
3. List the parameters which need to be tested as per IS code of practice in respect of a power cable. Describe any one test in detail. **(10 Marks)**

Dec. 2008

4. With a neat connection diagram, explain step by step a procedure to determine dielectric strength of transformer oil as per IS code of practice. What precautions are to be taken during the test? **(10 Marks)**
5. Explain loss tangent (tan δ) of a dielectric. Describe a method to determine to measure the loss tangent of an insulating material as per BIS code. Draw and label the connection diagram. **(10 Marks)**
6. List the parameters which need to be tested as per IS code of practice in respect of a power cable. Describe any one test in detail.
7. What is meant by partial discharge? Describe a method as relevant code of Indian standards to determine the partial discharge of dielectric of a capacitor.

May 2009

8. With a neat connection diagram, explain step by step a procedure to determine dielectric strength of transformer oil as per IS code of practice. What precautions are to be taken during test? **(10 Marks)**
9. How are cables tested? Describe any one test in detail. **(8 Marks)**
10. Describe in detail the procedure for measurement of dielectric strength of air as per relevant IS code practice. **(8 Marks)**
11. Explain loss tangent (tan δ) of a dielectric. Describe a method to determine to measure the loss tangent of an insulating material as per BIS code. Draw and label the connection diagram. **(10 Marks)**

Dec. 2009

12. With neat connection diagram explain a method of determining dielectric strength of transformer oil as per relevant IS code of practice. **(10 Marks)**
13. What is tan δ of a dielectric? Explain. Describe the method of measurement of tan δ of a dielectric by Schering bridge as per IS code of practice. **(8 Marks)**

14. With a neat connection diagram explain the method for measurement of dielectric strength of air as per relevant IS code of practice. What inferences will you draw from this test. **(10 Marks)**
15. What is partial discharge of a dielectric? Explain a method to determine the partial changes of a dielectric solid in the laboratory. **(8 Marks)**

May 2010

16. Explain tan δ of a dielectric. What is significance of higher tan δ? Describe the method of measurement of tan δ of a dielectric by using Schering bridge as per IS code of practice. **(10 Marks)**
17. With neat connection diagram explain a method for determining dielectric strength of a PVC sheath as per relevant IS code of practice. **(8 Marks)**
18. With neat connection diagram explain a method of determining dielectric strength of transformer oil as per relevant IS code of practice. What references will you draw from the test? **(10 Marks)**
19. Describe a method to test the high voltage bushing of a distribution transformer. **(8 Marks)**

Dec. 2010

20. How will you test transformer oil? Explain with neat diagram of test set-up. **(9 Marks)**
21. Describe any three tests on cable. **(9 Marks)**
22. Explain measurement of tangent of dielectric loss angle (tan δ) by Schering bridge as per IS code 13585-1994. **(9 Marks)**
23. Describe the measurement of dielectric strength of solid insulating material with reference to IS 2584. **(9 Marks)**

May 2011

24. With neat connection diagram explain method for determining dielectric strength of transformer oil as per relevant IS code of practice. What are the inferences from the test? **(10 Marks)**
25. With neat sketch explain how flux density is measured with help of Gauss-meter. **(8 Marks)**
26. What is loss tanget? Give its significance. Describe the method of measuring tan δ of a dielectric by using Schering bridge as per IS code of practice. **(10 Marks)**
27. With neat connection diagram, explain the method for measurement of dielectric strength of air as per IS code of practice. **(8 Marks)**

Dec. 2011

28. With a neat connection diagram, explain the method for determining dielectric strength of transformer oil as per IS Code of practice. What inferences will you draw from the test? **(10 Marks)**

29. What is partial discharge of a dielectric? Explain a method to determine the partial discharge of solid dielectric in laboratory. **(8 Marks)**

30. With a neat connection diagram explain the method for measurement of dielectric strength of air as per IS Code of practice. What inferences will you draw from this test? **(10 Marks)**

31. Explain loss tangent in dielectric materials. Describe the method of measurement of tan δ of a dielectric by Schering bridge as per IS code of practice. **(8 Marks)**

May 2012

32. Describe any three tests on cable. **(9 Marks)**

33. Describe measurement of dielectric strength of solid insulating material with reference to IS 2584. **(9 Marks)**

34. What is partial discharge of a dielectric? Explain a method to determine the partial discharge of a dielectric solid in the laboratory. **(9 Marks)**

35. How will you test transformer oil? Explain with neat diagram of test setup. **(9 Marks)**

36. List the parameters which need to be tested as per IS code of practice in respect of underground power cable. Describe any one test in detail. **(9 Marks)**

37. Describe in detail the procedure for determination of dielectric strength of air as per relevant IS code of practice. What precautions are taken during the experiment? **(9 Marks)**

38. Explain the loss tangent (tan δ) of a dielectric. Describe a method of measurement of tan δ of a dielectric by Schering Bridge as per IS code of practice. Draw and label connection diagram. **(10 Marks)**

39. With a neat sketch, explain how flux density is measured with the help of Gauss-meter. **(8 Marks)**

Notes

Notes

www.ingramcontent.com/pod-product-compliance
Lightning Source LLC
Chambersburg PA
CBHW081221170426
43198CB00017B/2679